P9-DEI-838

teach®
yourself

philosophy of religion
mel thompson

For over 60 years, more than
50 million people have learnt over
750 subjects the **teach yourself**
way, with impressive results.

be where you want to be
with **teach yourself**

For UK order enquiries: please contact Bookpoint Ltd, 130 Milton Park, Abingdon, Oxon, OX14 4SB. Telephone: +44 (0) 1235 827720. Fax: +44 (0) 1235 400454. Lines are open 09.00–17.00, Monday to Saturday, with a 24-hour message answering service. Details about our titles and how to order are available at www.teachyourself.co.uk

For USA order enquiries: please contact McGraw-Hill Customer Services, PO Box 545, Blacklick, OH 43004-0545, USA. Telephone: 1-800-722-4726. Fax: 1-614-755-5645.

For Canada order enquiries: please contact McGraw-Hill Ryerson Ltd, 300 Water St, Whitby, Ontario, L1N 9B6, Canada. Telephone: 905 430 5000. Fax: 905 430 5020.

Long renowned as the authoritative source for self-guided learning – with more than 50 million copies sold worldwide – the **teach yourself** series includes over 500 titles in the fields of languages, crafts, hobbies, business, computing and education.

British Library Cataloguing in Publication Data: a catalogue record for this title is available from the British Library.

Library of Congress Catalog Card Number: on file.

First published in UK 1997 by Hodder Education, 338 Euston Road, London, NW1 3BH.

First published in US 1997 by The McGraw-Hill Companies, Inc.

This edition published 2007.

The **teach yourself** name is a registered trade mark of Hodder Headline.

Copyright © 1997, 2003, 2007 Mel Thompson

Typeset by Transet Limited, Coventry, England.
Printed in Great Britain for Hodder Education, a division of Hodder Headline, an Hachette Livre UK Company, 338 Euston Road, London, NW1 3BH, by Cox & Wyman Ltd, Reading, Berkshire.

The publisher has used its best endeavours to ensure that the URLs for external websites referred to in this book are correct and active at the time of going to press. However, the publisher and the author have no responsibility for the websites and can make no guarantee that a site will remain live or that the content will remain relevant, decent or appropriate.

Hodder Headline's policy is to use papers that are natural, renewable and recyclable products and made from wood grown in sustainable forests. The logging and manufacturing processes are expected to conform to the environmental regulations of the country of origin.

Impression number   10 9 8 7 6 5 4 3 2 1
Year   2010 2009 2008 2007

contents

introduction   **vii**
   what is the philosophy of religion?   viii
   why study religion in this way?   ix
   what is involved?   xi
   what this book aims to do   xii

01   **religious experience**   **1**
   starting with experience   2
   what is religious experience?   4
   key features of religious experience   7
   induced experiences   16
   prayer   17
   mysticism   19
   charismatic experiences   22
   what can we know?   23
   conclusion   29

02   **religious language**   **32**
   a private language?   33
   knowledge and description   35
   faith, reason and belief   36
   the rational and the non-rational   39
   cognitive and non-cognitive   41
   interpreting language   43
   language games   50
   the limitations of language   54

03	**God: the concepts**	**56**
	eternal	57
	God as creator	59
	transcendence and immanence	62
	theism, pantheism and panentheism	62
	beliefs, language and religion	63
	basic beliefs	66
	a postmodernist interpretation	67
	exists?	69
04	**God: the arguments**	**73**
	the ontological argument	75
	the cosmological argument	82
	the teleological argument	90
	the moral argument	98
	the argument from religious experience	102
	conclusions	105
05	**atheism and humanism**	**107**
	atheism, agnosticism and secularism	108
	Nietzsche: God is dead	111
	secular explanations of God	112
	humanism	116
06	**the self**	**121**
	dualism	123
	materialism	130
	idealism	135
	a shifting identity?	136
	freedom?	139
	life beyond death?	141
07	**psychology and religion**	**149**
	is religion healthy?	150
	religion as therapy	153
	religion as spiritual development	155
08	**suffering and evil**	**158**
	the challenge and the response	159
	the problem	161

God as moral agent 174

suffering and the major religions 176

coming to terms with suffering 180

conclusions 183

09 religion and science 185

the problem science poses for religion 187

the changing world-view 189

the methods of science and religion 196

providence and miracles 204

the origin of the universe 215

evolution and humankind 218

some conclusions 224

10 religion and society 228

moral issues 229

the social impact of religion 238

political issues 242

religion and terrorism 245

social values and lifestyle 247

religion in a multicultural society 252

postscript 260

taking it further 262

glossary 265

index 269

God's gender

The Western monotheistic religions have, by tradition (and a male-dominated tradition it is, as any feminist will be quick to point out), referred to God as male.

Hopefully, this book will show that any attempt to reduce the idea of 'God' to a separate, existing entity in human (or any other) form is not only illogical, but fails to do justice to the best religious intuitions and philosophical arguments. Nevertheless, for reasons of convenience, 'God' is referred to in this book as 'he', with apologies to her/it, if she exists!

introduction

People long to make sense of life; to find the key that will unlock its mysteries and enable them to understand themselves and their place within the universe. Faced with their own fragility and death, they seek courage and comfort. Longing to develop and create, they seek inspiration.

In this human quest for meaning, some take to philosophy, others to the creative arts, and others – in fact the majority of humankind – take to some form of religion.

Almost every aspect of life – from sexuality to artistic creativity, or from the emotional trauma of prolonged suffering or bereavement to the spontaneous expression at the wonder of natural beauty – can become the raw material out of which a religious interpretation of life may be built.

But why? What are religious beliefs, and how do they relate to our general understanding of life? Can they be justified rationally? Are they a mental springboard, launching us into a deeper exploration and appreciation of life, or a mental prison, closing our minds to reason and evidence? Or are they neither, but only our use (or misuse) of them makes them so?

Each religion presents us with a particular view of life, expressed in its teachings, scriptures and traditions. But is it necessary to be committed to that religion in order to understand and appreciate what it teaches, or are religious questions and experiences open to all? By what criteria can we judge between competing claims made by religions? How do religious beliefs relate to lifestyle and morality? Should religions be judged by the way their followers behave?

These are just some of the questions we need to address: there will be many more.

What is the philosophy of religion?

The philosophy of religion examines the general ideas and principles upon which religion is based. It takes the beliefs that religious people hold to be true and tests them for:

Logical coherence: Does this belief make logical sense? Does it fit the evidence? Does it accord with other beliefs that the person holds? If it is true, what implications does it have?

Meaning: Is the language in which this belief is expressed meant to be taken literally? If so, what evidence may be given for or against its truth? If not, does it simply express the mental state or creative wishes of the person who makes it?

In other words, we can ask of any religious claim:

- How can we know whether it is true or false? Does it give the kind of truth with which science deals?

but also ...

- What does this claim mean for the person who makes it, and in the context of religion as a whole?

This second question is important, for it leads to a broader consideration of the philosophical issues that are raised by religion. The philosophy of religion is not just about logical arguments but about the meaning and significance religion has in people's lives, and what it is that leads some people to follow and others to reject a religion.

The task

The philosophy of religion takes religious beliefs and asks how they are to be understood, if they make sense, and if they fit with the rest of our knowledge of the universe.

In general, it does not promote one religion rather than another. Nor should it seek to promote belief in God over atheism. Its task is to probe and challenge religious beliefs with a measure of sensitive detachment, on the assumption that clarification and reason tend to support rather than destroy truth.

Very few people adopt a religion for purely rational reasons. It may have more to do with their family background, their culture, their love of religious music or art, their experience of being helped by religious people, or from a deep sense of meaning and purpose that they find expressed in religious language. On the other hand, most religious believers want to claim that their religion makes sense, and it is this claim that the philosophy of religion puts to the test.

Philosophy cannot show that a religion is either right or wrong. What it can do is to show that its beliefs are either logical or illogical, that its language is best understood literally or metaphorically, and the degree to which its beliefs are compatible with other things that people hold to be true.

Religion?

What do we mean by 'religion'? A dictionary definition as 'a system of faith and worship' leads in two different directions:

- A **substantive** definition will speak about the objects of faith – belief in God, miracles and so on. If so, is Buddhism a 'religion', since it does not involve belief in God?
- A **functional** definition will look at the part religion plays in a person's life – as providing an overall view of the world, along with the values and moral principles that spring from it. If so, should **Humanism** count as a religion?

In this book we shall try to get a balance between these two approaches to religion, by looking at religious beliefs and examining whether or not they can be justified rationally, but doing so in the broader context of the part that they play in people's lives.

Why study religion in this way?

For the sake of personal integrity, it is important that religious beliefs should be examined and tested out just like any other beliefs that one might hold – and that applies equally to the believer and the atheist, for thoughtless rejection is no better than thoughtless belief. The alternative is to claim that religion is an intellectual 'no-go area', to be left unexamined, private and mute. Not only is that unhealthy for a thinking being, it is also contrary to the great religious traditions, all of which have attempted to explain their beliefs to society as a whole.

But why should a non-believer study religion at all? Perhaps because it is an inescapable fact of life. It is difficult to overstate the global importance of religion and its impact on society:

- Western politics, culture and ideas are largely shaped by the Judaeo-Christian religious tradition. Even for a person who claims no religious allegiance, his or her thought patterns, language and concepts are therefore influenced by religion, even if that influence is no longer self-evident.

- Can one appreciate the social and political issues facing the Middle East without some understanding of Islam? Or India without Hinduism? Or the Punjab without Sikhism? Can one understand the life and culture of the Far East without some idea of what Buddhism, Confucianism and Taoism are about?

- The many tribal religions, the old Norse legends, the traditions of the Native American and Eskimo peoples, the deeply natural religions of Wicca, of the Druids and of the many early pagan cults – all have contributed to the rich, emotional, intuitive and artistic life of humanity.

- Conflict and terrorism are often linked to religion. Throughout history, wars have been fought either because of religion, or because of long-term differences between nations or groups that have their roots in religion. What is it about religious beliefs that leads people to die or kill for them?

- Many people now live in a multicultural, multi-faith society. Sensitivity to religious beliefs is therefore a crucial issue for social harmony and cohesion. While philosophy of religion tends to deal with general questions, rather than the details of each religion, it nevertheless gives a context within which religious dialogue can make sense.

Even those who claim to have no religion may still face issues with which the philosophy of religion has traditionally been concerned: the meaning of life; human fragility and death; the nature of the self; a sense of morality; the origin and end of the universe. The examination of such things is of universal interest. To take a practical example, one might want to consider what it is appropriate to say at a secular wedding or funeral. How might such significant moments in life be celebrated in a secular context?

What is involved?

As an academic subject in Western schools and universities, the philosophy of religion has generally focused on the truth claims of Christianity, although the issues studied are equally relevant to the other major monotheistic faiths, Judaism and Islam, while Eastern philosophy has tended to be studied separately, generally in the context of Eastern religions. It has been concerned with proofs for the existence of God, the problem of evil, the possibility of miracles, **providence** and other questions relating to the belief that God is active in the world, and particularly with the nature and status of religious language.

All philosophy is rational – it is the process of taking a careful look at some aspect of life and examining it in a logical way, exploring its dilemmas, attempting to clarify its ambiguities and resolve its apparent inconsistencies. In this sense, the philosophy of religion is concerned with the rational aspects of religion. But there is more to religion than rational beliefs. Religion has to do with the heart and will as much as with the mind. Religious people believe *in* things, they do not simply believe them to be the case. They tend to be committed to their beliefs, holding on to them even in the face of apparently overwhelming evidence to the contrary. This in itself is a phenomenon to be taken into consideration. Therefore, when we look at religious arguments, we need to be sensitive not just to **what** is being said, but to **why** and **how** it is being said. We may also need to ask 'What sort of experience of life would lead me to hold this belief, or to argue in this way?' Rational analysis alone may not be enough to discover the significance of a religious claim, it needs to be supplemented by a measure of empathy with the views of the person holding that belief.

Nor should beliefs be dismissed just because they are not capable of being justified rationally. Much of what is worthwhile in life is not rational – love, music, art, the whole world of the emotions. If a belief is held to be true, in spite of evidence to suggest it is false, we should at least pause to ask why. What does this belief *do* for those who hold it? Why is it so important to them?

Religion is concerned as much with integration as explanation. People become religious when, through some moment of personal insight, they sense their energies being harnessed and unified and their life given new direction. Some speak of the spiritual life in terms of a journey – a process of self-discovery and growth. In this sense, **religion is experienced as a process, rather than the acceptance of a set of propositions**, and its value should be judged according to the personal benefits it offers.

Whatever may be said about religion by philosophers, the phenomenon of religion will remain while people actually claim to feel its benefits. If religion did not actually give people a sense of purpose and value in their lives, it would not survive.

Too often religious argument has been carried on in a way that is rational but shallow. It has:

- caricatured a person's belief
- restated that caricature as a rational proposition
- shown that such a proposition is either false or meaningless
- therefore dismissed the original belief as unworthy of serious consideration.

That may be fine if the intention is to feel intellectually superior at the expense of another's beliefs, but it does little to explain the phenomenon of religion. The religious believer may appear to walk away vanquished, but continues to believe – for the power of that belief has neither been appreciated nor diminished by such a challenge. **By contrast, our task in this book is to try to probe beneath the superficial, to see what (if anything) in religious belief may be accepted as true on rational grounds alone, and what needs to be explained in terms of the non-rational factors.**

What this book aims to do

This book seeks:

- to introduce key concepts in the philosophy of religion
- to set out some of the arguments that have been put forward both for and against religious beliefs
- to point out the limits of rational debate in these matters.

This last point is important. To attempt to make oneself believe something for emotional or social reasons is quite hopeless – one either believes it or one does not. On the other hand, one can have a deep conviction that something is the case, and yet be unable to give evidence to back up that belief.

While every intuition is a step beyond reason, once it has been taken, reason returns and quickly tries to colonise the newly acquired insight and to integrate it into a rational view of things.

- I just feel that I shall like this person or this place; later I shall find my reasons.
- If you do not offer me your friendship until you know all about me, we shall remain strangers.

Emotion may be warm; reason is often portrayed as being detached or cold. The philosophy of religion thrives on reason that has acquired a little warmth, but that should not detract from the importance of thinking carefully and logically.

Some thinkers (for example, Alvin Plantinga) have pointed out that there are some fundamental beliefs that are held without being based on evidence or experience, like the experience of other minds or the reality of the external world. We simply know them to be true, without waiting to be convinced. So there may be some religious beliefs that form an unquestioned basis for the rest of our thinking. They may be based on 'faith' rather than on evidence. Nevertheless, it is perfectly reasonable that such beliefs should also be open to logical scrutiny.

As we examine these things, we shall need to keep in mind two different but related questions:

- Is religion reasonable?
- Is it reasonable to be religious?

The second is quite a different question, but one we should not ignore. Most important things in life are not undertaken on the basis of rational assessment alone. Hopes, fears, emotional attachments, memories and the longing to share activities with those we love and admire, all have their part to play. Considering one's life as a whole, it may be very reasonable to be religious, even if religion itself is not 'reasonable' in the sense of being based on logic and evidence.

For reflection

Proving that a play is not about real people, but a figment of the playwright's imagination, is not going to empty the theatre if the performance is enjoyable, moving or thought-provoking. Literal truth is not the only measure of value.

Some books are labelled 'fiction', but that is not regarded as a warning not to read them.

However, examining literature in order to point out what is fiction and what non-fiction, to prevent people being confused, is also a worthwhile activity.

The structure of this book

This book starts by looking at the nature of religious experience, and then at the language used to describe it. This is essential if we are to appreciate the beliefs and debates that are to follow. So, for example, there is little point in looking at arguments for and against belief in 'God' without some idea of what that word means and what sort of human experiences it relates to. Experience, of course, is always open to a variety of interpretations. A logical rejection of belief in God does not deny the experience that the word 'God' sought to express; indeed, a Buddhist or secular atheist might have exactly the same experience, recognizing it as personally or spiritually important, but find no need to use language about 'God' to explain it.

Chapters 03, 04 and 05 are concerned with 'God', since this is a central concept for Western religions. We start by looking at the terms used, then at the arguments that have traditionally been put forward for belief in the existence of God, and finally at the case for atheism and at the humanist view of life as one that expresses fundamental values without using the idea of 'God' to do so.

But religion is as much to do with the 'self' as it is about 'God', since religion is the means people have constructed for dealing with the relationship between the two, and there are interesting parallels between the relationship of the 'self' to the body and that of 'God' to the physical world. Concepts of the 'soul' or 'self' also impinge on the idea of life after death, which has an important place in many religious traditions. This is therefore the next topic to be examined, and it is followed by a brief survey of psychological views of religion and how it is related to emotional and other needs.

Religious belief faces two enormous challenges. The first of these is the fact of suffering and evil. Each religion needs to find some way of integrating this into its overall view of the world, particularly if it also wants to claim that the world is controlled by a loving God. The second is the impact of science and technology on our habitual way of understanding the world. Scientific method and argument is radically different from religious debate, and its overwhelming success in understanding how the world works, and in delivering technologies, suggests that it should be regarded as the norm. We shall therefore need to look at how religious beliefs fare in facing these challenges.

The final chapter looks at a range of issues under the general heading of 'Religion and society'. It is clear that religious ideas have influenced social and political life, as well as the more general questions of morality, values and lifestyle. At its most extreme, we have the phenomenon of terrorism carried out in the name of religion, but there are broader issues concerned with the way in which religion influences (and is influenced by) the assumptions about lifestyle and moral values in each society and era. In some ways, these topics go beyond the traditional debates in the philosophy of religion, but they are important if the relevance of those debates is to be appreciated.

Note

Philosophy of religion, as an academic subject, has been particularly shaped and influenced by the interaction between Christian beliefs and Western secular philosophy. This is reflected in the contents of this book, which is concerned primarily with the beliefs of the major Western religions.

But part of the value and fascination of the philosophy of religion lies in the way it addresses issues that are global and timeless. Different cultures and eras, faced with the same issues of life and its meaning, have come up with answers that may appear to differ radically from one another, but which also have common threads running through them.

For those interested in moving on to consider the philosophy that underlies the great Eastern religions of Hinduism, Buddhism, Confucianism and Taoism, there is *Teach Yourself: Eastern Philosophy* in this same series.

01

religious experience

In this chapter you will:
- examine different forms of religious experience
- see how they may be interpreted
- consider how they relate to people's beliefs.

Starting with experience

If there were no religion, there would be no philosophy of religion. If there were no 'religious experiences', there would be no religion. Religion, unlike most philosophy, starts with the interpretation of experience, with trying to make sense of life as a whole, or of particular things that happen.

Relatively few people who would call themselves religious spend their days reflecting on the logic of believing in the existence of God. What they are actually doing is living with a particular way of seeing things and a particular set of values. They take part in acts of worship and feel 'uplifted'. They claim to be inspired; to have moments of insight. They find that, even when not engaged in specifically religious activities, they have experiences that tend to reinforce their faith – they see a beautiful sunset, or experience childbirth; they face their own death or that of a loved one; they fall in love. At all these moments, their experience is informed by and in turn informs their religion.

For reflection

- You feel hot: they say you are running a temperature.
- You see stars: they point out that you have been hit on the head.
- You sense that the earth is moving beneath you: they say you are drunk, sexually over-excited, or have a disease of the inner ear.

The experience you have remains valid, whatever the explanation given for it.

Therefore a religious experience is not invalidated by an argument showing that God cannot exist. The most such an argument could show is that the explanation you may have given of your experience is not logically coherent.

In general, you can argue for or against an interpretation or a proposition; you cannot argue for or against an experience.

A major feature of philosophy in the second half of the twentieth century was the recognition that language is always used for a particular purpose and in a particular context and that its meaning is shown by its use. A philosophy of religion should therefore start where religion starts, with experience. It can then move on to examine religious language and beliefs, but it will have fundamentally misunderstood those beliefs if it takes them away from their religious context.

Towards the end of his book *The Varieties of Religious Experience* (1902) William James said:

> ... in a world in which no religious feeling had ever existed, I doubt whether any philosophic theology could ever have been framed.

In other words, however independent of actual experience some religious concepts may have become, and however rarefied a debate on them might appear, they owe their origin to the experiences of individuals and religious groups – experiences which those concerned have tried to describe, and whose descriptions have become the raw material of religious ideas and propositions. William James spoke particularly of 'religious feelings'; but are 'feelings' separable from things that are experienced? And what is it about experiences that lead people to have 'religious feelings' associated within them?

So, before looking at the various forms of religious experience, we need to consider a few basic things about experience in general.

What happens when you experience something?

Your sense organs – sight, sound, smell, taste, touch – register something, and this information is conveyed to your brain. But this raw sensation does not remain in a 'raw' state for long. As soon as it is received, four things happen:

1 The experience is registered as pleasant, painful or neutral. Something that is physically damaging (cutting your finger with a knife) is registered as painful. This is an essential part of the body's survival mechanism – painful feelings are warnings of danger. A cool drink on a hot day will immediately register as pleasant, since it represents the satisfaction of a physical need. The response is automatic; largely outside conscious control.

2 But memory also plays a part. Something is recognized, and the memory of the last encounter influences how it is now experienced. When you meet a stranger, you do not know how that experience will turn out. (Unless of course, previous meetings with strangers have been significantly pleasant or painful.) You meet that same person for a second time and,

although the actual sensations are the same, the whole experience is coloured by the first encounter. The person is now known, and his or her behaviour is anticipated.

3 The mind also starts to categorize what is experienced. It finds concepts and words to describe it. It experiences this thing *as* something. The more sensitive a person is to the thing experienced, the more sophisticated is this process of categorization. A connoisseur of fine wines distinguishes a particular grape and vintage; a less fussy drinker registers it as either white or red, sweet or dry.

4 As a result of all this mental and sensory activity, the body evaluates the experience and responds accordingly. A friend is recognized – there is a feeling of pleasure, a smile, a sudden wish to rush forward and greet the person, a feeling of relaxed warmth. An enemy is recognized – there is a tightness in the stomach, a clenching of the fists and jaw. One prepares for fight or flight; the adrenalin pumps, for the body knows that action is needed.

Every experience therefore involves sensation, interpretation and response. This process happens almost simultaneously and people seldom separate out its elements. Only when there is a mismatch between one process and the others do their separate functions come to light. If you register something as painful, but respond as if it were pleasant, the body objects.

Example

You can't stand the sight of these people, but they are customers and you have to be polite. Your smile feels taut and forced, your muscles tense ready for a fight, but you smile and give a friendly handshake. The integrity of the experience is lost – response does not match feeling or categorization – and the result is that the encounter is exhausting.

What is religious experience?

Religion is a complex phenomenon. It includes beliefs about the world, particular values and attitudes associated with them, and ways of responding and living which reflect them. It is likely to influence and be influenced by everything that we experience or remember.

In practice, this means that – for a religious person – a quite normal experience (looking at a beautiful scene, for example) may be profoundly religious. A non-religious person would describe the same thing as inspiring, uplifting, or beautiful, but would not want to go on to associate that interpretation with anything overtly religious.

However, certain experiences are profoundly influential in a person's life and are most likely to be given the label 'religious'. Although acknowledging that there may be a religious element in all experience, we shall therefore focus on these special experiences.

Where does the religious element come in?

If religion is to do with an understanding of life and responses to it, then it will influence the second, third and fourth parts of the experience process. It will matter less what actual sensations impinge on the body, and more on the way in which these are categorized, the way in which memory contributes to the feelings associated with them, and the responses that a person has to them.

With this in mind, we can now turn to some famous examples of religious experiences that have had a profound effect on the individuals concerned:

- Siddhartha seeing four sights (an old person, a sick person, a corpse and a holy man) and, struck by the harsh reality of life and death from which his comfortable upbringing had tried to shield him, started out on a spiritual quest that led him to become known as the Buddha.
- Moses at the burning bush, fascinated and awestruck by a phenomenon which led him to a profound sense of the holiness of that place and also challenged him to go back and lead the Children of Israel out of Egypt.
- The prophet Isaiah in the temple in Jerusalem, sensing the absolute holiness of God and the moral failures of humankind: 'Woe is me, for I am a man of unclean lips, and I dwell amidst a people of unclean lips, for my eyes have seen the Lord of Hosts.'
- Jesus in the desert, struggling with the temptation to misuse spiritual power for selfish ends.
- Paul on the Damascus road, having his views and his life totally changed; forced by a moment of insight to admit he

was wrong and to take the side of those whom he had sought to persecute.

- Muhammad in the cave hearing the words of the Qur'an and being told to recite them.
- Nanak, entering the river to bathe, and emerging later as a religious leader with insights that were to make him the founder of the Sikh faith.

We can never get to the historical basis of these accounts, for they have come down to us as stories that already bear a heavy burden of religious meaning and tradition. But what they do indicate most clearly is that, for all these great religious leaders, there were moments of such significance and insight that the response to them involved a radical disruption and upheaval in their lives. Muhammad was said to be terrified at the command to 'recite'. Moses was hardly taking an easy option in going back to Egypt from where he had already escaped in fear of his life. It is most unlikely that such experiences would have been induced artificially, at least on a conscious level. Their authenticity as experiences (irrespective of the religious interpretation given to them) is demonstrated by their unlikelihood and inconvenience.

But religious experiences need not always be so dramatic nor are they confined to those who are about to found a new religion! In general, religious experience involves:

- a sense of wonder
- a sense of new insight and values
- a sense of holiness and profundity.

Such experiences involve the whole person – mind, emotions, values and relationships – and seem to touch the most basic and fundamental sense of being oneself.

In other words

A religious experience is one in which a person says 'This is who I really am', 'This is what life is all about', 'This is so wonderful that it makes everything else worthwhile.' But exactly how that experience is interpreted depends on the culture, ideas and language of that particular time and place, and it need not be interpreted religiously at all.

Conversion

William James (1842–1910) was both a psychologist and a co-founder of Pragmatism, a school of philosophy that examined claims to knowledge in terms of their usefulness. He was keen to explore the way in which a 'conversion' experience could help a person to change and develop. In his *The Varieties of Religious Experience*, he sees it leading to:

- loss of worry
- truths not known before
- the sense that the world is changed as a result of the experience.

In other words, a conversion implies both a new view of the world and a new and integrated sense of the self.

As we saw above, all experience involved interpretation. (We shall look at this again in Chapter 02, when considering religious language. We experience everything 'as' something, and have a particular view – or 'blik' – which is our habitual way of looking at the world, colouring our interpretation of experience.) What happens when a person has a religious conversion is that he or she sees the world differently, interprets everything with new significance and responds accordingly. It is therefore possible to test out the validity of a claimed conversion by seeing if the person behaves differently as a result: a 'pragmatic' approach.

Example

You tell me that you now love spiders. I release a particularly juicy specimen in the room. Do you still jump up on a chair and scream, or do you pick it up and stroke it gently? By your response shall your new 'blik' be judged.

Key features of religious experience

In this section we shall look briefly at a number of different aspects of religious experience, each reflected in the work of a particular thinker.

Schleiermacher – a sense of the infinite

Friedrich Schleiermacher, writing at the end of the eighteenth century, was concerned to counter the view, prevalent at the time, that reason, aesthetic sensibility and morality between them were a sufficient basis for life, and that religion was entirely superfluous. He wanted to show that religious awareness was a profound and essential element in human life and culture. In his work *On Religion: Speeches to its Cultured Despisers* (published in 1806; trans. John Oman, Harper & Row, 1958) he describes religious experience in this way:

> The contemplation of the pious is the immediate consciousness of universal existence of all finite things, in and through the Infinite, and of all temporal things in and through the Eternal.
>
> (p. 36)

In other words, he sees the essence of religion as something that comes through immediate experience, not as the result of argument. It is an awareness, not just of the Eternal and the Infinite, but of every individual thing in the light of the whole.

He goes on, in an important passage, to show that this 'sense and taste for the infinite' underlies both science and art:

> True science is complete vision; true practice is culture and art self-produced; true religion is sense and taste for the Infinite ... What can man accomplish that is worth speaking of, either in life or in art, that does not arise in his own self from the influence of the sense for the Infinite? ... What is all science, if not the existence of things in you, in your reason? What is all art and culture if not your existence in the things to which you give measure, form and order? And how can both come to life in you except in so far as there lives immediately in you the eternal unity of Reason and Nature, the universal existence of all finite things in the Infinite?
>
> (p. 39)

Notice here that Schleiermacher is not talking about supernatural entities that might or might not exist. He is rooting religion in the experienced relationship between the individual and the universe. His argument is that an awareness of the unity of all things provides the starting point for religion:

> Such a feeling of being one with nature, of being quite rooted in it, so that in all the changing phenomena of life,

even in the change between life and death itself, we might await all that should befall us with approbation and peace, as merely the working out of those eternal laws, would indeed be the germ of all the religious feelings furnished by this side of existence.

(p. 71)

Comment

It seems to me, that what Schleiermacher was saying, in the context of the eighteenth and nineteenth centuries, was that the essence of life is destroyed by being analysed and compartmentalized into rational, scientific knowledge on the one hand, and morality and artistic expression on the other. **In modern terms, he thinks that religion is about taking a holistic view.**

William James – a psychological and natural approach

A classic study of religious experience (particularly mysticism, see below p. 21) is given in William James' *The Varieties of Religious Experience* (1902). James sub-titled his work 'a study of human nature', and he took a psychological approach to his subject. He examined the effect of religion on people's lives, without attempting to argue from this to any supernatural conclusions.

Natural or supernatural

It is interesting that James (and others) examine the nature of religious awareness without needing to argue for or against any supernatural content of religious belief. This enables him to explore the impact, and benefits (or otherwise) of religion without being distracted by metaphysical arguments.

Philosophers – for example, Daniel Dennett in *Breaking the Spell: Religion as a Natural Phenomenon* – may examine arguments for the natural origin and development of religion, but their question is still why it is that religion as a natural phenomenon leads people to believe in supernatural agents. Dennett even suggests – rather tongue-in-cheek – that believers might call themselves 'supers', to refer to their belief in supernatural entities. Similarly, in *The God Delusion*, Richard Dawkins is concerned with attacking the idea of the supernatural, and is not concerned with natural or mystical attitudes to religion.

It may be that a majority of religious people *do* hold supernatural beliefs but, in looking at religious experience, we can still ask whether an interpretation in terms of supernatural entities is *necessary*, or whether we can simply examine the 'sacred values' (to use Dennett's expression) that come from such experiences.

William James looked at the 'healthy minded soul' (the person who is naturally happy and positive) and the 'sick soul' (the person who is depressed and negative). To the 'sick' person, the 'healthy' soul is blind and shallow, not facing the realities of life; to the 'healthy' person, the 'sick' person is diseased and unable to enjoy normal life. James comments, however, that the morbid and depressed attitudes range over a wider range of life than the 'healthy', and that a religion is more complete if it can take these things into account. He cites Buddhism and Christianity as religions which have a great deal to say about suffering.

In looking at responses to religious experience, he points to the unification of the self, the sense of there being a higher controlling power, and the loss of cares as a result of it. There is also the sense that the world has objectively changed, and that truths are known as a result of the religious experience that were not known before.

He describes the positive side of religious experience as a process of moving from 'tenseness, self-responsibility and worry' towards 'equanimity, receptivity and peace'. Notice that he is not arguing for any supernatural interpretation – he is merely pointing to the effects that these experiences have.

Near death experiences

There is a considerable body of research into the experience of those who have been very near death but have subsequently been revived.

A common feature is a sense of moving away from the trauma surrounding the crisis that is threatening that person's life (for example, the medical technology in a hospital intensive care unit) into a state of calmness; of moving towards light and of being welcomed.

As a result, those concerned tend to speak of a new sense of values, of not being worried about trivia, of losing the fear of death. Such situations – whether or not they are interpreted religiously by the people concerned – illustrate the sort of psychological impact of religious experiences outlined by William James and others.

Rudolph Otto – the mysterious and threatening

In his book *The Idea of the Holy* (1917), Otto introduced the idea that religious experience is about the encounter with something totally other, unknowable; something awesome in its dimensions and power, but also attractive and fascinating. He outlined a whole range of feelings ('creeping flesh'; the fear of ghosts; the sense of something that is uncanny, weird or eerie) to illustrate this encounter.

Examples

1 You watch a horror film. You know that you are safe in your comfortable seat, yet you are drawn into the film. You feel your heart beat faster, you gasp, you shudder. You want to look away from the screen, but your attention is pulled back to it. Your rational mind tells you all this is nothing but projected images. The parts are played by actors; nothing is real. But still it stirs up in you some very basic emotions.

2 You climb upwards through woods, and then suddenly emerge into the sunlight at the top of a hill. There is a sense of wonder, of space, of light. You look out over the expanse of countryside and back down to the point from where you began your ascent. It gives you a 'tingle' – not fearful this time, nor irrational, but something that cannot fully be put into words. There is a sense of your own smallness in a large world, but even that fails to catch the exact feeling.

An encounter with 'the holy', according to Otto, is something like those experiences. Like them, it cannot be fully explained, only experienced.

Otto described the object of religious experience as *mysterium tremendum et fascinans*, to include the elements of awesomeness and fascination that it aroused. He spoke of this as an encounter with 'the **numinous**', based on the word 'numen', which he uses to indicate that particular quality of awe-inspiring holiness.

The problem is that it can only be described in words that have an ordinary, everyday meaning. But such ordinary language, taken literally, cannot do justice to the special quality of the experience. Many words (for example, absolute goodness, wonder, purity) approach it, but none describe the 'holy' itself. Otto used the work 'schema' for the set of words that attempt to describe the holy, and the process of finding a cluster of words which angle in on the experience is '**schematization**'. Religious language is just one such schema.

Otto's idea of schematization is important for understanding the limitations of what can be done by the philosophy of religion. Philosophy examines the concepts by means of which the religious experience is schematized, it cannot get back 'behind' them to examine the original experience itself.

Sören Kierkegaard – commitment

Kierkegaard, precursor of the modern existentialist thinkers, emphasized that religious experience was a matter of personal commitment and value – a matter of making a choice, of taking a risk.

He argued (in *Concluding Unscientific Postscript* Book 1, Part II, Chapter 2) that a person could be in one of two situations:

- convinced in faith of the truth of Christianity
- not a believer as such, but interested in Christianity.

The difference here is not in **what is believed**, but in the **way it is believed**. Kierkegaard argued that what mattered was one's relationship to a religious truth. He went so far as to welcome the paradoxical nature of some religious claims, stressing that one can only have the absurd as an object of faith.

For reflection

If something is absurd, one cannot accept it rationally. To believe it takes an act of commitment. But if something makes sense rationally, does that mean that one cannot also be committed to it in a personal way?

Commitment to what is beyond rational proof is a common phenomenon: totally rational people would never fall in love or make war; shopping for the latest in fashion would be suspect; rock climbing, bungee jumping and stamp collecting would cease!

Many religious experiences are actually of quite mundane things – what makes them religious is the way in which they are interpreted, the impact they have on the people experiencing them, and the depth or quality of the experience. **A superficial religious experience is almost a contradiction in terms.**

Kierkegaard's approach emphasizes another key feature of religious experience: that **it involves a relationship between the thing experienced and the experiencing subject.** Once that relationship is taken away and the object is analysed, it ceases to be 'religious'.

Kierkegaard's work is a reminder to us that intuition and risk play an important part in religion. They often provide a starting point for what develops into a serious commitment and new understanding of life. On the other hand, that should not imply that the rational is totally set aside (as Kierkegaard sometimes suggests) since the rational mind continues to work within the new framework provided by the intuition and one's subsequent commitment.

Examples

You fall in love (intuition and risk), settle into a serious relationship (commitment) and subsequently reflect on why this has become important for you (rational thought).

You experience a particular religious event and suddenly feel that this is right for you (intuition and risk). You become a member of the religion (commitment). You are then challenged to examine and test out the beliefs of that religion against your general understanding of life (rational thought).

Martin Buber – the personal encounter

In *I and Thou* (1937) Martin Buber argued that we have two different kinds of relationships: I–It and I–Thou. I–It relationships are impersonal; what is encountered is seen in a detached, objective, functional or scientific way. By contrast, I–Thou relationships are personal. Imagine meeting a good friend – that encounter involves emotions and a personal sharing. Now imagine that the friend was a stranger for whom one felt nothing, and with whom one had had only the most superficial of contact; something has gone from that relationship. I–Thou has moved towards I–It.

For Buber the relationship with God was an I–Thou relationship, he described God as 'the Eternal Thou'. What is more, he saw this Eternal Thou as present in every other 'Thou' that we encounter.

Paul Tillich – two essential components

Tillich, writing in the 1950s, described two essential components of a religious experience: 'ultimate concern' and 'being itself'.

Being itself

When you encounter something, your senses distinguish it as having a particular size and shape, colour, sound, smell or texture. These things enable you to distinguish and describe what you see. They enable you to think and speak of it as one thing, or being, over and against others.

In a religious experience, this is generally not the case. It is not just an experience of a particular thing or being, but of 'being itself', or reality itself, encapsulated in this particular moment.

Suppose, for example, a person is religiously moved by a particular scene, perhaps a sunset. He or she feels in that moment that something of value and meaning has been glimpsed, life will never be the same again. It might (or might not) be described as an experience of 'God', but it is certainly **more than** the information about that sunset that a photograph could capture. Someone might argue that there was nothing religious about that experience – it was just a pleasant mixture of colours produced by the light of the sun on the clouds and upper atmosphere. The essential point is that – for it to be religious – that particular thing must point beyond itself.

> **In other words**
>
> For something to be a religious experience, it needs to be about 'being itself' (life itself; reality itself) rather than a particular being. This is of crucial importance when we come to think about what 'God' means in this context.

Ultimate concern

Everything we encounter has some place within our overall scheme of things. A stranger glimpsed for just a fleeting moment makes little impact on us; he or she does not dominate our lives. On the other hand, a good friend may have a lasting and profound impression on us. A parent or child may shape our lives quite fundamentally. In a sense, each of these things has a place on a scale of 'concerns': superficial, important, essential.

Tillich argued that, for something to be genuinely religious, the concern must be **ultimate**. If a person attends religious worship because of lack of other entertainment, or because he or she is lonely and hopes to make new friends, or because of a love of ritual or music, it might be enjoyable and valuable, but it is **not** religious. It lacks that quality of ultimate concern.

> **In other words**
>
> Something is only religious if it encounters us in an ultimate way, challenging the very significance and meaning of our lives.

In this section we have looked at five thinkers, each of whom gives a particular perspective on religious experience:

- for Schleiermacher: the Infinite is seen in and through the finite
- for Otto: an experience suddenly reveals its numinous quality
- for Kierkegaard: the experience is personally challenging and involves commitment
- for Buber: the Eternal Thou is encountered in a personal way
- for Tillich: religion is a matter of our 'ultimate concern' and the only suitable object of that concern is 'being itself', not particular beings.

Of course, all of these thinkers have a great deal to say, and this section has merely touched on some key features of their work. But cumulatively, they build up a sense of what is involved in religious experience.

For reflection

Notice that none of these thinkers make supernatural claims about the object of religious experience, but they all probe the depth and quality of experience to see how it is that it becomes 'religious'. None offers a 'proof' of any external 'God'.

Induced experiences

Experiences that occur unexpectedly, totally reshaping the course of a person's life, are the exception rather than the rule. Far more common is the general 'religious experience' that occurs in the context of the worship, prayer or other rituals which are practised by followers of the world's religions. These experiences are deliberately encouraged, or induced, by their religious setting, words or ritual actions.

Although these experiences are induced, they are not produced automatically. You cannot guarantee that two people attending the same religious event are going to respond in the same way, any more than you can guarantee that two people listening to the same music are going to be equally moved by it. Following what was said above about the nature of all experience, it would be more accurate to say that religious rituals provide sensations (often with interpretations attached) in the hope that the people taking part will feel an appropriate religious response.

Example

A gesture or a word may spontaneously lead someone to feel forgiven for a wrong they have done, be able to regain their self-respect and tackle life with a clearer conscience.

In the induced equivalent of this, the priest makes a ritual gesture, adding to it words of interpretation which suggest that those who are present should feel that their sins are forgiven. What cannot be guaranteed is that those present will **actually** feel forgiven. The total experience will therefore vary from person to person.

taste for the mystical side of religious experience
lady mystics:

of Bingen was a twelfth-century abbess who led a
of nuns living about 25 miles south of Mainz. She
amazing woman, a composer of beautiful plainsong
a poet, a visionary mystic and one who was
y concerned about the environment. She was a
ter both on religious topics and on natural history
ine. Here she describes herself as a feather on the
God:

there was once a king sitting on his throne.
him stood great and wonderfully beautiful
s ornamented with ivory, bearing the banners of
g with great honour. Then it pleased the king to
small feather from the ground and he commanded
y. The feather flew, not because of anything in itself
cause the air bore it along. Thus am I ...

an of Norwich, a fifteenth-century English mystic, had
called a sequence of 'showings' (visions in which she
hat Christ showed her spiritual truths). In one of them,
he world as a cared-for whole:

showed me a little thing, the size of a hazelnut,
seemed to lie in the palm of my hand; and it was
und as any ball. I looked upon it with the eye of my
rstanding, and thought, 'What may this be?' I was
ered in a general way, thus 'It is all that is made.' I
dered how long it could last; for it seemed as though
ght suddenly fade away to nothing, it was so small.
I was answered in my understanding: 'It lasts, and
shall last; for God loveth it. And even so hath
ything being – by the love of God.'

lly, mystics are all 'one-offs'. Mysticism is not something
n be organized. What is remarkable, however, is that
from very different cultural and religious backgrounds
great deal in common.

nystical experience, there is a sense that the normal
nce between the experiencing subject and the external
experienced is overcome. You become at one with what
e. Bede Griffiths described it as 'losing oneself in an abyss
e' (1989, p. 253).

Some religious actions look strange, others are clear visual symbols. Take, for example:

- lying prostrate on the floor in front of a religious image
- washing the head of an already clean baby
- rows of people facing the same direction and bowing together
- lighting incense sticks at a shrine
- shaving the head of a young boy.

One can see why such things might be powerful for those taking part, whilst recognizing that, for others who are not involved, they might appear embarrassing, quaint or plain daft. But how do you judge their value? If they are emotionally satisfying for those taking part, is that not validity enough?

If such actions claim to do no more than induce a religious experience, perhaps also giving a sense of personal well-being, then fair enough. If, however, it is claimed that some special knowledge of the world is achieved through them, then it is fair to look at any such claims and examine them rationally (and this is one of the tasks of the philosophy of religion).

We need to recognize, however, that such rational examination may achieve little by way of agreement between the religious believer and the philosopher, since the believer is quite likely to claim that what is experienced goes beyond the rational and cannot therefore be assessed in terms of it.

Prayer

Prayer is a feature of those religions that are based on a personal relationship between individuals and a God or gods. It may involve:

- confession
- thanksgiving and celebration
- intercession (petitionary prayer)
- prayers for guidance
- acts of submission
- meditation.

Where these things are simply an expression of a religious commitment, they cause no problems for the philosophy of religion. Confession, thanksgiving and acts of submission logically follow from a belief in God. They are an appropriate thing for a believer to do whether or not God *actually* exists; it is enough that the person *believes* that he does.

Equally, meditation (in which a person quietly focuses his or her attention on a particular object or concept, allowing it to influence the unconscious as well as the conscious mind) presents no fundamental problems. Nothing is being claimed by the act of meditation – it is simply a process of encouraging a particular quality of mind. Neither do prayers for guidance create problems – they simply express the wish of the individual to act in accordance with his or her religion.

All the above forms of prayer can be understood in terms of human activity, and can be seen as valid in themselves, quite apart from any supernatural element.

The main problem comes with petitionary prayer, which raises questions about the existence and nature of God. If a person prays for something to happen, it is reasonable to want to know if, subsequently, the thing for which they prayed did or did not in fact take place.

- If it did, was that the result of the prayer, or would it have happened anyway?
- If it did not, was it because the act of prayer was done wrongly (for example, with the wrong motive)? Or is there no God to hear and answer the prayer? If there is a God, and the prayer was done in a way that he would find appropriate, perhaps God did not want what the person wanted. (This last option is usually covered by a 'nevertheless thy will be done' clause in some prayers.)

But there is a moral and metaphysical dilemma here, which touches on matters we shall be exploring later in this book:

- If God is wise, just and omnipotent, he is willing and able to know and do what is best in each situation.
- To ask God to do something that he would not do anyway, therefore implies that one is asking him to do something unjust or unwise!
- Belief in a wise, just and omnipotent God therefore renders all petitionary prayer unnecessary.
- To claim that a prayer has been answered implies that God's intended action has been changed, which means that either God was not originally wise and just, or that he has now been persuaded by the prayer to do something unwise or unjust!

To avoid such problems, a [...] of petitionary prayer is not [...] remind the person praying o[...] she should be concerned. In [...] mind with God's, rather tha[...] one's own. **If this is the [...] psychologically and religiou[...] its words suggest it is doing.**

In this last section we have [...] observation of religious exper[...] issues that such experience rai[...] what the person praying actu[...] doing. The question 'Do you th[...] asked of a praying believer, wi[...] God's existence, power, wisdom[...]

Mysticism

A mystical experience is one in w[...] underlying unity of everything, b[...] barriers between oneself and the [...] our normal awareness of the lim[...] can produce a very deep sense of [...] universe, of being at one with nat[...] cannot be put into words. There i[...] in both Christianity and other relig[...]

Gregory of Nyssa, one of the theol[...] saw the human person as an ico[...] knowledge of oneself brings with [...] thought that it was necessary to die t[...] to get beyond the particular thing[...] 'logos' or divine word which lay [...] phenomenal world. In this, his views[...] the Stoics – Greek philosophers who[...] principle of reason both in the human [...] as a whole.

His view highlights two key feature[...] ultimate (God, where that language is [...] the self, and that there is a fundamenta[...] beneath the separate things that we [...] However, mystics tend to say that t[...] expressed or defined in any way.

Let us get [...] through tw[...]

Hildegaar[...] communit[...] was a mos[...] melodies,[...] passionate[...] prolific w[...] and medi[...] breath of [...]

Listen[...] Aroun[...] colum[...] the ki[...] raise [...] it to f[...] but b[...]

Lady Ju[...] what sh[...] believed[...] she sees[...]

... h[...] whic[...] as r[...] und[...] answ[...] wor[...] it m[...] An[...] eve[...] eve[...]

Gener[...] that c[...] mystic[...] have [...]

In a[...] differ[...] thing [...] you s[...] of lo[...]

There is also a sense in which what is seen cannot be fully described, and it is this that has led to the general claim that mystical experience is ineffable (unable to be rationally articulated or understood). Meister Eckhart (c.1260–1327), for example, described God as incomprehensible light.

In his *Varieties of Religious Experience*, William James gives four qualities associated with mystical experiences:

1 Ineffability (they defy description, and are quite different from ordinary experience)
2 Neotic quality (they seem to convey knowledge of some sort, even if it cannot be expressed)
3 Transiency (they cannot be sustained for long)
4 Passivity (the person who has a mystical experience feels that he or she has received something, rather than done something).

To these, F. C. Happold, in *Mysticism: a Study and an Anthology*, (1970) added other qualities:

• a sense of the unity of all things
• a sense of timelessness
• a sense that there is an immortal, unchanging self, and that our 'ego' is not our true self.

William James also mentions two familiar features: a feeling of having 'been here before', and with it a sense that what is seen is familiar, but also seeing that familiar thing for the very first time as it really is – seeing it in quite a new way.

The problem with mystical experience, at least as far as a philosopher is concerned, is that it is difficult to know how one would either prove or refute anything that a mystic said. If what is being described is a mental state, then it cannot be contradicted, any more than one could contradict a person who honestly said that he or she felt unhappy. Claims can only be shown to be true of false if they refer to empirical facts that can be checked – in other words, if they are objective. The problem is that, when you encounter something outside yourself, you get information through your senses, but your actual 'experience' of it also includes your interpretation of it and your emotional responses to it. Your total experience is neither objective nor subjective, it is **both**. Without something external there would be no experience; without interpretation and response, the sense data would be meaningless. This is particularly true for the mystical experience, where subject and object appear to blur.

Note

To explore this further, one might look at St John of the Cross (1542–91) or St Teresa of Avila (1512–82) as classical examples within the Christian tradition. Within Islam there is the Sufi tradition, and within Hinduism and Buddhism meditation techniques aim at overcoming the distinction between self and other – so much of what is termed 'mysticism' in the West is central to those traditions.

The mystical sense of identity between oneself and the whole of nature is also found in the ancient 'pagan' religions – Wicca (Witchcraft) for example. Here there is the awareness of a divine spirit in both male and female forms and reverence for the earth and its life. Rituals which celebrate the changing of the seasons, or which call upon the spirit of a place, lead the worshippers to feel their own spirit being identified with its surroundings in a warm and accepting way. Druids in particular have a sense that the landscape is sacred, and that people can open themselves up to that sacredness. Many pagan groups express this sense of oneness with nature through care of the environment. In nurturing the earth, they are also nurturing their inner spiritual selves.

Charismatic experiences

Charismatic experiences are those in which people are inspired and enthused to the extent that they feel taken over by a spiritual power that acts within them but which seems to come from beyond them. They include 'speaking in tongues' (speaking in an unknown language), going into trance states, the laying on of hands in healing, and other signs of being caught up in a power greater than the individual.

Within the faith community, these experiences are attributed to the direct action of the Holy Spirit and therefore a proof of the validity of the ministry of the church. External observers may try to explain the phenomena in psychological terms (perhaps as group hysteria) or as a form of hypnosis.

It is particularly difficult for philosophy to engage with charismatic experiences. This is because the experience itself is not rational; the person concerned is ecstatic, literally standing 'outside' himself or herself, having let go of normal rational controls. Like the mystical experience, the charismatic is one that, however powerful and transforming for the person having it, it is not a source for reasoned evidence or propositions. Hence, any claims are made on the basis of personal experience, not reason. If such claims purport to be statements of fact, they can be examined in the light of reason and evidence, but the result of such examination is unlikely to satisfy the charismatic believer.

What can we know?

So far in this chapter we have looked at some of the varieties of religious experience. Now, because we are dealing with the philosophy of religion rather than just looking at religion as a phenomenon, we need to consider what sort of knowledge can be gained by it, and particularly whether it can provide evidence for the existence of God. We shall first look at a religious interpretation and then at a non-religious one.

Revelation

Revelation is the term used for knowledge that, it is claimed, is given by supernatural agency. In other words, as a result of a religious experience, a person claims that God made something known to him or her.

Since religious experiences tend to be authoritative for those who have them, such 'revelation' tends to be superior to knowledge given by reason, since it is believed to be direct and immediate.

Note

There are two ways in which the verb 'to reveal' may be used:

1 I may chip away the plaster from a wall to 'reveal' the brickwork underneath.

2 I may choose to 'reveal' something personal about myself to a stranger.

Religious experiences may claim to include revelations of both sorts.

- Where a person claims that (through meditation, for example) that he or she has become more sensitive to spiritual things, it would be possible to say that religion had 'revealed' truths about life not previously known. This is the equivalent of chipping away conventional plaster in order to reveal a brickwork of deeper reality. The person practising the religion is the active agent in bringing this about.

- A person may believe that he or she has had a direct and personal encounter with God (or an angel, or some other spiritual being) in the course of which God has taken the initiative to 'reveal' something of himself. Examples of this are found in the scriptures of many religions.

Notice also that:

- The first of these does not require belief in any supernatural agent. It is just a way of showing that a person has been in a position to allow life to 'reveal' something that was not seen before.
- The second implies the existence of one or more independent, active, personal and supernatural beings.

In terms of the philosophy of religion, revelation raises several issues:

- Whatever the source of knowledge, something can only be articulated using words that have a commonly understood meaning. Once described or written down, a revelation takes the form of descriptions and propositions that can be assessed rationally, but that assessment may reveal as much about the limitations of language and logic as about the original revelatory experience.
- Whatever rational assessments are made, the power of the revelatory experience is such that the person is unlikely to be convinced by criticism. Indeed, the 'revelation' may become normative for critically evaluating the scope of human reason, not vice versa!
- The fact that something is known through revelation, does not logically preclude it from being known by reason alone, unless what is 'revealed' goes directly against reason, in which case philosophy will be unable to endorse or accept it.

A distinction is made between *natural theology* and *revealed theology*. The former is based on human reason; the latter on the self-disclosure of God – revelation. The claims of natural theology can be assessed by looking at evidence and the logic of the arguments used. Assessing revelation might require:

Some religious actions look strange, others are clear visual symbols. Take, for example:

- lying prostrate on the floor in front of a religious image
- washing the head of an already clean baby
- rows of people facing the same direction and bowing together
- lighting incense sticks at a shrine
- shaving the head of a young boy.

One can see why such things might be powerful for those taking part, whilst recognizing that, for others who are not involved, they might appear embarrassing, quaint or plain daft. But how do you judge their value? If they are emotionally satisfying for those taking part, is that not validity enough?

If such actions claim to do no more than induce a religious experience, perhaps also giving a sense of personal well-being, then fair enough. If, however, it is claimed that some special knowledge of the world is achieved through them, then it is fair to look at any such claims and examine them rationally (and this is one of the tasks of the philosophy of religion).

We need to recognize, however, that such rational examination may achieve little by way of agreement between the religious believer and the philosopher, since the believer is quite likely to claim that what is experienced goes beyond the rational and cannot therefore be assessed in terms of it.

Prayer

Prayer is a feature of those religions that are based on a personal relationship between individuals and a God or gods. It may involve:

- confession
- thanksgiving and celebration
- intercession (petitionary prayer)
- prayers for guidance
- acts of submission
- meditation.

Where these things are simply an expression of a religious commitment, they cause no problems for the philosophy of religion. Confession, thanksgiving and acts of submission logically follow from a belief in God. They are an appropriate thing for a believer to do whether or not God *actually* exists; it is enough that the person *believes* that he does.

Equally, meditation (in which a person quietly focuses his or her attention on a particular object or concept, allowing it to influence the unconscious as well as the conscious mind) presents no fundamental problems. Nothing is being claimed by the act of meditation – it is simply a process of encouraging a particular quality of mind. Neither do prayers for guidance create problems – they simply express the wish of the individual to act in accordance with his or her religion.

All the above forms of prayer can be understood in terms of human activity, and can be seen as valid in themselves, quite apart from any supernatural element.

The main problem comes with petitionary prayer, which raises questions about the existence and nature of God. If a person prays for something to happen, it is reasonable to want to know if, subsequently, the thing for which they prayed did or did not in fact take place.

- If it did, was that the result of the prayer, or would it have happened anyway?
- If it did not, was it because the act of prayer was done wrongly (for example, with the wrong motive)? Or is there no God to hear and answer the prayer? If there is a God, and the prayer was done in a way that he would find appropriate, perhaps God did not want what the person wanted. (This last option is usually covered by a 'nevertheless thy will be done' clause in some prayers.)

But there is a moral and metaphysical dilemma here, which touches on matters we shall be exploring later in this book:

- If God is wise, just and omnipotent, he is willing and able to know and do what is best in each situation.
- To ask God to do something that he would not do anyway, therefore implies that one is asking him to do something unjust or unwise!
- Belief in a wise, just and omnipotent God therefore renders all petitionary prayer unnecessary.
- To claim that a prayer has been answered implies that God's intended action has been changed, which means that either God was not originally wise and just, or that he has now been persuaded by the prayer to do something unwise or unjust!

To avoid such problems, a believer may claim that the purpose of petitionary prayer is not to change God's mind, but simply to remind the person praying of the crucial issues with which he or she should be concerned. In other words, it aims to align one's mind with God's, rather than trying to align God's mind with one's own. **If this is the case, petitionary prayer may be psychologically and religiously useful, but it does not do what its words suggest it is doing.**

In this last section we have moved quite deliberately from an observation of religious experience to the sort of philosophical issues that such experience raises. The important thing is to ask what the person praying actually thinks he or she is actually doing. The question 'Do you think you can change God's mind?' asked of a praying believer, will set the context for the issue of God's existence, power, wisdom and justice.

Mysticism

A mystical experience is one in which a person has a sense of the underlying unity of everything, breaking down all conventional barriers between oneself and the external world, going beyond our normal awareness of the limitations of time and space. It can produce a very deep sense of joy, of 'being at home' in the universe, of being at one with nature and of seeing a truth that cannot be put into words. There is a long history of mysticism in both Christianity and other religions.

Gregory of Nyssa, one of the theologians of the early Church, saw the human person as an icon of God – so that true knowledge of oneself brings with it knowledge of God. He thought that it was necessary to die to the senses (in other words to get beyond the particular things experienced) to see the 'logos' or divine word which lay beyond the whole of the phenomenal world. In this, his views were not far from those of the Stoics – Greek philosophers who saw a single fundamental principle of reason both in the human mind and in the universe as a whole.

His view highlights two key features of mysticism: that the ultimate (God, where that language is used) is reflected within the self, and that there is a fundamental unity to be experienced beneath the separate things that we ordinarily experience. However, mystics tend to say that the ultimate cannot be expressed or defined in any way.

Let us get a taste for the mystical side of religious experience through two lady mystics:

Hildegaard of Bingen was a twelfth-century abbess who led a community of nuns living about 25 miles south of Mainz. She was a most amazing woman, a composer of beautiful plainsong melodies, a poet, a visionary mystic and one who was passionately concerned about the environment. She was a prolific writer both on religious topics and on natural history and medicine. Here she describes herself as a feather on the breath of God:

> Listen: there was once a king sitting on his throne. Around him stood great and wonderfully beautiful columns ornamented with ivory, bearing the banners of the king with great honour. Then it pleased the king to raise a small feather from the ground and he commanded it to fly. The feather flew, not because of anything in itself but because the air bore it along. Thus am I ...

Lady Julian of Norwich, a fifteenth-century English mystic, had what she called a sequence of 'showings' (visions in which she believed that Christ showed her spiritual truths). In one of them, she sees the world as a cared-for whole:

> ... he showed me a little thing, the size of a hazelnut, which seemed to lie in the palm of my hand; and it was as round as any ball. I looked upon it with the eye of my understanding, and thought, 'What may this be?' I was answered in a general way, thus 'It is all that is made.' I wondered how long it could last; for it seemed as though it might suddenly fade away to nothing, it was so small. And I was answered in my understanding: 'It lasts, and ever shall last; for God loveth it. And even so hath everything being – by the love of God.'

Generally, mystics are all 'one-offs'. Mysticism is not something that can be organized. What is remarkable, however, is that mystics from very different cultural and religious backgrounds have a great deal in common.

In a mystical experience, there is a sense that the normal difference between the experiencing subject and the external thing experienced is overcome. You become at one with what you see. Bede Griffiths described it as 'losing oneself in an abyss of love' (1989, p. 253).

There is also a sense in which what is seen cannot be fully described, and it is this that has led to the general claim that mystical experience is ineffable (unable to be rationally articulated or understood). Meister Eckhart (c.1260–1327), for example, described God as incomprehensible light.

In his *Varieties of Religious Experience*, William James gives four qualities associated with mystical experiences:

1 Ineffability (they defy description, and are quite different from ordinary experience)
2 Neotic quality (they seem to convey knowledge of some sort, even if it cannot be expressed)
3 Transiency (they cannot be sustained for long)
4 Passivity (the person who has a mystical experience feels that he or she has received something, rather than done something).

To these, F. C. Happold, in *Mysticism: a Study and an Anthology*, (1970) added other qualities:

• a sense of the unity of all things
• a sense of timelessness
• a sense that there is an immortal, unchanging self, and that our 'ego' is not our true self.

William James also mentions two familiar features: a feeling of having 'been here before', and with it a sense that what is seen is familiar, but also seeing that familiar thing for the very first time as it really is – seeing it in quite a new way.

The problem with mystical experience, at least as far as a philosopher is concerned, is that it is difficult to know how one would either prove or refute anything that a mystic said. If what is being described is a mental state, then it cannot be contradicted, any more than one could contradict a person who honestly said that he or she felt unhappy. Claims can only be shown to be true of false if they refer to empirical facts that can be checked – in other words, if they are objective. The problem is that, when you encounter something outside yourself, you get information through your senses, but your actual 'experience' of it also includes your interpretation of it and your emotional responses to it. Your total experience is neither objective nor subjective, it is **both**. Without something external there would be no experience; without interpretation and response, the sense data would be meaningless. This is particularly true for the mystical experience, where subject and object appear to blur.

Note

To explore this further, one might look at St John of the Cross (1542–91) or St Teresa of Avila (1512–82) as classical examples within the Christian tradition. Within Islam there is the Sufi tradition, and within Hinduism and Buddhism meditation techniques aim at overcoming the distinction between self and other – so much of what is termed 'mysticism' in the West is central to those traditions.

The mystical sense of identity between oneself and the whole of nature is also found in the ancient 'pagan' religions – Wicca (Witchcraft) for example. Here there is the awareness of a divine spirit in both male and female forms and reverence for the earth and its life. Rituals which celebrate the changing of the seasons, or which call upon the spirit of a place, lead the worshippers to feel their own spirit being identified with its surroundings in a warm and accepting way. Druids in particular have a sense that the landscape is sacred, and that people can open themselves up to that sacredness. Many pagan groups express this sense of oneness with nature through care of the environment. In nurturing the earth, they are also nurturing their inner spiritual selves.

Charismatic experiences

Charismatic experiences are those in which people are inspired and enthused to the extent that they feel taken over by a spiritual power that acts within them but which seems to come from beyond them. They include 'speaking in tongues' (speaking in an unknown language), going into trance states, the laying on of hands in healing, and other signs of being caught up in a power greater than the individual.

Within the faith community, these experiences are attributed to the direct action of the Holy Spirit and therefore a proof of the validity of the ministry of the church. External observers may try to explain the phenomena in psychological terms (perhaps as group hysteria) or as a form of hypnosis.

It is particularly difficult for philosophy to engage with charismatic experiences. This is because the experience itself is not rational; the person concerned is ecstatic, literally standing 'outside' himself or herself, having let go of normal rational controls. Like the mystical experience, the charismatic is one that, however powerful and transforming for the person having it, it is not a source for reasoned evidence or propositions. Hence, any claims are made on the basis of personal experience, not reason. If such claims purport to be statements of fact, they can be examined in the light of reason and evidence, but the result of such examination is unlikely to satisfy the charismatic believer.

What can we know?

So far in this chapter we have looked at some of the varieties of religious experience. Now, because we are dealing with the philosophy of religion rather than just looking at religion as a phenomenon, we need to consider what sort of knowledge can be gained by it, and particularly whether it can provide evidence for the existence of God. We shall first look at a religious interpretation and then at a non-religious one.

Revelation

Revelation is the term used for knowledge that, it is claimed, is given by supernatural agency. In other words, as a result of a religious experience, a person claims that God made something known to him or her.

Since religious experiences tend to be authoritative for those who have them, such 'revelation' tends to be superior to knowledge given by reason, since it is believed to be direct and immediate.

Note

There are two ways in which the verb 'to reveal' may be used:

1 I may chip away the plaster from a wall to 'reveal' the brickwork underneath.
2 I may choose to 'reveal' something personal about myself to a stranger.

Religious experiences may claim to include revelations of both sorts.

- Where a person claims that (through meditation, for example) that he or she has become more sensitive to spiritual things, it would be possible to say that religion had 'revealed' truths about life not previously known. This is the equivalent of

---

chipping away conventional plaster in order to reveal a brickwork of deeper reality. The person practising the religion is the active agent in bringing this about.

- A person may believe that he or she has had a direct and personal encounter with God (or an angel, or some other spiritual being) in the course of which God has taken the initiative to 'reveal' something of himself. Examples of this are found in the scriptures of many religions.

Notice also that:

- The first of these does not require belief in any supernatural agent. It is just a way of showing that a person has been in a position to allow life to 'reveal' something that was not seen before.
- The second implies the existence of one or more independent, active, personal and supernatural beings.

In terms of the philosophy of religion, revelation raises several issues:

- Whatever the source of knowledge, something can only be articulated using words that have a commonly understood meaning. Once described or written down, a revelation takes the form of descriptions and propositions that can be assessed rationally, but that assessment may reveal as much about the limitations of language and logic as about the original revelatory experience.
- Whatever rational assessments are made, the power of the revelatory experience is such that the person is unlikely to be convinced by criticism. Indeed, the 'revelation' may become normative for critically evaluating the scope of human reason, not vice versa!
- The fact that something is known through revelation, does not logically preclude it from being known by reason alone, unless what is 'revealed' goes directly against reason, in which case philosophy will be unable to endorse or accept it.

A distinction is made between *natural theology* and *revealed theology*. The former is based on human reason; the latter on the self-disclosure of God – revelation. The claims of natural theology can be assessed by looking at evidence and the logic of the arguments used. Assessing revelation might require:

- seeing if what is 'revealed' is consistent with other religious beliefs
- seeing what the effect of the 'revelation' has been upon the person who has had it, and upon others
- seeing if there are any special circumstances which might lead a person to claim as a 'revelation' something produced within his or her unconscious mind.

An extreme example

A person arrested for a string of murders, claims in his defence that he was commanded by God to carry them out. You may wish to ask:

- Is the command to murder consistent with other beliefs about God?
- Is murder consistent with the overall religious view of life?
- Does this person have a history of mental illness involving hearing voices (for example, schizophrenia)?

But this last point raises another problem. In schizophrenia, voices that originate in a person's own mind become disowned, split off, and therefore appear to come from someone else. How could you distinguish between a voice produced by mental illness, and one that genuinely 'reveals' something? And what would 'genuine' mean in this context?

Mystics have sometimes claimed supernatural knowledge through visions and voices. St John of the Cross, a sixteenth-century Spanish mystic warns (in his *Ascent of Mount Carmel*) against attachment to visions and voices, pointing out that they could come from the Devil as well as from God, and that there was a danger that they could give rise to pride. He also pointed out that one could not have a direct experience of God in this life, since God was not like other things, having no genus or species – and thus could not be encountered in the ordinary way. This view guards against claims to 'know' God in any literal sense.

Progressive revelation

Whatever the source of 'revelation', once a person describes what is revealed, he or she must do so in the language and thought forms of the day. Even if the revelation itself were valid for all time, the words used would soon become dated.

> **Therefore**
> - In considering a revelation one might ask: What must they have experienced to have expressed it like that?
> - To identify a revelation with a particular set of words or concepts, rather than with the insight itself, is to kill it. To be devoted to the words and concepts used to describe a revelation in the past, is a form of spiritual necrophilia!

But if words and concepts change, what happens to revelation? One answer to this is termed 'progressive revelation'. This is the idea that something is revealed for a particular age and may be superseded by subsequent revelations, which do not negate the earlier one, but bring it up to date. Here are some examples:

- Christianity regards the Old Testament as a revelation that is only made complete by the teachings of Jesus.
- Islam sees both Judaism and Christianity as expressing the teachings of earlier prophets, leading up to the final revelation given to Muhammad.
- Mahayana Buddhism regards the earlier 'Hinayana' tradition as an incomplete first stage in Buddhist teaching, given because people were not yet ready for the final form, which was only made explicit in the Lotus Sutra.

This approach is used as a defence against earlier beliefs becoming untenable due to changes in culture and language. It has implications for religion and science, since modern science reveals a world that is very different from that known at the time when the major world religions were 'revealed'. In general, if it is claimed that revelations from an earlier age are still valid, there needs to be a recognition that *all descriptions* of what is revealed will be partial and transient.

Non-religious interpretations

Any religious experience may be analysed and 'explained' in terms that are not themselves religious. For example:

- Freud noted parallels between religious behaviour and those of his patients who had obsessional neuroses. Such a psychological interpretation may see religious rituals as repeated attempts to cleanse sexual guilt.

- Sociologists may point out the social function of religion. It may mark particular stages in life and acceptance of an individual into society. It may be a way of holding a society together and giving it an identity and sense of purpose.

But what do such interpretations achieve? There is an old quip: 'Just because you're paranoid, doesn't mean they're not out to get you!' This applies to all such non-religious interpretations. A religious ritual may be used by a society to affirm its identity or by an individual to overcome sexual neuroses, but that does not in itself provide an exhaustive explanation of the experience.

If, as was said earlier, the result of a religious experience may be a new way of looking at life, then we might well expect social cohesion and sexual health to follow it. Having found some benefit, an individual or a society might want to induce those religious experiences again, through performing religious rituals. At that point, the reason for doing it may indeed be to get the desired benefit; but that does not imply that the whole meaning of the original experience is explained in terms of that benefit, any more than travel from one place to another is a sufficient explanation of the way in which a motor car works.

It is also possible to give a non-religious explanation for events that are recorded as being of religious significance. For example, a person's unexpected recovery from a dangerous illness may be hailed by the religious person as a miracle. A non-religious person may suggest a medical explanation, or may conclude that there is no known reason – and, for the non-religious person, there is no *need* to give an explanation. Things happen as they do, some are explained, others are not. There is no logical reason to make the leap from the failure to give an adequate explanation in scientific terms, to concluding that some supernatural agency was involved. That would only count as a valid explanation for someone who was already willing to accept the existence of supernatural agents.

In other words, religion is a phenomenon, and any phenomenon can attract perfectly ordinary or scientific explanations. If that secular explanation is adequate, it does not automatically invalidate any supernatural explanation, but it does place the burden of proof on the believer.

Objective and subjective

The philosopher Descartes, in attempting to establish what he could know for certain, doubted the validity of all sense experience, but came to the famous conclusion that he could not doubt his own existence as a thinking being – *cogito ergo sum* (I think, therefore I am).

Since Descartes, there has been a tendency in Western thought to make a fundamental distinction between mind and matter, subject and object, the world of thought and the world of experience.

When someone asks if your experience is subjective or objective, they imply that it is either:

- a record of external facts, gathered through your senses; facts that may be verified independently and which are not dependent upon your own feelings and attitudes (objective)

or

- the product of your own mind or imagination (subjective).

But religious experience cannot be either exclusively objective or subjective. Something is experienced (objective), but what is experienced is a matter of interpretation (subjective). Two people could experience the same thing; for one it would be profound, moving and 'religious', for the other it could be a matter of little interest. **The subjective aspect of experience is just as 'real' for the experiencing subject as the objective aspect.**

Example

I listen to a boring talk. I may vaguely be aware of what the speaker is saying, but I am far more aware of my own boredom. Boredom is a major part of that experience for me, and it cannot be denied just because the person next to me is sitting forward in his seat hanging on every word.

Boredom, irritation and happiness are things of which we are certain. They are as real as any other part of our experience of life, although there is no external sense experience that corresponds to them.

Although the subjective aspect of an experience may be just as real as the objective for the person who has it, it is difficult to demonstrate that reality to others.

One way to do this is to evaluate the way in which the person has responded to the experience. We may ask if their life has been changed, for example, or whether they live by new values – both of which will illustrate the significance of the subjective experience.

Generally, however, the philosophy of religion is concerned with the claims to special knowledge made by those who have had such experiences. Hence it will examine such claims in the light of reason and evidence – in the attempt to ascertain whether belief that the claim is true can be justified. In other words, it is primarily concerned with the objective aspects of the experience.

Conclusion

Religious experience can give a **new perspective** on life. Contemplating the impermanent nature of things, the Buddha said of the body that it was like the froth of a wave, Lady Julian of Norwich saw the world as a small round object in the hand of God. Then there comes a **response**, a new sense of oneself and an experience of being changed, converted or enlightened.

In terms of the relationship between the experiencing person and that which he or she experiences, there are three distinct but essential qualities:

1 There is a sense of the 'otherness' of what is experienced. It is something 'holy'. It gives a tingle, a sense of wonder, a feeling that the ordinary mundane world is small, limited in its scope and values, cut off from something far richer.

2 At the same time, there is a feeling of dependence – that the ordinary world is in some way resting on or rooted in something deeper. The religious experience is not of something 'out there', but of something 'within' and 'deep'.

3 The movement from the first to the second of these features continues into the third – a sense of being at one with the holy and the divine. Particularly with mysticism, as we saw above, but in all religions, there is the sense of God being within the self, or of the self being within God. There is, I believe, a Muslim saying: 'Allah is nearer to a man than his own breath.'

One way of expressing all this is to say that life is *self-transcending*. A particular thing, person or situation, may take on meaning beyond itself, may reveal something of Life itself (Truth itself, Being itself).

Let the last word on religious experience be with a poet rather than a philosopher. In Wordsworth's lines composed a few miles above Tintern Abbey he describes the energy of his earlier enthusiasm for nature and the way in which this has given way to something deeper:

> For I have learned
> To look on nature, not as in the hour
> Of thoughtless youth; but hearing often-times
> The still, sad music of humanity,
> Nor harsh nor grating, though of ample power
> To chasten and subdue. And I have felt
> A presence that disturbs me with the joy
> Of elevated thoughts; a sense sublime
> Of something far more deeply interfused,
> Whose dwelling is the light of setting suns,
> And the round ocean and the living air,
> And the blue sky, and in the mind of man;
> A motion and a spirit, that impels
> All thinking things, all objects of all thought,
> And rolls through all things.
> Therefore am I still
> A lover of the meadows and the woods,
> And mountains; and of all that we behold
> From this green earth; of all the mighty world
> Of eye, and ear – both what they half create,
> And what perceive; well pleased to recognize
> In nature and the language of the sense,
> The anchor of my purest thoughts, the nurse,
> The guide, the guardian of my heart, and soul
> Of all my moral being.

Here, nature is experienced as self-transcending – leading the mind to that which is 'far more deeply interfused'. Here is the raw material of religious experience.

Where does all this lead?

In his book *An Introduction to the Philosophy of Religion*, Brian Davies introduces religious experience after a consideration of the traditional arguments for the existence of God. His purpose in introducing it is given thus:

The question currently at issue is therefore this: does experience tell a reasonable man that God exists?

(p. 64)

In other words, having established what God is, he asks if religious experience can be used for evidence of his existence.

This is definitely **not** the approach taken in this present book. The questions we have been considering are:

• What is it in experience to which people ascribe the term 'God'?
• What has given rise to such a concept?
• What sustains people's interest in it?

Whereas Davies therefore considers objections to admitting experience as a valid argument for the existence of God, we need not concern ourselves about this. Even though experience is always ambiguous (and thus two people may experience the same thing in different ways) **it is nevertheless from the interpretation of this ambiguous experience that religion has developed.**

Religious beliefs continue, not because some intellectual conclusion has been reached about their validity, but because people benefit from them. One could say (following a line of argument taken by William James) that beliefs do not work because they are true, but that they are true because they work.

Of course, religious experience remains a private affair until someone attempts to describe it. This leads into the subject of the next chapter – religious language. But, as we examine it, we should be looking for those theories of religious language that allow this self-transcending quality of the religious experience to emerge. In other words, we should be looking for self-transcending language.

02 religious language

In this chapter you will:
- examine the different kinds of language used in religion
- explore the meaning of myth and symbol
- consider how religious language can best be interpreted.

In this chapter we shall be asking:

- What is the nature and status of religious language?
- Can a claim to religious knowledge be shown to be true or false?
- What function does religious language perform, and what are its limitations?

Anyone who wants to explain religion must use such languages and concepts as are available. This means that religious experience, once described, starts to be filtered through language and coloured by it. People are likely to experience things in a way that reflects their own culture – for every act of awareness takes with it a set of presuppositions and ways of looking. So it is **vital, in looking at religious beliefs, to appreciate the role that language plays in formulating those beliefs.**

Comment

You could argue that there is no such thing as religious language. There is simply language that is used for particular purposes – in this case, to express or describe religious experiences, practices or beliefs. How could the words used to articulate religious beliefs communicate anything if they did not have an ordinary, non-religious meaning?

Take the words 'revelation', 'transubstantiation' or 'incarnation'. Each of these has a very specific meaning within religion, and can form part of a religious argument. Yet none is simply a description of something with which science could deal. You cannot point to 'incarnation' in the way you might point to 'man' or 'tree', for something more than empirical evidence is needed to make sense of them. In order to communicate, each must therefore be defined in terms of other words – words that can be understood **outside** the religious context. Without some secular and universally understood words of explanation, religious terms are meaningless.

A private language?

Can there be such a thing as private language? You could mutter to yourself words that mean absolutely nothing to anyone else, and claim to know what they mean. But would that be a language? Indeed, Wittgenstein argued in *Philosophical*

Investigations that such a language would not be understood even by the speaker, for there would be no way of establishing meaning for its words – but that is debatable and beyond our present concern.

All we need to recognize is that language is about communication, and communication only takes place when two or more people use words and ideas that they have in common. If you devise your own language, you will not be able to communicate. Translating your private language will require you to use terms that others understand in order to give a shared equivalent of your private concepts.

There is a lot more that philosophers have to say on this matter, but for the purposes of the philosophy of religion, it is enough to notice that **religious language is used to express and communicate religion, and it cannot do this if it is private.**

Although this may seem obvious, it raises a crucial question: How does the 'religious' meaning of a word relate to its wider (non-religious) meaning?

For example, 'forgiveness' is a term used in religion, and it is understood because people know what it is to forgive and be forgiven in a normal human context. Thus the idea of a God who 'forgives' makes sense. But what of a word like 'God'? Can it be explained in terms that at least make sense to an atheist or sceptic? If not, does that word convey anything?

Comment

This is a serious issue for religious language. Two people may both use the term 'God' but may mean quite different things by it. One person may take it to refer to an objectively existing reality, capable of interacting directly with the physical universe. Another might reject that idea entirely, but still want to claim to believe in 'God' in a more personal or subjective sense.

You cannot have a sound argument until the meaning of the terms under discussion has been defined – or until the possibly conflicting definitions have been outlined and contrasted.

Knowledge and description

Some forms of language used in religion cause no problem whatever. For example, take the statement: 'Catholic priests usually wear vestments when conducting Mass.'

The word 'usually' covers any special occasions where Mass will be celebrated informally without vestments, or where Communion is given in extreme circumstances and it would not be expected that a priest could put his vestments on. Other than that the statement is purely factual. As long as you know what the terms mean, you could easily get evidence to prove that it is either true or false.

The reason there is no problem here is that the statement is *descriptive*. The test of its truth is empirical – just check the facts.

But what if a person says: 'I have just witnessed a miracle.' The truth of this may depend on what that person means by miracle, on the reliability of their senses (since they could have been mistaken) and on the way they have interpreted what happened. Someone might hear all the details and reply 'I appreciate what you saw and how you understood it, but I would not have called that a miracle.'

The issue here is that the statement claims to give knowledge which depends on a person's *interpretation* of facts. A miracle is not just a miracle, it is always something else as well! Therefore a person who does not believe in miracles will seek an interpretation of that 'something else' – be it an unexpected cure of a disease or avoiding an accident – in non-miraculous terms.

Nor will any additional evidence decide the matter one way or the other, simply because each person will interpret that evidence in the light of his or her prior idea about whether or not an event can count as a miracle.

Let us examine two other statements: 'I believe in God' and 'God exists'. These are by no means the same. The first can be right and the second wrong, or vice versa. Just because someone believes something, it does not mean that it is the case. The first is a description of what someone believes; the second is a claim to knowledge.

If religious people did no more than describe the observable features of their religion, and comment in a detached way on their own beliefs, there would be no problem. The problem arises when they make what amount to factual claims about the object of their beliefs – in other words, claims about God, or miracles, or about anything 'supernatural' and therefore beyond the normal bounds of scientific investigation.

Note

Much philosophy in the twentieth century was concerned with language. Indeed, many philosophers have seen the whole task of philosophy as one of examining language – so that political philosophy, for example, is not about politics (it doesn't tell you which way to vote) but about the meaning of political language, for example, 'What is democracy?'

That approach would limit the philosophy of religion entirely to a consideration of the meaning and use of religious language. Interesting though that might be, most people expect philosophy to help people reach conclusions about what is real, or what it is reasonable to believe, and that it should relate the subject under scrutiny (i.e. religion) to more general ideas about the world.

If it is to make any sense, religious language needs to break out of the closed loop of religious meanings, and explain itself in terms that may be universally understood. The philosophy of religion cannot therefore limit itself to describing religious language, but must try to give some account of that to which such language refers.

Faith, reason and belief

Once you reflect upon religious beliefs, however, you need concepts, and to use your reason to sort them out and relate them to one another.

- You can remember something without concepts, but you cannot think about it without concepts.
- You can paint a picture of something without concepts, but you cannot describe it without concepts.

As soon as religion gets beyond the area of personal religious experience, it encounters human reason. Once it does so, the result is language. The religious experience starts to be 'schematized' (to use Otto's term) in terms of concepts, ideas and beliefs.

Reason may contribute two things here:

- It may examine the logic of a statement. Does it make sense? If it does, fine. If not, are the words being used in an unusual way? Is there any other way in which the statement can be interpreted?
- It can look to see if this particular claim is compatible with the rest of a person's experience of life, and therefore come to a view about the likelihood of a statement being true or false. Which is more likely, that this is true or that I have been mistaken?

Experience, expressed through language, leads to propositions – statements about what is the case. Propositions that a person accepts as being true are the basis of his or her 'beliefs'. If you say 'I believe in God' it implies that you accept the proposition 'There is a God' as being true.

In other words

The philosophy of religion examines the logic and general coherence of religious statements and, by comparing such statements with other widely-held beliefs about life, assesses the appropriateness of accepting them as true.

But is it possible to have knowledge of God, for example, through reason alone? Is it possible to give a rational explanation of the meaning of 'God'? The view that human reason is incapable of knowledge of God, and therefore that God can only be known through faith or revelation, is termed **fideism**. Some Protestant Christians take the view that human nature – and therefore human reason – is 'fallen' and therefore inherently incapable of knowing God.

'Believing in' and 'believing that'

Faith is a matter of personal commitment and trust. A person's faith is not to be equated with a list of the things that he or she claims to believe. It includes them, or course, but it is more than that, for it describes the way in which he or she relates to them.

This can be expressed in terms of the difference between **believing that** something is true and **believing in** something. If you 'believe in' something, it implies commitment and trust. Believing 'that' something is true simply means that you think the statement is correct, whether or not it is of any personal interest to you. So, for example 'I believe that God exists' may be the logical conclusion of an argument, but does not imply that a person is in any way influenced by that belief, whereas 'I believe in God' implies that a person has a personal relationship with God, or at least believes that God in some way matters.

Experience 'as'

Whatever we experience, we interpret. Things are not just experienced, but experienced 'as' something. This aspect of religious language has been clearly set out by John Hick (for example, in 'Religious Faith as Experiencing-As' in *Talk of God*, Royal Institute of Philosophy Lectures, 1969) and it follows the work of Wittgenstein in his *Philosophical Investigations* (see also below p. 51).

It is best illustrated by the various visual puzzles in which the same image can be interpreted in two different ways. Best known ones include a duck that appears as a rabbit, a young woman that is also an old crone and a ornate chalice that become the silhouette of two people facing one another. There is no evidence to decide between the interpretations, it is simply a matter of choice, but considerable mental effort is required to shift one's view from one to the other.

The implication of this is that the religious way of interpreting the world is one valid 'blik' (view) alongside others. A person who has such a religious blik will interpret what is actually experienced in the light of it.

But what makes one person interpret a shape as that of a duck and another as a rabbit? What makes one person a theist and another an atheist? Their experience of the world (i.e. the sense impressions they receive) will be the same, so why do they interpret it differently?

The rational and the non-rational

There have been times when a rational approach to religion has been much in favour. So, for example, from the second to the fourth centuries of the Christian era, there were heated debates about Christian doctrine. It was the period during which the Creeds were formulated, and differences in wording (with the implied differences in meaning) were the cause of serious strife between members of different groups. Those who disagreed with the majority (or those with official backing) tended to be branded as heretics. But the language used would have been equally familiar to a secular Stoic philosopher and a Christian theologian.

Similarly in the thirteenth century there was a flowering of interest in Greek thought, and Aquinas set Christian doctrine within a scheme of thought derived largely from Aristotle, and using the best philosophical ideas available in the secular universities of his day.

In the eighteenth century, following the rise of modern science, there was once again a quest to present Christianity in a way that was acceptable to those for whom rational coherence was almost the sole criterion of truth, stripping it of superstitious and supernatural trappings.

In their different ways, each of these periods recognized the value of rational thought, and therefore sought to articulate religion using the best available philosophy.

Today the situation is rather different. In the early twentieth century there was a philosophical movement (**Logical Positivism**) that took the scientific, descriptive language and proof as the norm, and dismissed every statement whose truth or falsity could not be established either by logic or by reference to empirical facts as 'meaningless'. In response to that challenge, some religious thinkers sought to give a rational and non-literal interpretation of religious beliefs. Others sought to defend the literal truth of belief in the supernatural, even though such beliefs could be seen as irrational.

But what does it mean to say that something is rational?

Basically, the rational process is one in which conclusions are drawn from premises by a sequence of mental steps which can be followed, verified, and which others (provided they understood the meaning of the words used) would accept as being true – and true for everyone, not just for that particular individual.

Where then does this leave the complex web of elements that make up a religious experience? Can a religious experience be described in a rational way? Clearly, for there to be an experience at all there must be some empirical basis; for something to be experienced, the senses must be stimulated in some way.

But for an experience to be religious, it cannot be confined to that empirical basis, for otherwise it would just be a scientific description of what is seen or heard, with nothing to make it 'religious' or to convey anything of its importance and power. It is therefore important to recognize that religion can never be fully explained in terms that would satisfy a scientific observer, but nor can any scientific or rationalist interpretation of the evidence claim to be exhaustive. There is generally a 'something more' that eludes description. This does not go against reason (which would make it irrational) so much as *beyond* reason – taking a step which cannot be proved by logic or evidence, but which a person feels compelled to make.

Comment

Trying to understand a religion by rational means alone is rather like attempting to find a mate be means of a dating agency. It can sort out some of the basic groundwork for you, but unless you find in your computer-selected partner some spark of emotion, some willingness to take a risk, a leap beyond what is reasonable, you are hardly likely to embark on the most passionate relationship of your life!

Religions vary in the importance they place on a rational approach to belief:

- Of all the religions, **Christianity** is the most creedal. It attempts to define and explain what is to be believed. Although it accepts the non-rational (for example, in mystical experience) it keeps it in careful check.
- **Islam** too is concerned that its key doctrines are accepted universally. To do this it has to present its views in a rationally coherent form: all Muslims are expected to believe the same things and have the same confession of faith.

- When it comes to **Judaism**, there is more flexibility – with some basic tenets of belief, but also a wealth of rules for living the religious life. Judaism is a rich tradition, sometimes rational, sometimes poetic, rooting the spiritual in the physical stuff of life and emphasizing that spirituality is not simply a matter of the rational acceptance of beliefs, but a total way of life.

- **Hindu** religious traditions have a wealth of material that goes beyond the rational. This is seen in the great variety of its worship and in the colourful stories of its scriptures. On the other hand, Hinduism has not been without its rational, philosophical systems, for example, in the Upanishads.

- **Buddhism** too welcomes a balance between the rational and the non-rational. In this case, the rational approach is encouraged, and every follower is to test out teachings to see if they are able to be confirmed in his or her own experience. On the other hand, meditation and devotion, the chanting of mantras and ritual performances (especially within the Mahayana/Tibetan traditions) go beyond the rational.

For the purpose of our understanding of religious language, all we need to appreciate here is that religions present a balance between the rational and the non-rational. Without the former, nothing of the beliefs could be communicated. Without the latter, nothing of the power of the religion would be effectively conveyed.

Cognitive and non-cognitive

Language can perform many functions. It can describe what is experienced; indicate a particular emotion; express a preference; give a command; make a request. It can be the exuberant expression of joy – yelled in words with no meaning – or a vehicle of the deepest grief, where a name of one who has died or is lost is repeated over and over, conveying a lifetime of shared experience and of sudden isolation.

Some of these uses of language are **cognitive**, i.e. they convey information. Others are non-cognitive. So, for example, some utterances are described as '**performative**' in that they affect something by being used. When you marry, or take an oath in court, or agree to buy goods in a shop, your words are performative. 'Stop!' is not a statement of fact, to be analysed and proved right or wrong. In itself it is not cognitive – but it may be a matter of life or death!

Comments

If all language were of the cognitive variety, we would become overloaded with information but get nothing done!

Performative utterances are neither right nor wrong – they simply get things done!

Equally, we use language to express our own emotions and preferences, rather than to describe the external world. A. J. Ayer, while arguing that moral and religious language was meaningless, since it could not be verified by sense experience, suggested that it actually expressed the emotions and desires of the person using it. In other words, what appeared to be statements about objective, external realities were, according to Ayer, subjective, and therefore non-cognitive. This is called the 'emotive' theory of language. It is also possible to see moral language about right and wrong as a way of 'prescribing' one particular course of action rather than another.

Example

According to these theories, the statement 'This is right' would mean:

- In emotive terms – 'I like this.'
- In prescriptive terms – 'I want you to do this.'

These suggest that moral statements are non-cognitive. On the other hand, someone might want to claim that it is possible to base moral statements on pure reason or on some feature of the world, so that 'This is right' gave factual information. The crucial thing is to recognize that – whether based on fact or not – a moral statement is always **more than** a description.

So where does this leave us? Descriptions of religion are cognitive but uncontentious – you can always go and look and check if they are correct. But what of statements of religious belief? When someone claims to believe in God, or in miracles, or life after death, are they making a straightforward cognitive, factual statement?

In order to judge that, we need to examine how the language they use is to be interpreted, for we cannot simply assume that all language attempts to picture the world in a literal way.

Interpreting language

We now turn to various ways in which religious language may be understood and interpreted. It is essential to do this if we are to be able to judge whether a religious claim is true, and in what sense it may be true.

A literal picture?

The most straightforward use of language is as a means of literally picturing the world and giving information about it. Each word I use stands for something in my experience. A statement like 'There is a tree in my garden' is true or false to the extent that a person who understands the meaning of the words 'tree' and 'garden' can go and check if it is so.

David Hume (1711–76) in *An Enquiry Concerning Human Understanding* allows only two kinds of meaningful statement: abstract reasoning concerning quantity or number; experimental reasoning concerning matters of fact. In other words, all knowledge of the external world is based on sense experience – the 'matters of fact'.

Analytic and synthetic statements

Statements may be divided into two kinds – analytic and synthetic. An analytic statement simply unpacks the meaning of its own terms. The statement 'Two plus two equals four' is analytic. You don't have to go checking examples in order to prove it correct! A synthetic statement refers to external evidence. 'The cat is outside the door' is synthetic. No detailed explanation of the meaning of 'cat' or 'door' can ever prove the matter one way or the other – you have to go and look.

When it comes to a theory of knowledge, you can divide philosophers into two groups: those (like Hume) who base all knowledge on sense experience, and those (like Kant) who base it on the structures of thought by which we are able to experience and understand things. These two groups are generally referred to as **empiricists** and **idealists** respectively. It is the empirical tradition of philosophy which has emphasized the literal picturing function of language – because empiricist philosophers want to relate everything that is said to the 'facts' as they can be experienced.

The narrowest view of what constituted a meaningful proposition was developed in the 1920s by a group of philosophers known as the Vienna Circle. They produced a theory of meaning called the Verification Principle: that the meaning of a statement was its method of verification. Their ideas were influenced by the earlier work of Ludwig Wittgenstein (1889–1951) who had set out a radical view of the limitations of what we can know in a book called *Tractatus Logico-Philosophicus*, published in 1921.

Wittgenstein argued that the function of language is to picture the world. Something is said to be true if, on observation of the reality to which the statement refers, it is found to be the case. It is false if the evidence is against it. Truth is established by empirical verification.

Not everything can be checked. 'I saw your cat last night' is a statement that cannot now be verified. But it still has a basis in observation. What it means, in effect, is that if you had been where I was last night, you would have seen your cat.

This approach to language and its verification became known as Logical Positivism. Those things for which there was no means of empirical verification it considered meaningless.

The work of the Vienna Circle was made widely known by A. J. Ayer with the publication of his book *Language, Truth and Logic* in 1936. The impact on the philosophy of religion was quite traumatic, for what Ayer and the Vienna Circle was saying was not just that God did not exist, but that all talk about God was meaningless:

> No sentence which purports to describe the nature of a transcendent God can possess any literal significance.

> (p. 115)

For Ayer, the statement 'God exists' cannot be either true or false, because there is no empirical evidence that can be produced to prove the matter one way or the other.

This did not threaten all language about religion. Much is intended to be taken literally and causes no problems. 'Some priests wear black robes', for example, is simply *descriptive*, and can be verified by observation.

Note

The Logical Positivists of the Vienna Circle originally proposed what is termed the 'strong form' of the *verification principle*. This claimed that the meaning of a statement is identical with its method of verification.

It was soon recognized, however, that this was too limited. There were statements that could not be verified directly, but which nevertheless dealt with things that might be experienced, if circumstances permitted (going back in time, for example). This led to what is known as the 'weak form' of the verification principle: that, for a statement to be meaningful, it must be possible to say what evidence could count for or against it being true. It was this form that A. J. Ayer expounded.

One common criticism of the verification principle is that it cannot itself be verified. It is not analytic, so it cannot be shown to be true on logical grounds. Nor is there any piece of evidence that can count for or against its truth – a statement about what counts as factual or meaningful is not itself a picture of some sense experience. By its own argument it is therefore meaningless. But this criticism fails to recognize that the verification principle is not making a *factual* claim at all, but simply recommending the way in which such claims should be understood.

In many ways, the arguments of the Logical Positivists have not so much been refuted as bypassed. Towards the middle of the twentieth century, especially under the influence of later developments of Wittgenstein's work, there was a growing recognition that giving a literal representation of the world was a small part of the task of language, and that its many other functions (giving commands, expressing emotions, creating symbolic images, making jokes or caricatures) required a very different approach.

True or false?

In *New Essays in Philosophical Theology*, published in 1955, Anthony Flew presented a story (originally devised by John Wisdom) to examine the limits to which one could go in qualifying a statement whilst claiming that it was true.

In the story, two explorers come across a clearing in the jungle which has a mixture of flowers and weeds. One claims that there is a gardener who comes to tend it, the other thinks there is not. No gardener appears, so they set various tests to check for the presence of this invisible gardener.

In the end, the one explorer still thinks that there is a gardener – but an invisible, intangible, silent gardener who is insensitive to electric shocks and is in all other ways undetectable. The other, in despair, cannot see what the difference is between such a gardener and an imaginary gardener or no gardener at all! Hence, the claim that there is a gardener 'dies the death of a thousand qualifications'.

Clearly, the same thing happens with God. The claim that there is a God is qualified until nothing significant remains.

Several key themes have come out of this story and the discussions that followed its publication:

- Experience involves interpretation (as we saw in the first chapter). One explorer interprets the clearing as a garden, the other does not. Facts alone do not determine how something is interpreted.
- One's interpretation leads to a commitment. One chooses to see the world in a particular way, and is committed to that view, and that influences the way subsequent evidence is assessed. The one explorer is reluctant to let go of the claim that there is a gardener because, for him, it has become a matter of faith rather than just a hypothesis.
- The story implies that what is 'real' is what can be described literally – since the 'gardener' dies the death of becoming less and less literally a gardener. But when applied to God, many believers would say that a God who existed in a literal way (and therefore alongside other things that exist in the world) would not be the sort of God they are talking about. In the last chapter we saw, for example, that God could be described as 'being itself' rather than as 'a being'.

The limits of the literal

There are always problems when religious language is taken as literal. Here, the radical theologian Don Cupitt comments on the limitation of literal language:

> The critics urge that we should always give straight answers and admit what we believe. But I am saying that there is no such thing as literal truth and no such thing as

'the real meaning' of any text... Religious terms do not stand for, label or copy religious objects. Religion consists in a change in the way in which we see everything, a change in our whole life.

(*Radicals and the Future of the Church*, p. 111)

This point is absolutely central to a balanced understanding about religious language, and particularly language about 'God'. It would be very convenient for the atheist position if theists believed that God existed in the same way that individual physical objects exist. Refuting the logic or evidence for such a god would not take long!

However, as we shall see in the next chapter, such a god is certainly not what most thinking theists mean by the term 'God', and its dismissal does not really achieve much. But note that Cupitt's argument reflects what we have been exploring in terms of religious experience and language. It is *not* about particular things for which we might seek physical evidence. It is about a way of understanding life as a whole and its significance. That is not the sort of thing that can be evidenced by using literal language – for if it did not go *beyond* the literal and physical, it would not be religious.

Analogy

Particularly as a result of the influence of Thomas Aquinas, analogy has been important in the attempt to say positive things about God. When the same word is used to describe different things, its use may be univocal, equivocal or analogical:

- Univocal – I wear white shoes and a white hat. The word 'white' is used univocally; it has exactly the same meaning in each case.
- Equivocal – I have apple tart for dessert. If it lacks sweetness, I may describe it as a little tart, in quite another sense. Neither relates to my colloquial description of that young lady in a short skirt! The three 'tarts' are equivocal, having quite different meanings.
- Analogical – On a black night I may be in a mood that could (analogically) be described as 'black'. Or, to persist with the 'tart' example given above, the one might be tasty and the other might look tasty – which would be an analogical use of 'tasty', unless of course you were being intimately or cannibalistically univocal!

Clearly, univocal language is inadequate to describe God – for that would presuppose God to be a physical and limited thing, which theists do not accept. Equally, equivocal language achieves nothing, since any word used equivocally needs to be redefined before it can be understood, and therefore it conveys no new information.

That leaves us with analogy, and Aquinas argues for two kinds:

The **analogy of attribution** suggest that, if God is creator, then his creation will reflect his own qualities. Hence, if we know what it is to call a human being 'good' we must assume that we can use the term 'good' in analogous sense of his or her creator.

The **analogy of proportionality** argues that the meaning of a term is proportional to the nature of that which it describes. Hence – to continue the example given above – God can be expected to be 'good' in a way that reflects an infinite and all-powerful nature, whereas a human being is 'good' in a way that reflects a limited human nature.

Rudolph Otto (see above p. 11) argued that, in order to describe an experience of the numinous, we 'schematize' it – in other words, we find a set of words that most closely approach what has been experienced. This endorses analogy. We try to find words that reflect the nearest literal understanding we can find to that which – by definition, and according to accounts of religious experience – is really beyond description. Analogy is an attempt to bridge the gap between saying something literal and therefore false, and saying nothing at all.

Models and qualifiers

The language through which religious experience and insight is expressed will always be the common property of the culture within which it takes place. But words that are common property may have meanings which do not do justice to the thing being described. 'It is a bit like this, but more so ...!'

In *Religious Language* (1957) I. T. Ramsey used the terms **models** and **qualifiers** to explain the way in which religious language differs from literal, empirically based language.

A 'model' is a form of analogy – an image that helps a person to express what has been experienced. For example, if God is called a 'designer', it does not imply that the believer has some personal knowledge of a process of design carried out by God, simply that the image of human designers' relationship with their products is something like his or her sense of the relationship between God and the world.

On the other hand, having offered the 'model' it is then important to offer a 'qualifier' – God is an 'infinite' this, or a 'perfect' that. The model needs to be qualified, so that it is not mistakenly understood in a literal way.

In other words

If 'God' is described as 'Eternal Father': 'father' is the model, with all the overtones that experience of actual fathers brings to the concept; 'eternal' is the qualifier, making sure that the idea of father is transcended.

- Without models, nothing would be communicated.
- Without qualifiers, nothing would get beyond a literal description.

Symbolism

What is a religious symbol, and how does it work?

We need to distinguish between a sign and a symbol. A sign is something that points to something else. It can be conventional (like road signs); you can change one sign for another, as long as everyone agrees what it stands for. By contrast, a symbol is something that evolves and expresses and makes real the power of that which it symbolizes.

Example

A person waves the flag of his or her country: it becomes a symbol of patriotic feelings. Burning a flag is a great act of political defiance. It is not just a matter of burning a piece of cloth that happens to have a particular design on it; it is a sign of wishing to destroy the country and all that it stands for.

The theologian Paul Tillich held that religious symbols are the only means to pointing beyond individual beings to that which is 'being itself' (see above p. 14) for you cannot show 'being itself' directly. Equally, he held that a symbol is religious if it shows a person's ultimate concern.

Religion is about particular things, situations or people which reveal 'being itself' and which become a matter of 'ultimate concern' for us. Now these things become symbols, they point beyond themselves. **They also give rise to symbolic language, because the description of them, if it is to reflect the original experience, must also move beyond the literal meaning of the words used.**

At the end of Chapter 01, religious experience was described in terms of the 'self-transcending' quality of life. The religious symbol is the linguistic equivalent of this. It transcends its own literal meaning.

Myth

Myths are stories that express aspects of human self-awareness. Thus, some of the earliest myths are about creation, or about the expectation of life beyond death or of the end of the world. They present a range of symbols in a narrative form.

Myth should not be reduced to a literal form of language. In its literal meaning, a myth may or may not be true; that is relatively unimportant. What makes it a myth is the meaning that is conveyed through the narrative and the symbols it introduces. Myths, like individual symbols, or like poetry or fiction, can present many layers of meaning and have a power that is destroyed once it is taken apart and examined literally.

Language games

We have moved from literal to analogical language, and noted the way in which models and qualifiers influence religious description, and also the way in which language, like experience itself, can become self-transcending in the religious symbol.

We have also noted the way in which experience is 'schematized' in a particular language and philosophy and that (since all experience is 'experience as') description includes interpretation.

But so far we have only looked at cognitive language – language that attempts to describe the object of religious experience and devotion. In fact, language performs many other functions, and to these we must now turn.

For reflection

If you want to describe a moment of insight, you need to use words and concepts with which your hearers are familiar. You are starting to 'schematize' your experience (to use Otto's term). You are also starting to place it within a particular language, philosophy and social setting.

Later, other people will be able to look at your description and, on the basis of the words you have used, compare it with the thoughts and insights of others. What they cannot do is to get back behind the schema and reconstruct the actual moment of insight itself, free from the words that interpret it.

Except, perhaps, when reading a description, someone suddenly gets a tingle of excitement. Something in them says 'Yes, that's exactly how it is' – not because the words are logically compelling or soundly based, but because of an intuition that this description is of an experience parallel to their own.

In his earlier work (*Tractatus*) Wittgenstein had set out a theory that saw the function of language as picturing the world. His opening sentence was: 'The world is everything that is the case.' So language had to be checked against evidence for that which it pictured.

But we have seen the limitations of literal language, particularly from the point of view of religious experiences and ideas, and noted uses of language other than for description – expressing a view, emotion or choice, and actually performing a task. Language is far more flexible and creative than the Logical Positivists realized.

This was recognized by Wittgenstein himself, as reflected in his later work (for example, *Philosophical Investigations*). He expressed this by saying 'Don't think; look!' In other words, if you want to understand something, it is not enough to know the meaning of words and the way they logically fit together. Rather, it is important to look at how those words are used. Look at what that language means for people.

So, meaning is given by use, and language is a 'form of life' – it is a tool for doing something, and it takes on its meaning and significance from the context in which it is used. Wittgenstein gave the example of the builder who calls out 'Beam!' or 'More bricks!' to his assistant, who only needs to understand the significance of each request and act accordingly. The meaning of 'Bricks!' in that context is embedded in the activity of building.

Wittgenstein saw his task as a philosopher as essentially one of **description**. He famously argued (in *Philosophical Investigations* para. 123) that 'Philosophy may in no way interfere with the actual use of language, it can in the end only describe it.' The implication of this for religious language is clear. The meaning of a religious claim is not to be understood with reference to external or scientific data that might confirm or refute it – it can only be understood **from within that religion, by looking at how it is used.**

So, to know the meaning of a word is to know how to use it. Wittgenstein saw language rather like a game that we play according to a set of rules. There are many different games (ball games, card games etc.) and there are no actions that they all have in common. What makes them all games is the fact that they all follow rules. **Learning a language is like learning a game – it is a matter of getting to know how to use the words.**

Changing one's view of what language is about can have quite dramatic effects. D. Z. Phillips, a theologian who follows Wittgenstein's approach, argues that the statement 'God is love' is not a description, but a rule for how the word 'God' is to be used. This means that statements about religious belief are really descriptions of the grammar of the religious language game – and the implication of this is that something cannot be both a rule of grammar *and*, at the same time, a description of reality.

Finally, it is worth noting that for Wittgenstein (as earlier for Jeremy Bentham and Gottlob Frege) it is sentences and not individual words that are the primary bearers of meaning. **If you want to know what the word 'God' means, look at the sentences within which it is used.**

Comment

Followed to its logical conclusion, this approach leaves religious language going round and round within its own self-contained game, for ever defining its own rules. At which point I am tempted to ask 'What's the point? Why bother?'

If religious language does not in some way get beyond itself to explore a level of reality that is recognized by all, whether religious or not, does it have anything to say about life outside the closed circle of religion? And how did it get started in the first place, if not to perform some function of understanding or dealing with the world?

Language and truth claims

Unless we are going to limit all religious meaning to the grammar of the religious language game, we are likely to want at some point to claim that something is true or false. In other words, we are likely to relate religious beliefs to a general understanding of the world.

In doing so, care is needed to distinguish carefully between existential statements, which may express religious commitment, wonder or values, for example, 'Jesus is Lord' and apparently factual propositions, for example, 'Jesus is the unique Son of God'. Of course, it can be argued that the latter is in fact just another way of expressing the former. Once expressed as a proposition, however, an item of belief becomes limited by the language used, and with it a whole set of cultural presuppositions. This creates a problem for the dialogue between religions. Can truth claims from different religions be compatible, especially if they come from different cultures and eras?

Example

A Christian, examining Buddhist ideas, does so in the light of the central Christian experience and beliefs. From that perspective, Buddhist ideas are bound to be found wanting. But the same thing will apply the other way round. Ideas about sin and forgiveness, for example, which may be quite central to a Christian view of the relationship between humankind and God, may be seen as unacceptable and positively harmful to the Buddhist. This is not to deny the validity of the experience of these things on the part of the Christian, but simply that, from a Buddhist standpoint, a healthy spiritual life requires the setting aside of what is sees as unskilful attitudes such as guilt.

To guard against this, it is important to recognize that all truth claims are made in a particular context, using a particular language and set of ideas. In a different context, the same experience or conviction would have been expressed very differently.

However, where a religious proposition is put forward as a factual explanation, it is open to be assessed using the same criteria as scientific and other theories. In other words, we may ask of it:

- Does it fit the evidence?
- Is it coherent as a theory?
- Is it the simplest (or most straightforward) theory that may be given to account for the facts?
- Is it fruitful in producing new ideas and giving meaning for personal existence?

(For a further examination of this see, for example, A. Peacocke *Theology for a Scientific Age*.) Such an approach does not rule out religious questions on a narrow dogmatic basis, but allows them to be explored alongside questions raised by science.

The limitations of language

All the major religions accept that there is a fundamental limitation to what can be said. Every attempt to define God will be limited, offering at best a partial image, not a full definition or description. The same could be said of Buddhist ideas of 'the eternal', or the 'uncompounded', which in that religion is set in contrast to this world in which everything is compounded and liable to change and decay.

It could be that the experiences of a Buddhist and a Christian may be similar, but the whole structure of thought and language that has built up within each religion will ensure that the resulting descriptions will be different and possibly incompatible. This reminds us of the limitation of any attempt to express the essence of religion.

For a mystic (see Chapter 01) the sense of the transcendent is beyond language. The nearest language can get to describing mystical awareness is through symbols. Bede Griffiths, in *A New Vision of Reality*, points out that the intuitive mind is controlled by the right hemisphere of the brain, whereas the analytic and rational functions are controlled by the left. Clearly, mysticism is a right brain activity. He quotes Dionysus the Areopagite, a sixth-century neo-Platonist mystic, as saying that the Godhead is beyond name, thought and imagination. The Divine is seen by mystics as something to which one can point, but which cannot be described.

Western culture is dominated by literal language, particularly in the sphere of science. It is understandable therefore that religious beliefs are sometimes taken literally and examined as though they could be proved empirically, even if that was not the intention of those who originally formulated them.

We saw in the first chapter that an experience becomes religious when it somehow transcends the actual thing experienced, pointing to some 'deeper' or universal truth. For language to reflect this, it too needs to be self-transcending, taking words that have a literal meaning, but then indicating that what is referred to is more than the literal.

Comment

Religion is not unique in this. Writing about music is much the same; it attempts to convey what can generally only be experienced through the ear and the imagination.

But religions make claims, not least about God – so it is to these concepts and arguments that we now turn. In doing so, however, we need to be constantly aware of the origin of such ideas in religious experience, and the limitations of language.

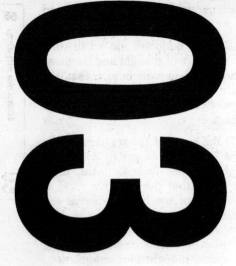

03 God: the concepts

In this chapter you will:
- examine what people mean by 'God'
- look at the implications this has for religious belief
- consider what it means to say that something 'exists'.

The next chapter will outline arguments that have been given for God's existence. But before these can be assessed, it is essential to consider what is meant by the word 'God' – because the claim 'God exists' is not at all straightforward.

In this chapter we will therefore start with a traditional Christian definition of God and explore the concepts generally used to describe him. We shall then look at the various philosophical options, and at the variety of religious beliefs associated with God or the gods. Only after that will we turn to the key question of what it means for something to exist, and therefore whether or not it is logical even to consider the possibility that 'God' might exist.

The basic definition

The Concise Oxford dictionary defines the word 'god' as 'superhuman being worshipped as having power over nature and human fortunes', whereas 'God' (with a capital G) is the 'supreme being, Creator and Ruler of universe'.

This is taken a step further by R. Swinburne:

'a person, without a body (i.e. a spirit) present everywhere, the creator and sustainer of the universe, a free agent, able to do everything (i.e. omnipotent) knowing all things, perfectly good, a source of moral obligation, immutable, eternal, a necessary being, holy, and worthy of worship. (*The Coherence of Theism*, p. 2)

As we unpack the various elements of this, a key question is whether – as a definition – it is logically coherent. Is the meaning of 'person' compatible with being 'present everywhere', since persons are usually recognizable and defined beings? Is a being who is able to do anything and knows everything able to be 'perfectly good' given the state of the world?

Eternal

There is an important distinction to be made between 'everlasting' and' eternal':

- Everything that exists within time can be thought of as having a beginning and an end. Even if it does not appear to change, it can still be said to be getting older. Now, something can be described as everlasting if its duration in time extends infinitely backwards into the past and forwards into the future. It is already very old and it will continue to get older indefinitely.

- If you want to describe a reality that is outside the ordinary world of space and time – the world in which all finite things can be said to exist – the correct word is 'eternal'. Terms like old, new, past and future cannot be applied to it. It is not part of the world that is known through the senses, for as soon as it became part of that world it is within space and time.

Within the tradition of classical theism (which originated from ideas in Greek philosophy and is found developed in the Christian tradition by Augustine of Hippo and Aquinas) God is definitely eternal rather than everlasting. He is not simply an ongoing part of the universe, but is beyond the whole process of change.

Note

This is reflected in the religious awareness of Schleiermacher (see above p. 8) who spoke of religion as a sense and taste for the infinite, and seeing the eternal within every moment.

By contrast, biblical language and much of the Liturgy of the Church speaks of God in terms that suggest he is everlasting rather than eternal. He is described as being in the past, as guiding the course of events: the one who was, and is and is to come. Such a god is involved with the process of change; he is described as acting within the world. But action implies change and limitation, doing one thing rather than another, and it is difficult to reconcile this with the idea of an eternal God who is beyond time and space.

Philosophers who regard God as eternal, generally see him as embodying the structure of reality, out of which emerges space, time and the world which we encounter with the senses. This is highlighted by the idea of creation out of nothing – not creation at some point in the past, but bringing into reality everything that exists here and now.

In other words

- To exist is to be in time and therefore to age.
- To act is to make a succession of changes with the passing of time.
- Therefore, if God exists and acts (in any literal sense) he cannot be eternal.
- An everlasting God may be seen as a counter (although by far the largest counter, the greatest imaginable counter) moving within the board game of the universe.
- An eternal God is the structure of the board game itself. That's fine, but you cannot throw dice and get him to move!

But note that some writers use the term 'eternal' to cover both the idea of being outside time, and also being unending but within time.

God as creator

God is said to be the creator of the world, and to have created it **out of nothing** (*ex nihilo*). This is an important feature of theism, for it implies that God is not an external force working with matter or coming in to animate it, nor is he an agent over and against other agents. Rather, he is the absolute origin of everything. There is no external material, no 'nothingness' out of which things can be made. Everything that comes into existence does so as a creative act of God.

But this radically challenges what we mean by 'God': if there is no matter external to God which he might use in creation, then God cannot be **separate from** creation. You cannot say 'There is something of beauty', and then point to something **else** and say 'There is its creator.'

The problem is that the word 'is' can be used in two quite different senses. Take the sentence 'God is the creative source of everything':

- Does that mean that I am giving the name 'God' to whatever it is that is the source of natural creativity? (In other words 'is' helps to *define* what we mean by God.)

or

- Does it mean that I have identified 'God' (a being who is known independently) as being responsible for natural creativity? (If so, 'is' is used to *identify* God.)

To take Swinburne's definition, one might argue that, if God is 'the creator and sustainer of the universe' then – in all probability – God is the process by which, at extreme temperatures, hydrogen is converted into helium. This conclusion *defines* God as creator and sustainer (so that he can then be described in scientific or other terms) whereas the clear intention in the traditional definition of God is to *identify* him as creator and sustainer.

So we need to take care to know whether any argument or concept is being used to *identify* God or to *define* God.

Omnipotent

If God creates out of nothing, his power is not limited. If his act of creation is not something that took place in the past, but an ongoing feature of life, it implies that God brings everything about, without being limited by the material that he uses to do so.

In this sense, the idea that God can do anything (i.e. is omnipotent) is implied in the doctrine of creation. It would be illogical to call God the 'creator' in this absolute sense and then to say that there are things he cannot do.

There is one exception to this: God cannot be said to do anything which is logically impossible. Once the meaning of the terms is understood, $2 + 2 = 4$; God cannot make $2 + 2 = 5$.

However, if God can do anything without limit, we must assume that he has ultimate responsibility for all that happens – for it would be in his power to change anything that might happen. That presents problems, as we shall see later.

Omniscient

If God is omniscient, he knows everything. There can be two ways of looking at this:

- If he is eternal, existing outside time, then his omniscience is also timeless. His knowledge of past, present and future is simultaneous. It is not that he correctly guesses what will happen in the future, but that – for him – there is no future. His knowledge is eternally present.
- If he is everlasting, then he will know everything that has happened in the past, and everything that is happening in the present. He will also be aware now of those things in the present which will determine what happens in the future. In

this sense, God might be said to 'know' the future, even though he hasn't been there yet!

The central problem with this concerns human freedom and responsibility. If God knows what we think we freely choose to do, our freedom is an illusion. Once someone correctly knows that something is going to happen, that thing is inevitable. If it is not inevitable, then he can't know it – at best he can make a reliable guess.

The perfect excuse

If God is omniscient, he knows everything.

He therefore knows that I will do X.

Therefore I am not free to choose not to do X.

Therefore I am not to blame for doing X.

But some thinkers (for example, Brian Davies in *An Introduction to the Philosophy of Religion*) would counter this argument by suggesting that God might know that at some point in the future I will freely choose to do X. In this case, my freedom is part of what God knows – therefore I remain free to choose.

But this seems to create a logical problem:

- I am free to choose if, and only if, there are at least two possible options at the moment of choosing.
- If God knows that I am free to choose, he must allow two possible outcomes.
- Therefore he cannot know which of those outcomes I will choose without denying me my freedom to make that decision.

One way out of this dilemma is to say that we freely make choices based on many factors, both conscious and unconscious. We do not fully understand these, and therefore do not fully appreciate why we make the choices we do. On the other hand, an omniscient God would understand all about us, and would therefore know exactly those factors (including our desire not to be predictable) which lead to our apparently 'free' choice.

An alternative approach (taken by Richard Swinburne in *The Existence of God*) is that omniscience implies that God knows all that it is **logically possible** to know. To know an undecided future event is logically impossible, so God cannot know it.

The problem of evil

The qualities of omnipotence and omniscience appear to be central to the traditional theistic view of God but, when taken together, they raise a central problem for belief in God, namely the problem of evil, which will be considered in Chapter 08. It seems incompatible with the idea of the goodness of God that he should both know about evil before it takes place (omniscient), be able to stop it (omnipotent), and yet choose not to do so.

Transcendence and immanence

When we looked at religious experience we saw that, although it took place in a particular place at a particular time, its meaning went beyond them. An experience became 'religious' when it said something about the meaning and purpose of everything. The same was true of religious language; it had a literal meaning, but went beyond it. A religious symbol – whether an event, an image or a word – pointed beyond itself and yet in some way participated in the power of that to which it pointed.

When we come to descriptions of God, this 'self-transcending' quality of religious experience and language needs to be appreciated. God is said to be within and yet also beyond our ordinary experience and the words we use. The words that describe this are **transcendence** and **immanence**.

The transcendence of God indicates that he is beyond any concept, language or experience. He cannot be limited or contained. A literal description of God is nothing but an idol, however sophisticated that mental idol might be.

But if God is infinite, there is no place where he may not be found, so there is no way to experience him without simultaneously experiencing *something else as well*. He is therefore described as **immanent** – found within everything.

Theism, pantheism and panentheism

Theism is the belief that there is a creator God who displays the qualities outlined in the definition given at the start of this chapter, who may be encountered within but is not limited to the material world. It reflects a balance of immanence and transcendence.

If God were thought to be immanent but not transcendent, he would be identified with the material world itself. This is termed **pantheism** (literally: everything = God).

Some philosophers and theologians use the term **panentheism** (literally: everything is within God). Panentheism does not really add anything to what is implied by theism – for the god of theism is already seen as immanent within everything – but it is a reminder of the need for both immanence and transcendence. It is the philosophical equivalent of the biblical idea that 'In him we live and move and have our being.' (Acts 17.28)

Note

Although we are mainly concerned with the Western concept of God, it is interesting to note that the Hindu tradition maintains a similar balance. **Brahman** is sometimes thought of as an impersonal term for God, something like 'absolute reality'. But, in fact, Hinduism has two terms: **Nirguna Brahman** (the eternal, self-existent reality of God) and **Saguna Brahman** (the personal aspect of God, seen in his relationship with his creation). God is also described as *satcitananda* (sat = absolute or true; cit = mind or consciousness; ananda = bliss). Although there are significant differences between Indian and Western philosophies, there is this same sense that the divine is encountered within and yet transcends human experience. (To explore some of these parallels further, see, for example John Hick *God and the Universe of Faiths*, or in this same series *Teach Yourself: Eastern Philosophy*.)

Beliefs, language and religion

So far in this chapter we have been looking at concepts by means of which people have tried to express their understanding of God. We need to recognize that language is always going to be inadequate for this task, for it generally deals with particular things that we encounter in life, things that can be described literally. That won't do, of course, for any reality that claims to be eternal. So there is always a balance to be struck between saying nothing, and trying to describe God in inappropriately literal language.

For the philosophy of religion (as compared with, for example, the theory of knowledge) there is an additional problem. People often feel very deeply about religious issues, and may not be willing or able to examine various philosophical options with detached objectivity. How does the asking of philosophical questions relate to the needs of those who are actually practising their religion? Indeed, **is a study of the philosophy of religion compatible with being religious?**

A view about the word 'God' that would be quite acceptable within the philosophy of religion debate, might be difficult to reconcile with the practice of religion. Indeed, we could ask whether some views are incompatible with attitudes of prayer and worship that seem essential to the religious way of life.

This question suggests that we should adopt a **pragmatic** test for religious language and beliefs: Do they work? Can a person think of God in this way and find an appropriate and emotionally satisfying way of engaging with that belief?

Comment

The dilemma for organized religion is this:

- How can you convey religious truth in a way that enables it to be passed on, without at the same time restricting its meaning?
- How can you capture the essence of an experience and put it into words or ritual actions without it becoming fossilized?

Religious alternatives to theism

Having introduced the idea of a pragmatic test for belief – whether a belief works in the context of religious devotion – it is worth reminding ourselves that not all religions require belief in the existence of God, and that there are forms of devotion which thrive without it.

- Four of the major world religions (Christianity, Islam, Judaism and Sikhism) are theistic – although there are significant variations in how their followers interpret 'God'.
- Hinduism appears to be polytheistic. In other words, a Hindu will accept the reality of many different gods and goddesses, each of which will reflect a particular aspect of life. This is how Indian religion appears to the outside observer and how it is expressed in popular devotion. On the other hand, at a deeper level, there is the concept of Brahman (the ultimate reality) which underlies all the individual deities.

- Whereas in theistic religions, the personal and the ultimate aspects of the divine are held together and presented in the form of a single being, in Hinduism the two levels remain distinct. At one level there are many personalities among the gods, and at a deeper level there is this single reality within which they all share.

- Buddhism is the only world religion which is non-theistic, in the sense that it does not require belief in God or in gods. It does not deny the existence of God or the gods, but regards arguments about the existence of God as irrelevant to the task of following a spiritual path towards enlightenment. There is worship and devotion in Buddhism, but this a matter of showing respect and gratitude to a spiritual ideal, not paying homage to a deity.

- In popular Buddhist devotion, however, there are many images of Buddhas and Bodhisattvas (enlightened beings), and in Buddhist scriptures there are many references to the gods. What Buddhism seems to manage to do quite successfully is to keep separate the emotional needs of worshippers for images that can act as the objects of devotion, and the more philosophical argument about the nature of reality.

These comments are, of necessity, over-simplified and should not be taken as a final statement about the Hindu or Buddhist views of 'God'. They are introduced here in order to make two important points:

- That there are forms of religion which do not require belief in God. So belief in God is not a **necessary** feature of religion as such, even if it is central to the three Western faiths.

- That both Hinduism and Buddhism tend to make a distinction between popular devotion and philosophical belief. The former is a means of engaging the emotions in worship, but it is not seen as being the final word. A person may want to go beyond the use of such images and engage reality directly.

The Christian concept of 'Trinity'

Judaism and Islam are strictly monotheistic religions. Neither will accept any direct representation of God, and neither will allow anything to be associated with God – indeed, the rejection of idolatry is fundamental to both religions, being enshrined in the first of the Jewish Ten Commandments, and the basic Muslim statement of faith that there is no God but Allah.

The Christian doctrine of God is more complex, and springs from the conviction of the early Christians that God himself was present in and through the life and activity of Jesus of Nazareth, and that the Holy Spirit of God had been poured out upon the disciples at Pentecost.

After a complex process of doctrinal debates during the early centuries, during which those who held minority views were regarded as heretics, the overall view of God that emerged was enshrined in the doctrine of the **Trinity** – that God is known as Father (creator), as Son (in the person of Jesus) and as Holy Spirit (acting through his followers).

This doctrine claims that there are three persons but one God. In Greek, this is expressed as one substance (*ousia*) and three persons (*prosopa*). The term *prosopa* may be explained by its use as the term for a theatrical mask – suggesting that God is encountered in three different forms. When translated into Latin, this became three persons (*persona*) in one substance (*substantia*). The term *persona* (and the concept 'person' that derives from it) implies a greater measure of separate reality than did the Greek theatrical mask.

The key thing, however, is to appreciate the experience that led to this doctrine – that 'God' was active in, and therefore encountered within, the community of believers. In other words, it was an expression of the *immanence* of God. The convoluted arguments in Christian doctrine are largely the attempt to square that experience of a 'God within' with the eternal God of traditional theism.

Basic beliefs

Most of those who believe in God are quite prepared to discuss religious concepts and will try to show that belief in God can be justified on rational grounds.

But not all philosophers are happy to do this. Alvin Plantinga, in a paper entitled 'Is Belief in God Rational?' (in *Rationality and Religious Belief*, 1979), argued that belief in God is quite beyond logical argument, and is a 'basic belief', something – like the existence of the external world or the reality of other people – that we assume to be the case, without needing evidence or proof.

Arguments for the existence of God may be useful – by showing that belief in God is neither impossible nor illogical – but they cannot either establish or undermine the basic belief, for such a belief expresses a fundamental commitment.

This approach is sometimes called a 'Reformed **Epistemology**', since it has parallels with the epistemology (theory of knowledge) that lay behind the arguments about faith, reason and knowledge of God that were set out at the Reformation, particularly by Calvin.

There is a strand of Protestant thinking that says that mankind is fallen and sinful, and that human reason is equally fallen and therefore cannot understand God. Knowledge of God can come only through God's own action (grace). Those who hold this view are unlikely to appreciate arguments about the nature of God or about his existence. If human reason is fallen, all such debate is likely to do more harm than good.

This view reinforces the argument that one needs to start with religious experience and how it can be articulated. Logic comes later and may be offered as a justification for, but not an complete explanation of, the beliefs that arise as a result of religious experience.

Perhaps that is why philosophers who take an atheist position find arguing with believers so frustrating. They know that, whatever arguments they produce, the believers will wriggle and then continue to believe just as before. The ground changes but the fundamental belief remains. That does not mean that the believer is necessarily being difficult or illogical, it is just that the 'basic belief' lies below the level of logical argument and touches an experience that is independent of subsequent interpretation. Why that basic belief is held is, of course, quite another matter, so in Chapter 05 we shall look at some attempts to account for the phenomenon of religion.

A postmodernist interpretation

Don Cupitt has argued for a radical and secular interpretation of Christianity. His philosophy is influenced by the movement known as **Postmodernism**. In brief, this is an approach which suggests there is no external reality to which our words refer and against which they may be checked. Words and concepts are their own reality. They form a closed system of signs, with their own value and significance – words have whatever meaning we choose for them. We live within a world of signs and words, and cannot step outside it. This is an enormous topic, beyond the scope of this present book, but we should at least be aware that the whole idea of language 'transcending itself' to express something 'more' creates problems for some modern philosophers.

Cupitt's point is that the traditional and 'realist' view of God – God as some being or force or invisible reality that actually exists in itself separate from the ordinary things we experience – is not acceptable to thinking people today. This is not presented in a negative way, but in a positive one:

> A modern person ought to be spiritually strong and healthy enough to live and die without superstition. Nothing is hidden. Everything is just what it appears to be and there is no occult reality. The world is ours and there is nothing conspiring against us. There is only the manifest, the world of appearances which is best analysed philosophically as a world of signs. There in only this beginningless endless flux, the human world of doings, meanings and feelings.

> (Don Cupitt, *Radicals and the Future of the Church*, p. 140)

The result of taking this view is that his religion is one that says 'yes' to life just as it is, affirms it in spite of its changes and suffering.

> ... I am advocating a religion of life in the sense of a spiritual discipline that enables us to accept and to say yes to our life as it is, baseless, brief, pointless and utterly contingent, and yet in its very nihility beautiful, ethically demanding, solemn and final.

> (p. 143)

Comment

In many ways, this comes close to the Buddhist view that spiritual happiness is possible and suffering may be overcome in spite of a realistic recognition of the limited and transient nature of life.

Cupitt also takes the view that gods are simply what they are within religion:

> The gods are just what people can be seen to be worshipping; they are our faith in them, and the things we say and feel about them and do for them. There is nothing extra. Gods have no existence outside our faith and practice.
>
> (*The Time Being*, p. 35)

In other words, for Cupitt, 'God' describes what happens in worship, it is not the name for something that exists independently.

This is a view of God with which many atheists and humanists would have no problem – for it is a term used to express an aspect of human life, that of wonder, worship, a sense of the eternal and universal perspective of which Schleiermacher spoke (see above p. 8). It does not require any supernatural, superstitious or occult beliefs.

This represents a radical departure for philosophy of religion, for much of the debate about God has taken the form of a quest for the single concept which can hold together the whole of reality. The ontological and cosmological arguments (which we shall look at in the next chapter) were just that – attempts to argue from meaning or from the structure of the cosmos to a single underlying reality. The assumption is that we can know (and want to know) a level of reality that is beyond our immediate experience. Cupitt's view denies that this is necessarily so.

The general approach of postmodernism is one that denies any reality that lies 'beyond' the actual words or images of a cultural artefact. There is no creative genius, only the words that are written, no 'thing' that the artist wants to capture, only the image within which he or she has captured it.

Thus God is what religion does, not something that exists separately. But that raises the absolutely fundamental question: What does it mean to say that something exists?

Exists?

The one thing that separates a believer from a non-believer (to divide people in a rather over-simple way) is whether or not they believe that there is something that corresponds to that word

'God'. Whatever else they have to say, believers generally accept that God **exists** and non-believers claim that he does not.

The next chapter will be concerned with the various arguments that attempt to show whether God exists or not. But before that, it is as well to set out as clearly as possible what we mean by 'exists'.

One thing is absolutely clear: **if God is infinite, he cannot exist in the same way that finite things exist.** I know ordinary things exist because I can define them, set boundaries to them, know what is them and what isn't. I can say, in effect, 'Go and look there and you will see what it is I am talking about.'

Once the definition of God as infinite is accepted, his existence or otherwise cannot really be debated in that crude way. Ordinary, limited things might or might not exist, and so it makes sense to seek evidence for whether they exist or not. God, by definition, cannot be such an optional thing. To say that God 'exists', in the normal, literal sense of that word, is therefore to deny God.

But if God does not exist in the same sense that finite things exist, does it make sense to say that he exists at all?

In thinking about this, it is worth reflecting that other concepts give us similar problems:

- Does 'space' or 'time' exist? Can you point to them, or set their boundaries?
- Does 'reality' exist?

Notice that these concepts form a kind of framework within which things are experienced. Might 'God' similarly be a framework for articulating religious experiences?

Even in the personal aspects of life, there are things that we might describe as real, or existing, but which defy separate existence:

- Does 'love' exist?

There are hormonal urges and acts of kindness, sexuality and social bonding, there is a sense of togetherness and gain in personal esteem. Many other things contribute to a description of the 'love' that binds people together. But is there any separate thing that is love and nothing else?

To speak of God as literally existing in a particular place, a being 'out there' in some way, either within or external to the world, is to limit him; and a being so limited cannot be God. So we need to be clear that any argument about an external, separate entity (as one might debate the existence of some remote star in the galaxy) is **not** about the God of the Christian, Jewish or Muslim traditions.

Even before we look at the arguments for his existence, it is therefore clear that God is not part of the universe. Nor is he outside the universe; for, if he is infinite, he cannot be outside anything. But we should recognize that much of what passes for belief in God in popular thought is, by the standards of the traditional concepts and arguments that we shall be examining, nonsense if taken literally.

There are three terms that need to be clarified:

- An identification of God with the physical universe is **pantheism,** but it is not pantheism to say that God is everywhere or within everything.
- The idea of an external designer God who created the world, but is not immanent within it, is **deism**. This form of 'external explanation' God is often the target of those who oppose any supernatural or occult ideas. Again, it is important to remember that it is not the 'God' of traditional theism. The other significant difference between deism and theism is that the former is generally justified by human reason alone, as an answer to the question about why the universe exists at all.
- The literal identification of God with any individual thing or concept is **idolatry**. Although most obviously applied to a physical image, idolatry can also apply to mental concepts or doctrines.

For reflection

Anyone who claims that there is a possibility that God exists, denies God. A possible god cannot be 'God'. So agnosticism is atheism without adequate conviction.

It may be worth looking back now at what was said about religious experience in the first chapter. It involved a sense of awe and an awareness of the fragility of human life in the face of the dimensions of the universe. What was encountered in such experiences was not a separate, defined entity, but a level of reality that could not be described literally. We need to keep this in mind as we consider what 'God' means and whether he exists.

Comment

'Does Mozart exist?' is not a question to ask in the middle of a performance of one of his symphonies. There may be some historical arguments for or against the authenticity of a particular composition; but this performance, this present experience, is what 'Mozart' is. If you enjoy Mozart, it becomes little more than an academic game to start arguing about whether Mozart exists. There are instruments being played; there are musical notes on sheets of paper; there is a conductor waving his baton; there is an audience whose eardrums are helping to convert vibrations into electrical impulses; there is a great deal of recognition, memory and other mental activity going on. Where then is 'Mozart'? Dead! But that's irrelevant. 'Mozart' is now the whole thing: Mozart is the vibration of eardrums and the scraping of hair on strings; Mozart is a manuscript and a tradition of interpretation.

Mozart used to exist as a human being, but does so no longer. 'Mozart' is the word we now use for the whole experience that embodies sheet music, recordings, performances and so on. There is no one thing that is 'Mozart' that is not also something else (paper, instruments, sound waves etc). **Might the same apply to 'God'?**

The task of this chapter has been to point out that the concepts used to describe what is meant by 'God' make the question 'Does God exist?' far from simple. As might be expected of a philosophical approach, the answer you give to that question depends on what you mean by 'God' and also what you mean by 'exists'.

We need to keep in the forefront of our minds the subtlety of both terms if we are to appreciate the traditional arguments about the existence of God, to which we will now turn.

04 God: the arguments

In this chapter you will:
- explore the logic of the ontological argument for God's existence
- examine the claim that the world and its design points to a creator
- see how morality and religious experience can lead to belief in God.

Is it possible, by a logical argument, to prove that God exists? That is the basic question we need to tackle in this chapter, and we shall do so by examining some traditional arguments to see whether they are conclusive and what they contribute to our understanding of what belief in God means.

Immanuel Kant (1724–1804) argued, in his *Critique of Pure Reason*, that there were three types of argument for the existence of God:

- based on reason alone
- based on the general fact of the existence of the world
- based on particular features of the world.

These are called the **ontological**, **cosmological** and **teleological** arguments, and he set about giving a critique of all three. He then introduced a fourth one, the **moral** argument.

We shall examine all four of these in this chapter, and will also add a fifth line of approach, based on religious experience.

Note

In looking at the arguments, it is important to keep in mind the concepts of God outlined in the last chapter. The relevant question to ask may not be 'Does this prove that God exists?' but 'What sort of "God" does this argument present? Does this argument address what religious experience or organized religion mean by the word "God"?'

So, for example, pantheists will have no problem with this argument for the existence of God:

- God is everything that exists.
- Everything that exists, exists.
- Therefore God exists.

But what has this argument achieved? It is just saying that, when the pantheist uses the term God, he or she means by it 'everything that exists'. It illustrates the meaning of a word, it does not argue for or against the actual existence of anything.

In evaluating these arguments, we may ask:

- Does this argument prove without doubt that God exists?
- If it does not, does it at least suggest that the existence of God is either possible or probable?

The outline of the traditional arguments set out in this chapter is an expanded version of that found in the philosophy of religion chapter in *Teach Yourself: Philosophy*.

After examining all five of the arguments outlined in this chapter, you may conclude that, individually, they fail to prove God's existence, but that the force of their arguments is cumulative, and that – taken together – they are persuasive.

On the other hand, you may feel that the whole attempt to argue for God's existence is fundamentally at odds with the ideas about God and religious experience that we have been thinking about in Chapters 01 and 03. In that case, you may conclude that it does not matter whether the arguments are persuasive or not, for belief in God is not a matter of logical deduction at all.

Equally, you could come to the conclusion that the arguments not only fail to prove that God exists, but that – if that is what their authors meant by God – then the conclusion from the failure of the arguments is that God certainly does not exist. In that case, you may either dismiss the notion of God completely, or may hold that 'God' is a meaningful idea for religious people, but that he does not have external, objective existence.

The ontological argument

The ontological argument is not based on observation of the world, or on any form of external evidence, but simply on the definition of the word 'God'. It argued that, by its definition, the word 'God' refers to something that has necessary existence.

The argument was set out by Anselm (1033–1109), Archbishop of Canterbury, in the opening chapters of his *Proslogion*. He is not putting forward the argument in order to be able to believe in God – that is never in doubt (indeed, the argument is addressed to God) – but because his belief in God leads him to understand God's existence in this particular way: a way which leads him to the conclusion that God **must** exist.

The argument is based on the idea that God is, *aliquid quo nihil maius cogitari possit* – 'that than which no greater can be thought'.

Note

This does not refer to something that just happens to be greater than anything else. He has not lined up a whole range of things and happened to decide that God is the greatest of them. Rather, the phrase 'that than which no greater can be thought' expresses his idea of 'perfection', or 'the absolute', the most real thing (*ens reallissimum*).

Here is the logical structure of the argument he presents in the second chapter of *Proslogion*:

- God is a being 'than which none greater can be thought'.
- Can it be that there is no such being? (Since, in Psalm 14:1, 'the fool hath said in his heart, "There is no God"'.)
- But this 'fool' understands 'a being than which none greater can be thought', and what he understands is in his understanding, even if he does not think that it actually exists.
- But 'that than which a greater cannot be thought' cannot exist in the understanding *alone*. For, if so, it could be thought of as existing also in reality, and *that is greater*. Therefore to believe that it exists in the understanding alone would involve a contradiction.
- Therefore, there exists, *both in the understanding and in reality*, something 'than which a greater cannot be thought'.

In other words
- When it comes to spending power, the real pound or dollar in your pocket will always be greater than the imaginary wad of notes!
- So something is greater if it exists than if it doesn't.
- If God is the greatest thing imaginable, he must exist. For if he didn't, you could imagine something greater – something with all his qualities, but which did actually exist.

One of the clearest criticisms of this argument was made by Kant (in his *Critique of Pure Reason*) in response to a version of it set out by Descartes (1596–1650). Descartes had maintained that, just as it was impossible to have a triangle without having its three sides and angles (since they were qualities that belong to being a triangle), so it was impossible to have God without having the quality of existence.

In other words, Descartes was arguing that existence was **a necessary predicate of God**, and that it would be illogical to believe that God had every possible perfection, but then to say that he did not exist.

Kant's argument may be set out like this:

- **If** you have a triangle
- **Then** it must have three angles (i.e. to have a triangle without three angles involves a contradiction)
- **But** if you do not have the triangle, you do not have its three angles or sides either.

In the same way, Kant argued:

- **If** you accept that there is a God, it is logical to accept also that his existence is necessary (as opposed by contingent – something that happens by chance)
- **But** you do not **have** to accept that there is a God.

To appreciate the force of Kant's argument, it is important to remember that he divided all statements into two categories – *analytic* and *synthetic*:

- **analytic statements** are true by definition
- **synthetic statements** can only be proved true or false with reference to experience.

For Kant, statements about existence are synthetic; definitions are analytic. Therefore, the angles and sides of a triangle are necessary because they are part of the definition of a triangle. But that says nothing about the **actual** existence of a triangle.

> ### In other words
>
> For Kant, necessity is a feature of logic and definition (2 + 2 must always = 4). When it comes to describing what exists, we depend upon experience (there may be four things, but there could have been five). Therefore existence cannot be a matter of necessity. All statements about what exists are 'synthetic' and need to be confirmed by either directly by our own experience, or through the reports of others.

Kant gives another way of expressing the same idea. He says that **existence is not a predicate**. In other words, if you describe something completely, you add nothing to that description by then saying 'and it has existence'. Existence is not an extra quality – it is just a way of saying that there is the thing itself, with all the qualities already given.

Norman Malcolm (in *Philosophical Review*, January 1960) agreed with Kant's view that existence is not a predicate, but did not think that this adequately refuted Anselm's argument. In particular, he pointed to the difference between existence and 'necessary existence', which was introduced by Anselm in another version of the ontological argument that he presented in Chapter 3 of the *Proslogion*:

- Something which *cannot* be thought of as not existing is *greater* than something which can either exist or not.
- Therefore 'that than which a greater cannot be thought' cannot either exist or not, but much exist *necessarily*, and cannot be thought of as not existing.

In other words, Anselm points out that we can imagine limited things coming into existence and passing out of existence, simply *because they are limited*. But if God is 'that than which no greater can be thought', then his existence cannot be a matter of chance. Thus he claims that **necessary existence** is part of the idea of God, but of nothing else.

Anselm was challenged by a fellow monk, Gaunilo, who used the idea of the perfect island. He claimed that, if Anselm's argument were true, then the perfect island would also have to exist. Anselm rejected this. An island is a limited thing, and you can always imagine better and better islands. But he held that 'that than which a greater cannot be thought' is unique. If it could be thought of as nonexistent, it could also be thought of as having a beginning and an end, but then it would not be the greatest that can be thought.

Note

It is important to distinguish between logical necessity and factual necessity.

- If 'God exists' is a logical necessity (i.e. if it is an analytic statement) then 'God does not exist' would be self-contradictory.

- If 'God exists' is a factual necessity, it implies that it is impossible for things to be as they are if God did not exist, and therefore that it is actually not possible for there to be no God.

The ontological argument is about *logical* necessity. The question remains whether its unique definition of God means that his existence is also a *factual* necessity.

Norman Malcolm's comment depends on this distinction. The necessity of a triangle having three angles is a **logical** necessity; but it is not **factually** necessary for there to be a triangle at all. Malcolm suggests that Anselm's definition of God means that, even if existence is not a necessary predicate of God, 'necessary existence' logically is. So one might think that a triangle either exists or doesn't, but if it does, it must of necessity have three angles; but one cannot think that God either exists or doesn't, but that – if he does – his existence is necessary. Anselm's argument depends on the idea that one cannot think of 'that than which no greater can be conceived' as not existing. In other words, as Malcolm presents it, God's existence is either necessary or impossible – not being contingent, he cannot simply come into existence or cease to exist. Yet God's existence cannot be logically impossible unless the statement 'God exists' is self-contradictory.

But we still have to decide whether Anselm was concerned with logical necessity or factual necessity. Clearly, he was not interested simply in the word 'God', for in Chapter 4 of *Proslogion* he makes the distinction between thinking of a word and thinking of the thing itself to which the word refers. His claim is that, if you understand the reality to which the word 'God' refers, you will understand that it must exist.

So what did Anselm understand by speaking of God as 'that than which none greater can be thought'? In another work, *Monologion*, he spoke of degrees of goodness and perfection in the world, and that there must be something that constitutes perfect goodness, which he calls 'God', which causes goodness in all else.

This idea of the degrees of perfection was not new. Aristotle had used this idea in *De Philosophia*, and it is also closely related to Plato's idea of **Forms**. Indeed, Anselm uses the idea of God in a way that is very similar to Plato's use of the 'Form of the Good' – as the source of goodness. Plato argued that you could only recognize and evaluate goodness because of a prior knowledge of the Form of the Good. In his *Monologion*, Anselm is effectively saying the same thing – that the idea of degrees of goodness, or of any other quality, makes no sense without some prior knowledge of that which is perfect, and for Anselm that perfect being is what he calls God.

Plato's cave

In Plato's 'cave' allegory in *The Republic*, prisoners in a cave are chained to face the back wall. Behind them there is a fire, and between them and the fire are various objects, which cast their shadows onto the wall. The prisoners take these shadows for reality, since they have known nothing else. One prisoner, released from his shackles, turns round and sees first the objects casting the shadows and then the source of the light. He makes his way out of the cave, painfully blinded at first by the brightness of the sunlight beyond the entrance to the cave. He now sees reality, and recognizes the shadows below for what they were.

For Plato, this image reflects a key feature of his understanding of reality: that individual things, like the shadows in the cave, are but imperfect copies of their 'form'. Thus we only know things to be trees because they share in the qualities of the 'form of the tree', the ideal concept by which individual trees are to be understood. Chief of these forms is 'The Form of the Good'.

So how does this affect the ontological argument?

- Imagine you have an assortment of apples. You can arrange them according to quality and size, absence of defects and colour. You can set them in rank order, but you will always be able to imagine an apple that is just a little better than any existing apple.
- Now imagine 'the perfect apple'. It has qualities that go beyond any one existing apple – and so, in that sense, it does not exist. But without that concept of the perfect apple, how would you be able to judge the quality of all the existing apples?
- If you tried to argue that 'the perfect apple' existed in the same way that the other apples existed, you would be following Gaunilo and his argument for the perfect island.
- By contrast, the argument in *Proslogion* Chapter 4 underlines the fact that the existence of God, for Anselm, is *not* like the existence of other things. God is a unique but necessary

concept. The word 'God' may be dismissed, but the reality which that word signifies for Anselm is something that he cannot deny.

So:

- 'God', for Anselm, is not a limited object, and therefore does not 'exist' in the way that other objects exist.
- Anselm's idea of God springs from his awareness of degrees of goodness in the world.

> **Note**
>
> One of the great debates in philosophy is whether individual things are 'real' and the ideal representations of them are merely intellectual abstractions – 'names' we give to groups of similar things (this view is termed **nominalism**) – or whether those ideals or 'forms' are real, and individual things are merely derivative of them (**Platonism**, or **realism**).

In her book *Metaphysics as a Guide to Morals*, Iris Murdoch claimed that the argument about necessary existence can only be taken in the context of this Platonic view of degrees of reality. She pointed out that the ontological argument is not simply a piece of logic, but something that points to a spiritual reality that transcends any limited idea of God. It is also something that goes beyond individual religions:

> An ultimate religious 'belief' must be that even if all 'religions' were to blow away like mist, the necessity of virtue and the reality of the good would remain. This is what the Ontological Proof tries to 'prove' in terms of a unique formulation.
>
> (p. 427)

And this, she claims, is a necessary part of our understanding of life:

> What is perfect must exist, that is, what we think of as goodness and perfection, the 'object' of our best thoughts, must be something real, indeed especially and most real, not as contingent accidental reality but as something fundamental, essential and necessary. What is experienced as most real in our lives is connected with a value which points further on. Our consciousness of failure is a source

of knowledge. We are constantly in process of recognizing the falseness of our 'goods', and the unimportance of what we deem important. Great art teaches a sense of reality, so does ordinary living and loving.

(p. 430)

Comments
- If we think of the ontological argument simply in terms of 'existence is a predicate' then Kant was probably right, and Anselm wrong, for to say that something 'exists' is quite different from anything else about it.
- But Anselm's argument can also be taken to illustrate the belief that some idea of 'that than which no greater can be thought' is a necessary part of the way we understand the world.
- The ontological argument is about how we relate the ordinary, conditioned, limited things we experience to the idea of the perfect, the absolute and the unconditioned.

Where does that leave God? Well, if Anselm's second form of the argument, and Malcolm's interpretation of it, are correct then God's existence, if he exists, cannot be a matter of chance: it is either necessary or impossible. What seems certain is that God does not exist in the sense that other contingent, physical things exist. Whatever else he might be, he is not part of the world in that sense. But we knew that already, from the qualities ascribed to God in Chapter 03: God is simply not that sort of thing.

The cosmological argument

In his *Enquiry Concerning Human Understanding*, Hume said:

.. we can never ascribe to the cause any qualities, but what are exactly sufficient to produce the effect.

Which was, in some ways, to repeat an older philosophical principle, known as Ockham's razor, that when there are a number of equally possible explanations for something, one should accept the simplest.

We need to keep this principle in mind as we turn to the Cosmological argument – which is the attempt to argue from the fact of the world's existence to a transcendent creator. In seeking an explanation (if one is needed) for why the world is, one is not justified in positing a God with qualities other than those required for the purpose of creation.

It is, of course, possible to come at the question of the existence of the world from quite a different angle. Richard Swinburne, for example, starts with the idea of a personal God and then asks if such a God would have a reason for making the world the way it is. So, for example, in considering the fact that human beings can choose to understand the world and to act, he says:

> It is because it provides these opportunities for humans that God has a reason to create a world governed by natural laws of the kind we have.

> (*Does God Exist?* p. 51)

Indeed, he can go on to say:

> God has reason to make an orderly world, because beauty is a good thing ...

> (p. 54)

If you start from such a view of a personal God who shares your views about giving individuals responsibility, about the moral challenge posed by suffering, and your taste in beauty, then it is, of course, possible to interpret the world to fit.

It is more of a challenge to start with the raw facts of the world as we experience it, and see if its existence *requires* belief in a creator. It might then be equally possible to conclude that the universe is 'just there' as a brute fact which requires no further explanation, or that any explanation would be beyond the understanding of humans, since their whole way of reasoning is part of the universe and cannot get outside it, or achieve a view of the universe as a whole.

The Kalam argument

There are two forms of the cosmological argument. The better known is that of Aquinas (1224–74) which he set out in the first three of his famous 'Five Ways'. The other, known as the Kalam argument, was set out by the Muslim philosophers al-Kindi (ninth century) and al-Ghazali (1058–1111).

Note

For a fascinating discussion of cosmology and the Kalam argument, see W. L. Craig *The Kalam Cosmological Argument*, Macmillan, 1979.

The Kalam argument is that, looking back in time, the universe must have a first cause. It may be set out like this:

- Everything that begins to exist has a cause for its existence.
- The universe began to exist.
- Therefore the universe must have a cause.

This argument throws up a very basic question: If you have a sequence of events, each one caused by another that precedes it, stretching back in time, can that sequence be infinite?

Although a theoretical infinity (as used in mathematics) may seem a straightforward idea, actual infinities cause all sorts of problems. Infinity plus one, equals infinity; infinities cannot grow. Since the time of Aristotle, philosophers have argued that an actual infinity cannot exist. Even if it did, how could you know that something was infinite? It is not the same as being without discernable limit.

You can therefore present the Kalam argument like this:

- an actual infinite number cannot exist
- therefore the series of causes for the world being as it is now cannot be an **infinite** temporal sequence
- in other words, the sequence of causes must be finite
- therefore the world began to exist at some point in the past
- there was a time in the past when one of two states was possible – that there should be, or should not be, a universe.

Al-Ghazali argued that when two states of affairs are equally possible the one that comes about must be willed by a personal agent.

Comment

A circle provides an infinite journey. The surface of a sphere provides for infinite movement in all directions.

Therefore, it is possible to think of a universe that is limited both in terms of space and time, and yet appears infinite to those within it.

Aquinas' versions

From the age of five, Thomas Aquinas had been brought up in the Benedictine monastery of Monte Cassino, but because of the war between Frederick II and the Pope, he moved to the secular university at Naples when he was 14, to continue his studies there. That was a crucial move for Aquinas, for the University of Naples taught the philosophy of Aristotle, and he was able to use Aristotle's ideas as an intellectual vehicle for setting down his own religious philosophy.

Aquinas presented **Five Ways** in which he believed the existence of God could be shown. They are:

1 The argument from an unmoved mover.
2 The argument from an uncaused cause.
3 The argument from possibility and necessity.
4 The argument from degrees of quality.
5 The argument from design.

The fourth of these has already been considered, for a version of it came in Anselm's *Monologion*. It concerns the way in which we understand goodness and perfection – and moves from them to the idea of a source of goodness. In *Summa Theologiae* (Book 1, Chapter 1, 5:1) Aquinas speaks of goodness as *achieved actuality*.

This idea comes from Aristotle, for whom everything has a potential (a **final cause**) and it is considered 'good' to the extent that it fulfils that potential. For example, a good knife is one that cuts well – its goodness comes from actualizing its essential nature. Hence the idea of value or perfection is related to degrees of existence and actuality; the most real is also the most valuable and the most good. To be good without qualification is to be absolutely real.

If goodness is completeness, then within a world of limited, fallible things, goodness is likely to be rather lacking. Nothing will display perfection. (This is rather like the Buddhist idea that everything is 'unsatisfactory' – we can always look beyond what exists for something more, our craving for perfection in particular things can be a source of frustration.) For Aquinas, goodness and completeness are qualities that belong to God alone, whereas finite things have only a partial share in them.

The last of the arguments, based on the idea of **design**, will be examined in the next section. For now, however, we are concerned with the first three, which are forms of the cosmological argument. Unlike the ontological argument, which was based on logic, Aquinas' cosmological arguments are based on the observation of the world.

The first may be presented like this:

- everything that moves is moved by something
- that mover is in turn moved by something else again
- **but** this chain of movers cannot be infinite, or movement would not have started in the first place
- **therefore** there must be an unmoved mover, causing movement in everything, without itself actually being moved
- this unmoved mover is what people understand by 'God'.

Although referred to as the 'unmoved mover', the movement that Aquinas is thinking about is more a matter of change than of physical displacement. Everything that changes is changed by something else. His example is of fire causing something potentially hot to become actually hot, and therefore changing. But the thing that does the changing must itself be changed by something else. Now, we must stop somewhere, otherwise there will be no first change, and, as a result, no subsequent changes. This first cause of change, itself not changed by anything, is what he understands by God.

The second argument has the same structure:

- everything has a cause
- every cause itself has a cause
- **but** you cannot have an infinite number of causes
- **therefore** there must be an uncaused cause, which causes everything to happen without itself being caused by anything else
- such an uncaused cause is what people understand by 'God'.

A possible objection to this argument is that you might indeed have an infinite number of causes or movers. Instead of stretching back into the past in a straight line (with all the problems that the idea of an actually infinite number can cause), the series of causes could be circular, or looped in a figure of eight, so that you never get to a first cause, and everything is quite adequately explained by the one cause that comes immediately before it. But this image of circularity does not really help, for it is unlikely that Aquinas was thinking of a series of causes (or movers) stretching into the past. His argument actually suggests a hierarchy of causes here and now. This is the crucial difference between the Kalam argument and Aquinas's version.

Example

Of the two versions of the cosmological argument, Aquinas' is the one which most closely reflects that actual nature of the cause of particular events. For example, I sit at a computer typing these words. What is the cause of this action?

- One might trace back the muscular movements to electrical impulses in my brain. In turn these physical systems might be related to oxygen, food and drink that I consume in order to maintain them.
- There is also the chain of causes that have put this computer on this desk, including those who have developed the software and hardware. This will touch on many lives of people I will never know.
- Then there is the publisher of this series of books and the whole tradition of reading and buying books.
- There is also the fact that ideas have been written down and discussed over the centuries. This forms another chain of causes, linking thirteenth-century thinkers like Aquinas to twenty-first-century writers.
- And then there are the causes in my personal history that have led me to the point at which I have chosen to write this particular book.
- But I also need gravity to keep me in my chair, and heat from the sun to make life on planet Earth possible. Without the huge gravitational pull of the planet Jupiter, the Earth would long since have been destroyed by incoming space debris.

Thus the causes of this simple action of keying words spread outwards to include the size of the Earth, the Sun and Jupiter. The mind reels!

Causes grow exponentially. Each action has a theoretically infinite number of causes. Equally, each action may produce a theoretically infinite number of results. At any moment, we move within a seamless web of causality that goes forwards and backwards through time and outwards through space.

The key point

Everything is only fully understood in terms of the whole. But how is the whole to be understood? **That** is the cosmological question.

The third argument follows from the first two:

- individual things come into existence and later cease to exist
- therefore at one time none of them was in existence
- **but** something comes into existence only as a result of something else that already exists
- **therefore** there must be a being whose existence is necessary, and that all would understand to be 'God'.

This further unpacks the points raised by the second argument. There is nothing in the universe which can account for the universe as a whole, for everything is limited. To get an explanation for the whole, you need to get outside the normal chains of cause and effect and therefore beyond the universe.

Comment

The problem we face concerns our imagination and the implication of the word 'beyond'. The universe is theoretically infinite – however large we imagine it, we can always imagine something more. Therefore, to imagine (in the sense of getting a mental picture of) a cause 'outside' the universe is simply to extend the universe to include that cause.

Our conceptual ability is limited to the picturing of actual entities. We can develop concepts that get beyond those conceptual limitations (for example, a theoretical infinity) but when we try to integrate them into the rest of our thinking, we have to take great care.

'God' is a concept that has suffered from being visually conceptualized and therefore 'placed' within the universe in a way that is quite inappropriate.

Perhaps attempting to think about an uncaused cause beyond the world is something that our minds are not designed to do. The philosopher Kant argued that the whole notion of cause and effect was one of the ways (along with the concepts of space and time) in which our minds interpret the world – we cannot help but impose causality upon our experience. If Kant is right, then an uncaused cause is a mental impossibility.

A rather different objection to the cosmological argument came from David Hume (1711–76). He based all knowledge on the observation of the world. Something is said to be a cause because it is seen to occur just before the thing that is called its effect, and the linking of cause and effect depends on the observation of them as two separate things.

But, in the case of the world as a whole, we have a unique 'effect', and therefore cannot observe its cause. We cannot get 'outside' the world to see both the world and its cause, and thus establish the relationship between them.

Nor, since this is the only world we know, can we say that in the case of all **other** worlds there was seen to be a cause, and that therefore there is likely to be one in the case of **this** world.

If, like Hume, you consider sense impressions to be the basis of all knowledge, then the cosmological proofs cannot be accepted as giving proof of the existence of a God who is outside the world known through the senses.

An important limitation

Aquinas was well aware of the possibility of taking this sort of argument in a crude way, and he was at pains to guard against using the argument to defend a simplistic idea of God. In *Summa Theologiae* (Book I, Chapter 1, Section 2:2) just before introducing the Five Ways, he says of the arguments that he is about to produce:

> ... any effect of a cause demonstrates that its cause exists: it could not occur unless its cause first existed. In such proofs the central link is not what the cause is (since we cannot even ask what a thing is until we know that it exists) but what the name of the cause is used to mean; and, as we shall see, what the word *God* means derives from his effects. God's effects then are enough to prove that God exists, even if they are not enough to help us comprehend what he is.

So Aquinas never intended that his arguments should be used to **define** 'God' – merely to illustrate the existence of something to which that word could be applied. They do not **prove** that there is a God who is the uncaused cause or unmoved mover, for (as Hume or Kant would readily show) that is beyond the possibility of human reason. However, they do point towards the sort of reality that a religious person is thinking about when he or she uses the word 'God' – not a particular thing within (or, imaginatively, outside) the universe, but a reality which underlies and sustains everything. Not one cause among the myriads of others that determine every event, but that which lies within and yet beyond all of them.

The Copleston–Russell debate

In 1948, the BBC broadcast a debate between the Catholic theologian and philosopher F. C. Copleston and Bertrand Russell. In it, Copleston presents his version of Aquinas' third argument – the Argument from Contingency – and Russell responds to it. Russell's view is that while individual contingent things require a cause or explanation outside themselves, the world as a whole does not.

The debate is valuable in that is covers many of the key issues here, including the distinction between necessary and contingent, *a priori* and *a posteriori*, analytic and synthetic, and it touches of the broad issues of 'sufficient reason' and whether we should expect the world as a whole to be intelligible.

The arguments presented are concise and densely packed, and a further summary here cannot do them justice, any more than Russell's comment that 'the universe is just there, and that's all' (frequently cited by students in examination essays as though his final and only comment) does justice to his position!

The debate is reproduced in Russell's *Why I am not a Christian*, published in 1957, and transcripts are available on-line – just key 'Copleston Russell' into a search engine.

The teleological argument

The Teleological argument is concerned with the sense of a 'telos' (meaning 'end' or 'purpose') in the world. It argues that the sense of purposeful design we see in nature suggests that the world has a designer – God.

In *Summa Theologiae*, Aquinas links the idea of causation to that of purpose. First of all, he makes the point that causation gives things their perfections:

Something therefore causes in all other things their being, their goodness, and whatever other perfections they have. And this is what we call *God*.

Then he links this to the idea of purpose:

Goal-directed behaviour is observed in all bodies obeying natural laws, even when they lack awareness ... But nothing lacking awareness can tend to a goal except it be directed by someone with awareness and understanding; the arrow, for example, requires an archer. Everything in nature, therefore, is directed to its goal by someone with understanding, and this we call *God*.

David Hume (in his *Dialogues Concerning Natural Religion*) presented a form of the teleological argument and offered several important criticisms of it. In the dialogue, the argument is presented by Cleanthes:

Look round the world, contemplate the whole and every part of it: you will find it to be nothing but one great machine, subdivided into an infinite number of lesser machines, which again admit of subdivisions to a degree beyond what human senses and faculties can trace and explain. All these various machines, and even their most minute parts, are adjusted to each other with an accuracy which ravishes into admiration all men who have ever contemplated them. The curious adapting of means to ends, throughout all nature, resembles exactly, though it much exceeds, the productions of human contrivance – of human design, thought, wisdom, and intelligence. Since therefore the effects resemble each other, we are led to infer, by all the rules of analogy, that the causes also resemble, and that the Author of nature is somewhat similar to the mind of man, thought possessed of much larger faculties, proportioned to the grandeur of the world which he has executed. By this argument *a posteriori*, and by this argument alone, do we prove at once the existence of a Deity and his similarity to human mind and intelligence.

Hume (in the guise of Philo summarising Cleanthes) makes the key point that matter cannot arrange itself in this way:

Stone and mortar and wood, without an architect, never erect a house. But the ideas of the human mind, we see, by an unknown, inexplicable economy, arrange themselves so as to form the plan of a watch or house. Experience, therefore, proves that there is an original principle of order in mind, not in matter.

Before moving on to look at Hume's objections to the argument, we should pause to consider whether this assertion – that matter cannot arrange itself according to a design or purpose – is correct.

Evolution

Darwin's theory of natural selection provides an alternative explanation for design, and one that does **not** require the aid of any external designer. He argued that those members of a species whose characteristics were best suited to enable them to survive in their environment, went on to breed. Those ill suited were more likely to die off before doing so. This mechanical process of selection meant that whenever an advantageous characteristic appeared, those who displayed it had a natural advantage which they could pass on to a proportionately larger number of offspring. In this way a species could gradually evolve without the need for any external agency.

- Darwin therefore offered a mechanical explanation for what had previously been thought of as possible only through the agency of mind (in this case, the mind of God).
- Therefore Aquinas' and Cleanthes' assertion that an arrow requires an archer, or that bricks can't arrange themselves into a house, is challenged by natural selection.

Although Darwin saw how natural selection worked, he did not know the process by which tiny variations arose in a species. Now, thanks to an understanding of genetics, we know that, within living things, damage occurs in a random way to the genetic information coded on DNA molecules, causing these random mutations. Where such a mutation is beneficial, those displaying it breed more successfully and therefore pass it on to a proportionately larger number of offspring, and thus the species gradually changes. Life progresses because what is randomly produced subsequently takes advantage of its situation. Genetics therefore endorses Darwin's theory, and it is now possible, by examining genetic material, to trace back the process of differentiation by which species develop and separate off from one another.

Genetic mutations may occur randomly, but that does not imply that the process of evolutionary change is a matter of chance. There has been considerable debate on the whole issue of random change and its implications. In 1970, Jacques Monod published *Chance and Necessity* in which he argued that creative developments could arise on the basis of random chance. The key feature of Darwinism, however, is that tiny changes provide opportunities which gradually build up into apparently 'designed' features that could not have happened as a result of a one-off chance.

In recent years, there has been considerable interest in the ability of 'open' complex systems (i.e. those that interact with the world around them) to self-arrange and develop. All that takes place without any need to posit an external agency or controlling mind.

A clear exploration of this is found in Richard Dawkins book *The Blind Watchmaker* (1986). He illustrates the way in which random changes can lead to am amazing variety of apparently 'designed' forms. Particularly in his *The God Delusion* (2006) he has criticized any notion of external supernatural agency to account for the 'designed' appearance of things, and has pointed out that natural selection is certainly not the result of chance, but that the evolution of complex forms takes place through a systematic process of small steps.

Hume's objections

Hume (in the guise of Philo) argues that our concepts of design are limited and cannot be applied to the world as a whole. He asks:

> Have worlds ever been formed under your eye …?

In other words, the analogy between a designed object and its designer and the apparent design in the world and God cannot hold. We do not know what it would be like to design a world – so how can we be sure of a designer?

But Cleanthes continues:

> Consider, anatomise the eye, survey its structure and contrivance, and tell me, from your own feeling, if the idea of a contriver does not immediately flow in upon you with a force like that of sensation.

In other words, common sense leads to the idea of a designer, in spite of the fact that one is not able to stand back and observe the act of design.

Hume argues that a supposed cause need only be proportional to its effect. The world is limited therefore it cannot be the basis for arguing for an infinite or perfect God. Also, when observing the world:

> ... it is impossible for us to tell, from our limited views, whether this system contains any great faults or deserves any considerable praise if compared to other possible or even real systems. ... Many worlds might have been botched and bungled, throughout an eternity, ere this system was struck out; much labour lost, many fruitless trials made, and a slow but continued improvement carried on during infinite ages in the art of world-making.

A key feature of Hume's first comment here is that, even if you find that there is order in the world, all that it enables you to say is that there is order in the world. It does not justify the leap from that sense of order to the idea of a concept of a God. This point is brought out clearly by Mackie in *The Miracle of Theism*, who says:

> The further postulation of a god ... is a gratuitous addition to this solution, an attempted underpinning which is as needless as it is incomprehensible.

(p. 251)

He makes this point in contrast to Hans Kung (in *Does God Exist?*) who sees God as the 'ground and support of reality' and who claims that:

> 'If someone affirms God, he knows why he can trust reality.'

(p. 572)

Kung contrasts this basic sense of trust with an atheistic nihilism. Against this, Mackie wants to say that you can also have a basic trust in reality on intellectual grounds, and that humans make their own values. In other words, like Hume, he argues that you do not need to take a further step and go beyond what is required by the actual experience of an ordered world.

For reflection

Someone has to win a lottery, even if there is an almost infinite unlikelihood of any particular person doing so. The winner might claim it to be a miracle, wrought by a supernatural designer. But what of all the rest of us who have not won?

- Design is easy to see in retrospect, and with a selective view of the facts.
- Design is also easy to see if you make your own existence the centre and purpose of the universe.

If any one particular design **were** a matter of chance, it would still not justify the notion of an external designer, but natural selection has shown that design is **not** based on chance, but on the cumulative result of small changes.

Hume makes three other important points:

> The world plainly resembles more an animal or a vegetable than it does a watch or a knitting-loom. Its cause, therefore, it is more probable, resembles the cause of the former.

> ... we have no data to establish any system of cosmogony. Our experience, so imperfect in itself and so limited both in extent and duration, can afford us no probably conjecture concerning the whole of things.

> I would fain ask how an animal could subsist unless its parts were so adjusted?

For reflection

Consider the last point made by Hume. In order to live, all the various parts of your body need to be working together. If you had no lungs, you could not breathe, and the rest of your body would fail for lack of oxygen. Without a digestive system, you could not get nourishment to provide the energy to maintain all your systems. Does this imply a careful designer?

You could argue that any creature that needs oxygen and nourishment is going to die quickly if it is born without lungs or a digestive system. Such creatures therefore cannot exist. This argument works by simple logic:

- Everything is as it is.
- If anything were different, everything would be different.
- Everything contributes to everything else.
- If everything else were different, everything would contribute differently.

Projected design

Kant argued that our minds impose the concepts of time, space and causality upon experience. They are regulative concepts. We experience everything as having a cause and as existing in space and time because that is the way we look at things.

Now this has implications for both the cosmological and teleological arguments. We could argue that, if we see the universe as an ordered place, it is because our minds are predisposed to interpret events in an orderly way. Indeed, modern philosophers of what we generally term a 'postmodernist' approach, would see the very act of talking or writing about the world as a process of creating order. Order and design are a feature of the world that we create.

Hence, it could be argued that, if we see design in the natural world, it is because our minds are predisposed to project order and design upon it.

Redundant watchmaker?

Is the world constructed like a watch, where each piece is constructed to move in exactly the right way to enable the watch to achieve its overall purpose in telling the time? This image and question was raised by Hume, and was taken up a little later by William Paley (1743–1805). In what is probably the best-known version of the teleological argument, he suggests that, coming across a watch on the ground and examining its workings, one would be led to assume that it could not be the result of chance, but required the hand of a skilled designer. With the same logic that led Aquinas to say that an arrow needed an archer, Paley argued that the intricate design of the world (in which, like the watch, particular parts worked together in ways that suggested complex design and planning) led inescapably to the conclusion that the world itself had to have a designer, God.

Whereas the logic of the argument had been both set out and challenged by Hume, Paley's version, published at the beginning of the nineteenth century, set the scene for the debate that arose later in that century as a result of Darwin's theory of natural selection.

Clearly, natural selection provides a mechanism by which species appear to design themselves, thus making the watchmaker redundant. However, natural selection was put forward as a theory to account for the phenomenon of the variety of living things. It was not an attempt to discredit religion, nor to oppose the sense that nature reflected God's design. Indeed, towards the end of *The Origin of Species*, Darwin wonders at the way in which species have evolved, from the most simple to the most complex, and describes the powers of nature as having been 'breathed by the Creator into a few forms or into one'.

Faced with the fact of evolution, one possible line of argument for a theist is to say that natural selection is the tool by which God brings about his chosen design. However, in that case the burden of proof is on the theist for taking a step beyond the evidence of design by natural selection. If natural selection sufficiently accounts for design, why posit the existence of a creator god?

Comment

In the chapter on religious language (see p. 46), we discussed the dilemma of whether or not you could prove that there was a gardener attending to the flowers and weeds. The conclusion was that there was no direct evidence for the gardener, and so the hypothesis died the 'death of a thousand qualifications'. The situation here is rather similar. Since God cannot be observed in the act of designing, whether directly or through the tool of natural selection, there can never be sufficient evidence to settle the matter by looking at the 'flowers and weeds' in the world.

The choice of whether to see the world as designed, or as the product of a natural mechanism, is therefore a matter of religious commitment, rather than the outcome of a scientific or logical examination.

Within the philosophy of religion, one topic naturally leads on into another. Evolution will need to be considered again under 'religion and science'. Equally, because evolution only progresses through the huge loss of life required for natural selection to be effective, one might well consider whether a God who used such a 'tool' could be considered to be good – a topic to consider under what is generally termed 'the problem of evil'.

To sum up

- Religious common sense tends to see the intricacies of nature as pointing to a designing and purposive creator – God.
- We do not have the evidence or the perspective to justify an analogy between human creativity and the idea of a divine creator. As a logical argument, the teleological approach cannot be sustained.
- The most we can say is that the world appears to have order and purpose. But even that may be challenged on two major fronts:

  1 The observation of the way in which open complex systems appear to organize themselves provides an alternative to a design made by an external agent.

  2 Design and purpose may be seen as projections upon the external world of aspects of human creativity.

- For a person who already believes in God, the cosmological and teleological arguments may provide support for that belief. On the other hand, for the person without such a prior commitment, they are logically inconclusive.

The moral argument

If pure logic (the ontological argument), the fact of the world's existence (cosmological arguments) or the apparent design and purposefulness of the world (the teleological argument) cannot give definitive proof of the existence of God, where might one look for such proof?

It seems reasonable that the next step should be to examine those aspects of human experience which relate to religion. In other words, is there anything in the way in which people respond to the idea of God that can be used to prove that God exists?

There are two possibilities here:

- the experience of morality
- religious experience itself.

We looked at religious experience in the first chapter, and will return to it shortly to see to what extent it can be used as a basis of proof for the existence of God. For now, we need to consider if there is a valid argument for the existence of God based on morality.

Where do moral rules come from? There are three possibilities:

- They may be God's commands (but this makes any attempt to argue from morality to the existence of God circular, so we may set it aside for now).
- Moral rules may spring from the basic features of human nature, and our biological or social needs. If there are such rules, they may well be absolute, since they would apply to all people at all times. Rules in this category may or may not require the support of belief in God.
- Moral rules may be the product of human society and human choice – such as promoting general welfare and the need for co-operation, for example. Such rules are unlikely to be absolute. They are devised to meet the needs of a particular situation.

We start with the second of these options:

Aristotle related morality to his idea of a final cause (a concept which we shall examine in Chapter 09). Basically, he held the view what we ought to do that which would lead to our maximum self-fulfilment. Once we understand our true nature, we will act accordingly – this is termed a **'natural law'** approach.

Taking this approach, we may say that morality is rational and objective: it depends on our understanding of our own nature and goals, and does not depend upon the any rules imposed upon us by a god.

Within ancient Greek philosophy there was a debate between the Stoics and the Epicureans on how morality related to happiness. On the one side was the conviction that to do your duty was the way in which you would achieve true happiness, and on the other was the idea that the pursuit of happiness was your duty. Both sides of this debate require some linkage between duty and happiness; if the world is a rational place, the one ought to result in the other.

This attempt to give an objective basis for morality was approached from a rather different angle by Kant. He believed that the cosmological arguments could never prove the existence of God, but that, by getting rid of those arguments, he could make way for an understanding of God based on faith, rather than reason. He did this by examining the idea of moral experience, and in particular the ideas of virtue and happiness with which the Greeks had been concerned. He argued that, in an ideal world, they should follow one another, so that doing what is right (virtue) should ultimately lead to happiness. But, as we look at the world around us, it is by no means certain that virtue will lead to happiness. Why then should anyone be moral?

Kant started from the fact that people do actually have a sense of moral obligation: a feeling that something is right and must be done, no matter what the consequences. He called this sense of moral obligation the **categorical imperative**, to distinguish it from a **hypothetical imperative** (which says, 'If you want to achieve this, then you must do that').

In *The Critique of Practical Reason* Kant explored the presuppositions of this categorical imperative. He asked, in effect: What do I actually believe about life if I respond to an absolute moral demand? Notice that he did **not** expect that one should accept the rational argument for these beliefs **before** being moral. Rather, he argued that, if a person responds to a moral imperative for reasons rational or otherwise, that response **implies** certain fundamental beliefs. He came to the conclusion that three things (which he called the *postulates* of the practical reason) were presupposed:

- freedom
- immortality
- God.

If you experience moral obligation, it implies that you are free to act (even if someone observing you claimed that you were not), that you will eventually experience happiness as a result of your virtue even if you will not do so in this life (as when someone sacrifices his or her own life for the benefit of others) and that, for this to be possible, there has to be some overall ordering principle which will reward virtue with happiness – and this might be called 'God'.

In other words, Kant is saying that you cannot **prove** the existence of God, but that your sense of morality implies the world is ordered in a moral way – and that, in turn, implies belief in God.

Note

The link between morality and belief in God is not without its difficulties. There are some (for example, Bertrand Russell in *Why I am Not a Christian*) who have argued that human maturity requires that we get rid of religion. They point out that a truly free rational choice is incompatible with religious concepts like sin and the idea of rewards and punishments. To obey out of fear, or in the hope of gaining some reward, is not the same as making a free moral choice.

In looking at an objective basis for morality, let us return for a moment to Kant's argument. If the idea of one thing causing another is something that our mind imposes on external reality, it cannot be used as the basis for a proof for the existence of God. This was the reason why he rejected the cosmological argument. So:

- **If** our minds impose the ideas of space, time and causality onto our understanding of the world, **then** to argue from these things to something outside the world is impossible.
- God, freedom and immortality are postulates of the practical reason, not things that we discover **in** the world that we experience. They are to do with **the way in which** we experience the world.
- God is therefore a **regulative** concept (part of our way of understanding) not a **constitutive** concept (one of the things out there to be discovered).

Kant's moral argument amounts to this:

If we know what it is to behave morally (to do what we believe to be right, even though it may be against our own immediate interests) then, in the very act of being moral, we presuppose the idea of God. This is not a God who exists within the world of phenomena, but a regulative concept – an overall idea of a divinely guaranteed moral order, that we use to help us make sense of life.

Let us be clear about the second option for morality – the idea that there is an objective moral order. It may be used as a way of introducing God as the upholder of a moral order (as Kant) but equally it may be used by the atheist to show that there can be a rational basis for morality that does **not** depend on God.

The third option is that morality is a human construct, a product of the individual's or society's needs for protection and regulation. This is a 'naturalistic' approach, and does not require belief in God. It is taken by, for example, Hume, and is widespread in modern thinking. It is particularly appropriate where there are a number of different sets of moral rules competing with one another, for example in multi-ethnic or multi-faith situations. Moral principles are seen as the products of particular social groups, and they may be changed by mutual agreement.

Summary

If you believe that there is an objective moral order, it may be used *either* to suggest that the world is created by a moral being (God), *or* to show that morality is well established on objective moral grounds and no idea of God is needed.

On the other hand, if morality is a human product, no God is required to account for moral experience.

On balance then, the moral argument cannot prove the existence of God.

The argument from religious experience

In Chapter 01, we examined some features of religious experience. We saw that a key feature was what was called the 'self-transcending' quality of an experience. In other words, something which could have been experienced in quite an ordinary way (and for which there might be a rational explanation) pointed beyond itself to reveal something about the meaning of life as a whole.

The various forms of language in Chapter 02 mirrored this self-transcending quality: language which had a straightforward, literal meaning could also go beyond that meaning in order to express the religious dimension.

But can such religious experience by used as an argument for the existence of God?

Someone who has a religious experience may say simply 'I have experienced God.' In one sense, that claim is irrefutable, for you cannot argue that someone has not had the experience that they claim to have had. **If that's what they call 'God' and that's what they've experienced, then no further proof is needed.**

On the other hand, there may be various ways of interpreting what is experienced. One person may call it 'God', another may say simply that it is a sense of beauty, or grandeur. One person may feel that he or she has been encountered by a reality that is in some way 'out there', another may say that it is all psychologically generated, or the result of drink or drugs.

In *An Introduction to the Philosophy of Religion*, Brian Davies asks if it is possible to be mistaken about what one experiences. If so, then it must also be possible to be correct about it. So, if someone could be mistaken about an experience of God, they could also be correct. The implication of that, he suggests, is that knowledge of God through experience is at least *possible*.

But notice the presupposition of such an argument. It requires a prior knowledge of what God is. If you do not know what God is, then there would be no grounds for saying that an experience of him was either correct or mistaken.

In other words: if you accept belief in God on other grounds, then religious experience may help to confirm it. If you do **not** then accounts of religious experience will tell you no more than what a person means by 'God'.

There is an additional problem. Davies asks whether we can know if someone is experiencing God or something else (p. 125–7). But there is a difficulty with such a question. How is it possible to experience God other than through experiencing something else as well? If God is infinite, he is not located in a particular place, nor does he have boundaries. Yet all sense data is of particular places – things are known only because they have boundaries. Sense data is the result of chopping up reality into segments: this is one thing; that is another.

So arguments about whether one has or has not experienced God all require prior knowledge of God. This follows from the general point that *all* experience involves interpretation (we experience 'as'). Prior beliefs influence what is experienced. A believer experiences 'God' – but is that a matter of sense data or of interpretation?

In terms of logical argument, there is a further problem:

- In order to be able to say that a person has or has not experienced X, one needs to know what X is (i.e. to have information about X that is independent of the present experience).

- But in the case of God, there is no such unambiguous, independent or objective information. If there were, then there would be no reason to be debating whether or not God exists!

- You could take the view that God is whatever a person chooses to call 'God'. If so, religious experience is a source of knowledge of God, but it remains convincing only for that individual, or those who accept or share in that experience.

- But that view will not satisfy a philosopher, who aims to understand the terms 'God' and 'exists' in such a way that the proposition 'God exists' can be shown to be either correct, incorrect or meaningless.

- Religious experience can therefore only become the basis for an argument about the existence of God, once there is the common acceptance of what the word 'God' means.

There are many descriptions of religious experiences from widely differing cultures. If you recognize in them some common core of experience, some reality to which they are all pointing, then you can say that religious experience contributes to your understanding of the meaning of the term 'God', and therefore to the reality to which that word refers.

On the other hand, if you feel that these experiences, however personally interesting for those who have them, do not point to a level of reality which is theoretically available to everyone, then you will remain unconvinced by any argument from religious experience.

The argument from religious experience may therefore be enlightening and persuasive, but it is not a logically compelling argument. For this reason, philosophers may not like it much. However, they need to recognize that, for religious people, it is probably the most persuasive of all arguments, because it relates 'God' directly to their own experience and that of the religious tradition within which they stand.

Conclusions

In considering all the arguments about the existence of God, it might be worth keeping the whole exercise in perspective by reminding ourselves that 'God' is hardly the sort of thing which might or might not happen to exist. Of course, this was an important feature of the ontological argument, but it is relevant to consider it in the context of the arguments in general. The theologian Paul Tillich, in *Systematic Theology* (Vol. I p. 262) says:

> ... the question of the existence of God can be neither asked nor answered. If asked, it is a question about that which by its very nature is above existence, and therefore the answer – whether negative or affirmative – implicitly denies the nature of God. It is as atheistic to affirm the existence of God as to deny it. God is being itself, not a being.

This reinforces what has been implied throughout the ontological and cosmological arguments: that what is being claimed is not the existence of one entity alongside others, but a fundamental way of regarding the whole universe. It is about the structures of 'being itself' (to use Tillich's term) not the possible existence of a being.

Of course, it is always possible to define 'God' simply in terms of the intuition of meaning and personal value that come through religious experience. If so, there is really nothing to discuss – 'God' is simply the term used for a particular way of engaging with and interpreting the world. On the other hand, if you adopt this personal and experiential interpretation of 'God', you will almost certainly fall foul of those who insist that God must exist in some objective sense.

Worth a bet?

Perhaps the last word in any discussion of the arguments for the existence of God should go to Pascal. In his *Pensées* (Section III, Number 233) he sets out his famous wager. He points out that you cannot decide the question of God's existence, therefore it is advisable to look at what you gain or lose by your belief or disbelief.

- If you believe in God and he exists, then you stand to gain infinite happiness as your reward.

- If you believe in God and he does not exist, you lose nothing.
- If you deny God's existence and he does in fact exist, then you lose your chance of infinite happiness.
- If you deny God's existence and he does not exist, you gain nothing.

Given these options, according to Pascal, for practical purposes it is better to bet on God existing! On the other hand, the very idea that it might be worth putting up with the minor inconvenience of religious observances for the possibility of a reward after death, must surely rank as one of the saddest arguments ever put forward by a religious writer!

So what has been achieved by the arguments?

- The ontological argument highlighted the logical problems in speaking about God as 'that than which no great can be conceived', and made the important distinction between logical and factual necessity.
- The cosmological and design arguments suggest that there are features of the world which lead the mind to that which goes beyond experience: What is the cause of everything? Why is the world as it is?
- The Kantian moral argument suggested that we all presuppose God (along with freedom and immortality) every time we experience a sense of moral obligation.
- The argument from religious experience could not be conclusive, since all experience is open to interpretations, but it did highlight the fact that there is an awareness at the heart of religion which struggles to find expression in beliefs, including belief in God.

Even if these arguments are not conclusive, they have value in indicating the sort of thing a religious person is thinking about when he or she uses the word 'God'. For a believer, they may reinforce faith. For an agnostic or atheist, they are unlikely to convince, but can at least illustrate the real differences in perspective that belief in the existence of God implies.

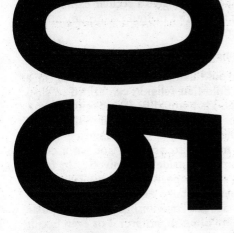

05

atheism and humanism

In this chapter you will:
- distinguish between atheism, agnosticism and secularism
- consider the appeal of humanism
- examine secular explanations of religion.

So far, in looking at religious experience, religious language and the concepts and arguments concerned with 'God', we have recognized that it is quite possible to give a secular explanation for the phenomenon of religion, and to find the arguments for the existence of God unpersuasive.

Those taking that view come from two very different camps:

- There are those who would call themselves religious, in a general sense, but who hold that religion can afford to shed its supernatural elements. That would be the position of, say, Don Cupitt (see above p. 67). It is also reflected in the widely held view among theologians that 'God' language is not literal, and that it is a mistake to present 'God' in a crude sense as 'a being' within or outside the universe. In fairly conservative terms, this was the position of Paul Tillich (see above p. 14). Indeed, there is a huge gap (seldom recognized by those who argue against religion) between popular religious beliefs, which are often supernatural or even occult in nature, and the arguments of liberal theologians and philosophers of religion.

- There are also those who see religion as either unnecessary or positively harmful. They offer secular explanations of religious phenomena, and choose to understand life according to the established principles of reason and evidence. Of those mentioned so far, Russell (see above p. 90) and Dawkins (see pp. 9 and 109) would take that view.

In this chapter we shall outline this second, non-religious perspective on religion, and also the positive claims made on behalf of humanism.

Atheism, agnosticism and secularism

Let us start with something of a caricature:

You regard religious people as guilt-ridden, cringing wimps, afraid to take responsibility for their life or face the reality of their own annihilation at death. At best, you see religion as a set of fairy tales, acted out to make the feeble feel better about themselves. At worst, you see it as an agent of emasculation, preventing growth and maturity. You regard their 'God' as a fiction behind which the religious hide. You are therefore likely to call yourself an atheist. That does not mean that you deny that the word 'God' has meaning for religious people – indeed you are the first to point out that it is a powerful but harmful idea. What you mean is that you do not see what they call 'God' as an inevitable, correct or desirable interpretation of reality.

This raises a fundamental problem:

- We have seen that a religious believer, faced with a logical argument about the existence of God, is going to be inclined to consider only those elements that favour the conclusion that God exists.
- But it is equally true that the atheist, as caricatured above, will equally come to religious arguments with the intention of dismissing any conclusion that does not fit his or her perspective.
- It is therefore very difficult (perhaps impossible) to consider arguments in the philosophy of religion in a completely objective or unbiased way.

Example

Richard Dawkins, a most lucid exponent of natural selection, of the benefits of science and of the wonders nature, is opposed to religion and presents a case against it most forcefully in *The God Delusion* (2006). He is keen to illustrate the crude supernatural beliefs of some believers, contrasting them with the logic and evidence that he sees as key to understanding the world. However, at the beginning of the book, he touches on those (including Einstein) who hold beliefs that could be termed 'religious', but whose concepts of God are not supernatural in nature. He sets aside such beliefs as irrelevant to the argument he wants to make – which is fundamentally to oppose what he sees as traditional supernatural beliefs.

Now that makes for a lively and straightforward argument, but it does not start to do justice to the subtleties of the philosophical concepts involved. For a philosopher like Aquinas, battling in the thirteenth century with Aristotelian concepts (the best available philosophy and science of his day) in order to understand how the universe can be causally sustained, the God that Dawkins rejects would have been quickly dismissed as crude and even idolatrous.

Let us clarify terms:

Atheism is the view that there is no God. It is defined negatively as a rejection of 'theism' and – by implication – the rejection of other beliefs involving God or gods. In terms of the arguments in the philosophy of religion, atheism is a position that rejects the arguments for the existence of God, and/or argues that the concept of God is illogical.

As used in the West, atheism is non-religious. However, it should be recognized that there are forms of religion (for example, Buddhism and some branches of Hinduism) which are compatible with atheism or agnosticism.

A caricature of atheism is that it is concerned only with physical reality and has no place for the subtleties of the human mind, beauty, awe at the wonders of nature, moral values and so on. But atheists do accept all these things – the difference being that they see them arising naturally out of this present, physical world. They do not require their origin to come from any supernatural source.

Agnosticism is rather different. It is the claim that there is no conclusive evidence upon which one can decide whether God exists or not. In many ways this is the least satisfactory position to take in the philosophy of religion, since – depending on how 'God' is defined – it neither follows reason and evidence rigorously (which may lead to atheism), nor does it yield a conclusion that is compatible with the articulation of religious experience. In other words, if someone is religious, they know what they mean by God, and it is at least part of the task of the philosophy of religion to tease out that meaning. Agnosticism is the conclusion that it is impossible to know whether that belief refers to an existing entity (God) or is simply a way of describing this element in human awareness.

Positive agnosticism

Of the various positions, agnosticism sometimes appears reasonable but least appealing, since it is generally not presented as forcefully as either religious belief or militant atheism. However, it can be seen as a positive and creative alternative, as is presented in a very readable and personal way by Mark Vernon in *Science, Religion and the Meaning of Life* (2007). This book also makes the important point that the supernatural God against which the atheist argues is unlikely to be accepted by the theologian either.

Agnosticism allows for a sense of wonder and for the intuition that there is a reality beyond what we can grasp intellectually. It can explore what religion is trying to grasp, without being wedded to religious doctrines.

Secularism is a phenomenon that exists over and above atheism and agnosticism. It is the view that the real concern of humankind is and should be with this world, rather than with metaphysical questions such as the existence of God.

An **abductive argument** is one that seeks the simplest and most coherent explanation. Thus, when it comes to explaining the way the world is, an abductive argument would favour atheism, since it does not require any additional supernatural causes. This follows Ockham's razor – that, when two explanations are equally possible, you should always accept the simplest. Abductive arguments may show that a belief is unnecessary as an explanation – they do not, however, show why the explanation may be favoured, even if an adequate but simpler one is available.

Nietzsche: God is dead

In *Thus Spoke Zarathustra* Friedrich Nietzsche (1844–1900) describes the prophet Zarathustra coming down from his mountain retreat and marvelling that the people he encounters do not yet recognize that God is dead.

Nietzsche saw that the world of his day was breaking away from all the former certainties and fixed structures of thought (which included the idea of God). He therefore proclaimed the death of God as an inescapable fact. God was no longer there; the world was drifting freely towards an unknown future.

One should view Nietzsche against the background of the nineteenth century. He was reflecting the shifting times within which he lived. His atheism was in part a rebellion against what he saw as the emasculating effect of the Christian religion – showing concern for the welfare of the least fortunate rather than promoting the welfare of the strongest and the leaders.

But he also saw that, in place of God, there needed to be some goal, some sense of direction for humankind, without which it would simply languish. The model he uses is that of evolution, reflecting a nineteenth-century optimism about the future of the species. Once humankind is free from belief in God, it can seek its ultimate meaning and purpose in terms of its own future. But how is such a future to be conceived and articulated? Nietzsche explores that future using ideas that stem from the Classical Greek view of the qualities to be cultivated in the good life, rather than those embodied in the Christian Gospel. For him it was the appearance of the *Übermensch* – the 'superman' – who would represent the next step forward in the progress that had led from the animal world up to humankind. Man is something to be surpassed.

In a way, Nietzsche was calling for courage – courage to see the world exactly as it is and to affirm it. In his idea of 'the eternal recurrence' he throws out the challenge of being prepared to say 'yes' to living this same life, exactly as it is now, over and over again. For him, religion was an escape from the task of building the future, and a failure to accept present reality.

Nietzsche is a difficult but fascinating and challenging writer. All we can do here is note that it is not enough to get rid of God, one has to consider the implications – including what one puts in place of God in terms of an overall goal and understanding of life.

Secular explanations of God

Whether God exists or not, it is an undeniable fact that many people believe in him. Why? Is there a rational, scientific explanation for the idea of God or for the persistence of belief in God?

For reflection

The fundamental issue is this: if there is a sufficient explanation of the idea of God in secular terms, is it not an unnecessary complication (in the absence of any other evidence) to claim also that he exists?

A question to ask of any secular explanation is this: if the idea of God is effective (i.e. that people find it religiously satisfying, that it provides a useful way of interpreting the way the world is, or that it helps them to find meaning and purpose in their lives), does this explanation give a satisfactory account of that effectiveness?

Of course, we need to recognize that all explanations for religion arise at a particular time and for a particular purpose; Feuerbach and Marx, for example, represent radical thinking in the nineteenth century, and their views need to be seen against the religious and social attitudes of that time.

Feuerbach

In *The Essence of Christianity* (1841) Ludwig Feuerbach (1804–72) described God thus:

> God as a morally perfect being is nothing else than the realized idea, the fulfilled law of morality, the moral nature of man posited as the absolute being.

> (translation: Evans, p. 46)

In other words, God is a projection of the human moral idea. He is our idea of what the perfectly moral person would like to be, freed from all the limitations that apply to individual human beings:

> God is the self-consciousness of man freed from all discordant elements.

> (p. 97)

All actual individuals and societies are limited, so they can never completely exemplify the ideals and hopes we have of them. (In a way, this reflects Plato's theory that individual things are pale, imperfect copies of an eternal 'form' or ideal.) But we still have these hopes and aspiration for something perfect. Feuerbach argued that God was a projection of those ideals; to believe in him was to believe in a moral order freed from all conflicts and limitations. He is a way of describing the highest aspirations of our own self-consciousness.

In the nineteenth century, such thoughts were regarded as threatening and unacceptable to many, and when Feuerbach first challenged belief in personal immortality and belief in a transcendent God, at the age of 26, he effectively ended his academic career.

Feuerbach argued that the natural world, known through the senses, is the sum total of reality. Hence 'God' is seen as part of that world only by being a projection of an aspect of humankind. In this sense, religion becomes a feature of humankind that should be studied by anthropologists – a phenomenon like any other. That did not imply that religion had not played an important part in human self-awareness, since it was through religion that a sense of the world as a whole and humankind's part in it had been developed. However, Feuerbach argued that it had already performed that task. It should now be recognized as a projection of ideals, and should give way to a humanism which would allow those ideals to be developed in this world, rather than projected out into another realm. He accepted the need for human spirituality, and saw the benefits of celebrating human and natural qualities, but argued against these being associated with supernatural beliefs.

For reflection

It is surprising how close this comes to some modern, liberal approaches to religion. The minister at a baptism who speaks of the life-giving benefits of water, and its ability to wash away impurities, as an introduction to the ritual for cleansing an individual and giving him or her new life, is following a line that is pure Feuerbach – giving spiritual significance to what is natural!

In other words, for Feuerbach, people create gods to express the spiritual significance of life, just as the artist creates a work of art in order to express his or her awareness of beauty. But for Feuerbach, it was better to celebrate life directly, as encountered in this world.

Marx

In his most famous passage, in *Introduction to the Critique of the Hegelian Philosophy of Right*, Karl Marx (1818–83) says of religion:

> Religion is the sigh of the oppressed creature, the feelings of a heartless world, just as it is the spirit of unspiritual conditions. It is the opium of the people. The people cannot be really happy until it has been deprived of illusory happiness by the abolition of religion. The demand that the people should shake itself free of illusion as to its own condition is the demand that it should abandon a condition which needs illusion.

This continues the line of argument presented by Feuerbach. Its implications would seem to be:

- that religion may be effective: but only because it serves as a consolation for intolerable conditions in this world.
- that the happiness it offers is illusory, not real, since it does not remove from people's lives those conditions that cause them to suffer.
- that people would be better freed from illusion, and that this can only be effected by the abolition of religion.
- that only once people are freed from illusion will they set about taking responsibility for abandoning those conditions which cause them suffering.

You may wish to reflect on these things again when we come to consider the problem of suffering and evil. As far as secular explanations of God are concerned, we should notice that, whereas Feuerbach offered quite a positive interpretation of God's role as a projection, Marx offered an entirely negative one.

The reason it is negative is that Marx believed that real happiness is possible if people can change the conditions that cause them suffering, but that this is unlikely to happen until religion (offering illusory happiness in the future as a consolation) is abolished.

In this, Marx comes close to Nietzsche, since it is only in shaking off the emasculating restriction of Christianity that, according to Nietzsche, one is able to take the positive step of self-determination and follow the path of the 'supermen', accepting and affirming life just as it is.

Of course, there is another element to this – that it is useful to rulers if their subjects are prepared to accept otherwise unacceptable living conditions on the basis of future religious compensation. This is reflected in the often quoted comment by Seneca: 'Religion is regarded by the common people as true, by the wise as false and by the rulers as useful.'

Durkheim and functional analysis

An alternative approach to explaining the phenomenon of religion is to examine the function that it performs within society. This is exemplified in the work of the sociologist Emile Durkheim (1858–1917) who saw religion as embodying the beliefs of a particular society, and therefore as a cohesive force within society. Durkheim's approach, and those that have developed from it, are generally termed 'functionalist', in other words, religion is to be understood by examining the function that it performs.

If religion can express the values that are held by a society, then it can function to hold that society together, particularly when threatened either from outside or by a sense of meaninglessness. Religion can also give a 'cognitive' answer to some of life's tragedies. In other words, if someone is trying to make sense of, say, the death of a partner or loved one, religion offers a set of beliefs that can suggest answers. We shall look at some of these in the context of the 'problem of evil' in Chapter 08.

This approach raises many issues concerning the way in which religion relates to society. If those within a religious group are given comfort and a sense of purpose through its beliefs, it suggests that those who are outside the religious circle are seen as 'profane'. Hence the cohesive forces of religion have both advantages and disadvantages in a complex society, for the existence of more than one religious group may lead to the establishment of divisions and barriers, of which the world is full of tragic examples.

Functionalism – as a way of understanding what religion does in society – is an important reminder to the philosophy of religion, that religion itself is not merely a set of propositions to be accepted or rejected on rational grounds. Beliefs are held for functional reasons – whether true or not, they persist if they are experienced as working to help individuals or society cope with the challenges of life.

For reflection

Notice that this functionalist approach does not, in itself, argue for or against the factual truth of what is believed. It simply examines its social and functional context – i.e. whether the belief is true or not, it examines what the belief does for the person who holds it.

Many secular arguments against religious belief fail to take this into account. Showing something to be illogical is only half the battle; more significant is showing *why* that belief continues to be held.

Humanism

A useful definition of humanism is given on the website of the British Humanist Association:

> Humanism is the belief that we can live good lives without religious or superstitious beliefs. Humanists

make sense of the world using reason, experience and shared human values. We seek to make the best of the one life we have by creating meaning and purpose for ourselves. We take responsibility for our actions and work with others for the common good.

Notice first of all that this is a positive statement about the human potential for living the good life. Unlike atheism, it is not defined negatively in terms of rejection of the idea of God, but its positive message implies that religion is unnecessary.

Whether religion is helpful or unhelpful in terms of human development is a secondary matter. Some (for example, Richard Dawkins, as mentioned above) point out the damage that religion has done. Others see it as having a limited but positive role, rather along the lines set out by Feuerbach. Here, for example, is what Professor Sir Raymond Firth has to say in *Religion: a Humanist Interpretation* (1996, p. 214):

> In the sophisticated major religions, for example, concepts of the divine, of 'ultimate reality', and of the extremes of knowledge, wisdom, morality and power associated with the divine, are just a summation of the absolutes of human imagination ...

> It may seem harsh to say that God is an example of the fallacy of misplaced concreteness. But while at an abstract, figurative level the ideas of God, Yahweh, Allah, Brahma can provide spectacular symbolic expressions and penetrating thoughts upon the human condition, at bottom they are just essentially human constructs.

He sees them as offering explanations of the world, guides for conduct which can offer patterns for human conduct, but – in terms that exactly reflect Feuerbach – he says:

> Therefore I would argue that there is truth in every religion. But it is a human, not a divine truth. In every society the beliefs and practices of religion are modelled on secular beliefs, desires, interests, fears and actions. These are raised by religion to a higher power, given an alleged external authority and legitimacy, because in their abstract, figurative, often symbolic form they are ultimately an outcome of the human condition and at attempt to remedy its difficulties.

> (p. 215)

If religion is a projection, then it is likely to reflect both positive and negative aspects of human life. So, Firth is able to say:

> Many of the values of these religious faiths are true values, in the sense that if honestly adopted, they make for a more viable social life – self-sacrifice, thought for others, avoidance of deceit, care for more vulnerable members of society, integrative meaning of rituals, strength in co-operation.
>
> (p. 215)

Whereas, on the other side of the balance, Dawkins is able to point to many stories in the Bible where people are ordered by God to carry out acts that, by any civilized standards, are regarded as cruel and barbaric (see, for example, his chapter entitled 'The "Good" Book and the Moral *Zeitgeist*' in *The God Delusion*).

There is an issue here for humanism:

- Humanism presents a positive view of the human potential.
- It may sometimes criticize religion for being unreasonable or taking a line on moral issues that it finds unpalatable.
- But, if religion is a projection of human values, it may be expected to reflect both the kind and the cruel aspects of human life – both self-sacrifice for the good of others and the murderous defence of a minority group's interest.
- The question may then be raised: does humanism take sufficient account of the negative aspects of human life? Would the abolition of religion really lead to a world where reason and shared human values guided every decision?

This question is not really fair to the humanist position, for humanism is not commenting on how human life *is* lived, but on how it *should* be lived, or is *capable of* being lived. It believes 'in' a life lived by reason and shared human values, not 'that' humans always live by reason and shared human values.

Humanism points to the human potential, and offers a clear set of principles by which to live. These include examining everything according to reason and evidence, taking responsibility for one's actions, taking account of the needs of others within society, and recognizing that we have only one life and that we should therefore live it to the full.

The fact that many people do not live by those values is something to be regretted, and humanists may blame religion for that. The fundamental question, however, is whether religion is the cause or the symptom of this predicament.

Comments

Much of what passes for belief in God in popular religion is not theism at all, but **interactive deism**. In other words, it is a belief in an external deity who somehow enters the world and interacts with it. The humanist position does religion a great service by pointing out the folly of this form of belief.

But we have already argued that 'God' should not be taken to refer to a crude 'out there' entity. Religious experience is rather more subtle than that, and the language used to convey it should not be taken literally. Religion, as a response to the self-transcending quality of experience is, of course, a human construct. It is an attempt to articulate, reproduce and live out what is perceived as of ultimate value.

But a humanist also has fundamental values that reflect an understanding of human life and its place within the universe. They are described as 'human' values, but they transcend any individual human being and any individual society. The values themselves are not the product of any one society (if they were, they could not be used to judge society's constructs, like religion) or individual, but transcend them.

But the transcending of human experience by values that are encountered within individual situations, but are not limited to them, is exactly what religion is (or should be) about. **In that sense, humanism mirrors the best aspects of religion, but does so without the need for projection. Its transcendence is natural, not supernatural.**

Religion has traditionally offered three things:

- a set of values by which to live
- a set of beliefs (metaphysical ones, popularly regarded as supernatural)
- a set of practices in terms of worship or social customs.

Humanism clearly offers a secular version of the first of these. If it is argued that most people do not live by its high ideals, that is no different from the complaint that most people (including religious people) do not live up to the ideals of their religion.

It regards the second as unnecessary and as potentially harmful. However, this needs to be qualified. There are some belief systems (for example, Buddhism) which do not require belief in supernatural agencies (i.e. gods). Hence there is no reason, in principle, why a humanist and a Buddhist might not find themselves in substantial agreement. It is also the case that some followers of religion hold beliefs that are not 'supernatural' in any crude sense, but are simply an expression of ultimate purpose and value. Again, the difference between this and humanism may not be substantial, although humanism would claim to be universal, whereas religions are related to a particular historical tradition.

Although without the trappings of worship, some humanists meet regularly to discuss and share their common values and perspective. Many more regard themselves as humanist, without actually belonging to any recognized humanist organization. Although this is parallel to those who attend religious worship and those who are only nominal in their religion, the key difference is that humanism does not require any beliefs or practices. In other words, anyone who accepts humanist values can call himself or herself 'humanist', whereas most religions require some formal act of commitment.

A challenge

Given the humanist option and the strength of arguments against literal acceptance of religious beliefs, a key question for humanism is why religion continues to flourish. Clearly, it can only do so if it meets human needs that are not met elsewhere.

The challenge for humanism (and indeed for all who take an atheist or agnostic view) is to understand the mechanisms by which supernatural beliefs and religious observances appeal to and meet the needs of so many people. It does not appear to be sufficient to show that they are illogical or divisive, for example, for that may only strengthen the determination of some believers.

Those addicted to drugs generally come off them only when an alternative (either a drug-substitute, or changed emotional or social circumstances) is provided. If – from a humanist perspective – it is desirable to wean people off the drug of religion, what needs to be provided to meet those needs previously met by religious belief and practice?

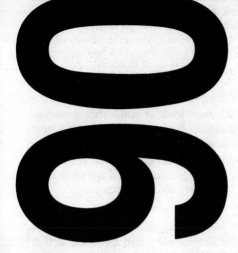

06

the self

In this chapter you will:
- explore different views of how body and mind are related
- consider whether we are free or determined
- see how views of the self have implications for life beyond death.

In the West, religion is primarily about the relationship that people claim to have with God – along with the morality, attitudes to life and self-understanding that go with it.

This being the case, the philosophy of religion is as much concerned with the nature of the self as it is about God, for it needs to understand the relationship between the two. This chapter will therefore consider three questions:

- Who and what am I? (We shall look at some theories about the relationship between minds, bodies and souls, in order to see what kind of 'self' it is with which religion is concerned.)
- Are we free or determined by physical laws? What has shaped us, and what can we do to change ourselves if we wish to do so? How does our freedom relate to our identity?
- Is there life beyond death?

> Some of the material in this chapter may also be found in the chapter on The Philosophy of Mind in *Teach Yourself: Philosophy*, but for a more detailed consideration see *Teach Yourself: Philosophy of Mind*.

One of the key issues discussed within the philosophy of mind (otherwise known as 'philosophical psychology') is how the mind is related to the body. This is also relevant to the philosophy of religion, both because religion is concerned with 'selves', 'souls' or 'minds' and also because the issue of how the mind is related to the body is a similar problem to considering the way in which God might be related to the world. Like God, the mind or self is invisible, and arguably it should not simply be identified with the body any more than God should be identified with the world.

This issue is made more complicated because of the questions related to the terms used:

- What is the 'self'?
- Is it the same as the 'soul'?
- And are both of them simply ways of describing the 'mind'?
- Does 'mind' simply refer to the thinking side of a human being, or to something more?

It would be ideal if we could simply define these terms from the outset, but this is not possible because what is meant by 'mind' or 'self' is only revealed in the course of examining theories about how minds and bodies are related. There are three broad possibilities:

- that minds are unreal; there are only bodies
- that bodies are unreal; there are only minds
- that there exist both bodies and minds, distinct from one another, but linked together in some way.

The first of these is termed **materialism**, the second **idealism** and the third **dualism**. Of these three, dualism in various forms has rather dominated Western thinking, whereas materialism and idealism have been put forward largely in response to problems it has posed, although materialism has received a considerable boost from the implications of modern cognitive science, including pharmacology, neuroscience and computing.

Dualism

We shall first examine the self/body dualism of Plato, Aristotle and Aquinas, and then look at the rather different dualism of a thinking mind/physical body as presented by Descartes.

Plato and Aquinas

In general, Plato was concerned to understand how the ordinary things in life related to eternal realities. He noted that people were naturally able to grasp mathematical principles and general concepts and thought that this went beyond what they could have deduced from their limited experience. He therefore considered that they must have known such things prior to birth, existing in an eternal realm, to which the self could return after the death of the physical body. He considered that a human being had three parts – a physical body, a natural life of awareness, sensations and so on (like all animals), and a thinking mind (distinctive to humans). The 'soul' or 'self' (*psyche* in Greek) is immaterial, including both emotions, actions and intellect, but it is linked to (he saw it as being entombed within) a physical body.

Aristotle took a very different approach, seeing the self as that which gave form to the physical body, organizing it as a living being, and – uniquely for humans – the ability to think. For him, you could no more separate mind and body than you could separate wax from the shape given it by a seal. In many ways, therefore, Aristotle tends to oppose the kind of dualism that we see in Plato and later in Descartes. For our purposes now, we simply need to recognize that in Ancient Greece the issue was not a straightforward one of dividing thinking mind from physical body, but was rather more complex, as can be seen by the different terms used:

Greek terms

sarx   – the physical body (flesh and blood)

soma   – the organized body, with its activities and characteristics

psyche – the sensations and emotions (also found in animals)

pneuma – the rational, spiritual aspect of humankind; mental activity

nous   – the thinking mind.

In Greek thought there is no distinction between your inner state of consciousness and the thing of which you are conscious. In other words, suppose you experience something as cold, your experience is of the coldness of that thing. There is no separate thing called 'an experience of coldness' that goes on unobserved in your mind. They did not ask (as Descartes and later philosophers did) 'How does my experience of cold relate to the cold I experience?' For the ancient Greeks, the distinctive thing about humans was their ability to reflect on 'coldness' as a universal concept, not the location of some ghostly 'coldness' going on in their heads!

Note

The important thing here is to note the distinction between psyche (in the sense of animal life, awareness, sensations etc.) and *pneuma* (mental activity):

• For the Greeks, sense perception was on the 'body' side of the body/mind dualism.

- Descartes (in the seventeenth century) included in 'mind', all the feelings and sensations that he could describe but not locate physically.

So we need to be aware that, within Western thought, there have been two distinct forms of dualism – the pre-Cartesian form, with mental activity distinguished from the body and its sensations, and the Cartesian (i.e. from Descartes) where everything non-physical becomes part of 'mind'.

Thomas Aquinas followed Aristotle, in seeing the soul as that which **animated** the body, giving it form and life (indeed, Aquinas uses the Latin term *anima* for the soul). He also saw it as 'the primary source of all those activities that differentiate levels of life: growth, sensation, movement, understanding' (*Summa Theologiae* Vol II 76:1).

So we have two distinct but compatible ideas:

- that the soul is what 'animates' the body, giving it life and form
- that reason is what distinguishes humankind from other species.

Note

The term used for 'soul' in the Hebrew Scriptures (the Old Testament) is *ruach*. This can perhaps best be translated as 'breath'. God breathes life into an inanimate body; he gives it breath. Your soul therefore, in Old Testament terms, is what makes you a living thing.

In the later Old Testament writings, there is more emphasis on an other-worldly destiny for the soul, a religious theme that was developed particularly in response to persecution and martyrdom. But in the earlier period, the emphasis is very much on this world.

In the New Testament the Greek terms used for the self are as set out above. It is important to distinguish between *sarx*, which has a very physical and earthy connotation and *soma*, which is an ordered body.

The Greek influence is more clearly seen in Gnostic writings, where people are divided up according to their spiritual disposition, the most elevated of whom were the *pneumatikoi* (from *pneuma*) or spiritual ones.

This is a huge and complex subject, and there is no scope to pursue it here, other than to note where the body/soul division comes. For most biblical writers, the soul is concerned with feelings and actions – with the whole process of living – it is **not** simply the rational mind.

Descartes

Descartes' starting point in the quest for knowledge, 'I think, therefore I am', implied a radical distinction between the world of matter, known to the senses, and the world of thought, known (at least in one's own case) directly.

Descartes recognized that the mind is able to control the mechanical working of the body, and therefore needed to find some point of interaction between mind and body, because in all other respects he considered the body to be controlled by mechanical forces. He suggested that it was done through the pineal gland, lodged between right and left hemispheres, for which he could find no other function.

There is a danger of presenting Descartes' view of 'mind' as being of some kind of subtle, invisible body, existing in the world of space and time, yet not subject to its usual laws of cause and effect. This, of course, is a rather crude caricature of what he and other dualists have actually claimed. (It is also an important caricature, having been used by Ryle in *The Concept of Mind*, see below p. 133.)

Notice what a radical change came about with Descartes:

- Plato's 'Forms' were **out there in the world**, although they were capable of being understood by the rational mind. The Greek term used for 'form' was 'idea'.
- The distinctive thing about human reason was that it was able to appreciate the 'idea' rather than just responding to particular things in the physical world.
- By contrast, for Descartes, 'ideas' were **in the mind**, not out there in the world waiting to be grasped. He saw them as **the contents of the mind**.

Descartes therefore introduced a radical dualism of mind and body; with all feelings, sensations and thoughts on one side (things known only to the person experiencing them) and the physical (publicly observable) body – including the brain – on the other.

This radical, 'Cartesian' dualism came to dominate the philosophical debate, but it was not the mind/body dualism of the Greeks, nor of the Bible, nor of Christian belief.

A note of caution

We need to look at these theories about how the mind is related to the body, simply because they have influenced thinking about religious beliefs, and it is clear that some of the options are incompatible with, for example, ideas of immortality or free will. But in doing so, we should keep in mind that the mind/body 'problem' presented here is largely a response to Descartes. Hence, even if it is relevant to modern discussions of religious beliefs about the self, it was **not** an issue during the formative period of any of the major world religions.

Some dualist theories

It is clear that thoughts and emotions gives rise to physical change – the most obvious examples being depression, fear or sexual excitement. Equally, if the body is damaged, there is a sensation of pain, or if it lacks food or oxygen, the mind will become dull and muddled. So dualism needs to account for the fact of this **interaction**.

Descartes strained to establish a point of mind/body contact and, as we noted above, believed that the pineal gland was the point at which the mind and body acted upon one another. But this interaction itself is very curious, given the radically different natures of mind and body. The pineal gland is definitely part of the body, even if it was to Descartes a sensitive and mysterious part. How then could its physical nature respond to that which was not physical at all?

There have been various theories to attempt to explain the mind/body interaction, one of which is termed **occasionalism**. On the occasion of my being hit over the head with a cricket bat, there is a simultaneous but uncaused feeling of pain! The two systems (physical and mental) do not have a direct causal connection. The philosopher Malebranche suggested that whenever he wanted to move his arm, it was actually moved by God.

This seems a very curious theory and it relies on God to link the physical and the mental. However, it serves to highlight the problem. We know that everything in the universe, including the brain and the pineal gland, is part of a single web of causes and conditions, it is physical and can be examined by science. At the same time we are well aware that the mind is not open to examination in the same way. I know what I'm feeling at this moment, but you cannot see it directly. Unless I choose to reveal it to you, it must forever remain hidden. Thoughts can express themselves in actions and words, but they are not **the same thing** as the actions and words. We know that minds and bodies interact – thoughts lead to actions and so on; yet radical dualism allows for no mechanism by which this can happen – so Malebranche tried to import God to solve the problem.

Geulinx, a Dutch follower of Descartes, and Leibniz held a theory known as **pre-established harmony**. Leibniz thought that everything physical could be divided again and again until you arrive at 'monads' – simple entities without physical extension. These monads cannot act upon one another, for each develops according to its own nature, but a complex being comprises countless monads. How do they all work together to produce intelligent activity? Leibniz argued that there must be a pre-established harmony, organizing the otherwise independent monads. As far as human persons are concerned, Leibniz held that there is a dominant monad (a soul) and that God had established that the other monads that form this complex person work in harmony with it.

Note

'Pre-established harmony' may seem one of the most bizarre of the mind-body theories, but in Leibniz it has a very specific purpose, and one which has implications for both **metaphysics** and the philosophy of religion. Leibniz was concerned with preserving the idea of teleology (i.e. that the world is organized in a purposeful way) in the face of the mechanistic science and philosophy of his day. If everything is locked into a series of causes, what room is left for a sense of purpose or for God? Leibniz's answer is that the individual monads, of which everything is composed, do not actually affect one another. Rather, God has established a harmony by which they can work together.

Epiphenomenalism is the name given to the view that the brain and nervous system are so complex that they give the *impression* of individuality and free choice. Although totally controlled by physical laws, we 'seem' to have an independent mind. This is the closest that a dualistic view comes to materialism. The essential thing here is that mind does not influence the body – what appears to us as mind is no more than a product of the complexity of the body's systems.

The various things that I think, imagine, picture in my mind are *epiphenomena*. They arise out of and are caused by electrical impulses that move between brain cells, but they are not to be identified with those phenomena themselves (i.e. they are not electrical impulses), rather, they are 'above' (epi-) those phenomena and produced by them.

Example

Imagine a robot, programmed by computer. A simple version could be the source of amusement, as it attempts to mimic human behaviour. But as the memory capacity of the computer is increased, the process of decision-making that the programme makes possible is elaborated to the point at which it becomes so complex that the computer takes on a definite character.

In this case the character is distinctive (you don't see it by looking at the memory chips) but it is entirely produced by and dependent upon the computer's memory: that is epiphenomenalism.

Another approach is to think of mind and body as two different ways of looking at the same thing. This **double aspect theory** was set out by Spinoza and is sometimes called the 'identity hypothesis'. According to this theory, ideas and brain activity are simply two aspects of the same thing. Thinking is thus the **inner** aspect of which brain activity is the **outer** aspect.

Comment

There are many other things to which a double-aspect theory could be applied. Music could be seen as the inner, cultural aspect of which sound waves of particular frequencies are the outer, physical aspect. Without sound waves, no music. But music is not something else, caused by the sound waves. Music is the sound waves, but experienced and described in a different way.

Spinoza argued that everything is both conscious and extended; all reality has both a mental and a physical aspect. The mind and body cannot be separated, and therefore there can be no life beyond this physical existence. Spinoza also held that freedom was an illusion, caused by the fact that we simply do not know all the real causes of our decisions.

But is the 'double aspect' a matter of reality or of description? In other words, how do we tell the difference between two ways of describing the same thing and descriptions of two separate things?

Another problem is how you account for the private sensations that people have. In *Philosophy and the Mirror of Nature* (an important book for anyone wanting to look further into these issues), R. Rorty, comments:

> 'The neo-dualist is no longer talking about how people feel but about feelings as little self-subsistent entities, floating free of people in the way in which universals float free of the instantiations.'

(p. 30)

For reflection

It seems that Rorty has touched on a major theme here: that, in a dualist way of describing feelings, an aspect of human experience (the feelings) are somehow detached from the act of experiencing them, and are allowed a separate existence. For example: I feel happy on several occasions, but I am then described as experiencing 'happiness' as though it were something separate from what I actually felt. Once separated, we ask how happiness (mental phenomenon) is related to the body and to the original situations. This is another example of the issue about Plato's 'Forms' – is there a 'form' of a tree over and above all the particular trees? So: are there feelings (like happiness) that exist independently of my feeling happy on occasions?

Materialism

You can avoid all problems of relating minds to bodies if you explain everything in terms of physical objects. For a materialist, the mind or self is nothing more than a way of describing physical bodies and their actions, including their brain activity. We may experience something as a thought or emotion, but in fact it is nothing more than electrical impulses in the brain, or chemical or other reactions in the rest of the body.

Some situations tend to confirm this materialist view. If a person suffers brain damage, his or her character may be changed. In severe cases he or she may not appear to be a person at all, but merely a living body, devoid of all the normal attributes of mind.

Materialism generally takes what is called a **reductionist** approach to mental activity – which suggests that a person is 'nothing but' a brain attached to a body and nervous system, so the person is 'reduced to' these things.

> **Note**
>
> The 'nothing but' distinguishes materialism from other theories, for nobody would deny that, in some sense, a person is related to a brain, in the same way as a symphony is related to vibrations in the air. The essential question is whether or not it is possible to express a 'something more', if a strictly materialist position seems inadequate.

Richard Rorty (see above) argues for 'eliminative materialism'. This claims that, when we speak about mental phenomena (thoughts, hopes, emotions) there is nothing that corresponds to these things, other than physical states. In other words, if we knew everything it was possible to know about brain functioning, there would be no place in that explanation to correspond to mental phenomena. Along with that goes the idea that everything that we have in our minds comes from outside – from what we accept as logical conventions or learn from experience. In other words, the brain just acts as a data store, processing and responding to what it receives.

This approach is endorsed by the increasing body of knowledge about how different parts of the brain function. It is now possible to identify areas that are concerned with speech and language, for example, or hearing. Damage to that part of the brain affects the relevant function. This suggests, that – however the experience of our senses suggest that the mind is not material – there is a most intimate connection between the human mind and the physical brain. Whether that is thought of in terms of the mind being an 'epiphenomenon' (see above p. 128), or simply a confirmation of the materialist identity of physical and mental, is another matter.

Another fascinating way to relate religion and morality to brain function is to look at the development of emotions. Natural selection favours those who have an advantage in a competitive environment. Early hominids developed visual communications and emotions – displaying to one another their intentions, and enabling a whole range of social co-operation to develop. In a world in which they lacked the physical strength and speed of some other species, this gave them an advantage. It is therefore possible to explore the way in which communications of emotions developed into systems of shared signs and rituals for bonding people together. Rational thought and language followed. Neurology can show the way in which parts of the brain have developed to express these functions, giving us individuality and communication networks that may start to explain phenomena such as morality and religion. This is set out in Jonathan H. Turner's book *On the Origins of Human Emotions* (2000).

It is also clear that, as computers increase in power, they can do things that previously could only have been done by human brains. This, of course, can be explained by the fact that computers are programmed by human beings, but it also shows that – once it receives the appropriate data – a machine can simulate brain activity. This suggests that the basic processes going on in the brain and in the machine are similar. And if that is so, it endorses a materialist view of the mind.

Behaviourism is the term used for the theory that mental attributes are in fact descriptions of physical phenomena. Crying out and rubbing a part of the body is what pain is about. Shouting and waving a fist is what anger is about. All mental states are reduced by the behaviourist to things that can be observed and measured. Thus the behaviourist psychologist (for example, Pavlov observing the salivation of his dogs) observes and records behaviour, and shows how animals can be trained to respond to stimuli in a particular way.

Comment

I can think before I speak, or before I write; but for a behaviourist there is nothing other than the words or the writing – to know a feeling one must observe behaviour.

Ryle

A particularly influential form of behaviourism is 'logical behaviourism', which is based on our use of language and was presented by Gilbert Ryle, in *The Concept of Mind* (1949). He suggests that to speak of minds and bodies as though they were equivalent things is a 'category mistake'. To explain what he means by this he uses the example of someone visiting a university and seeing many different colleges, libraries and research laboratories. The visitor then asks, 'But where is the University?' The answer, of course, is that there is no university over and above all its component parts that have already been visited. The term university is a way of describing all of these things together – it is a term from another category, not the same category as the individual components.

In the same way, Ryle argued that you should not expect to find a 'mind' over and above all the various parts of the body and its actions, for 'mind' is a term from another category, a way of describing bodies and the way in which they operate. This he claims is the fundamental flaw in the traditional dualistic approach to mind and body, which he attributes to Descartes and terms the 'ghost in the machine'.

He does not deny that there are mental processes – his examples are doing long division or making a joke. But he insists that they are not the same sort of thing as physical processes, so it makes no sense to conjoin them. In other words, he will not allow that one can speak about both physical and mental causes of an action.

Ryle is primarily concerned with language: his book is about what we mean when we speak about the 'mind'. And in this, his argument matches our ordinary experience, for when we speak about the mind of another person we are not claiming to have any privileged information about their inner mental operations; all we are actually describing are activities performed by the body.

Clearly, we can get to know another person, but, if Ryle is correct and there is no 'inner' self to be found, in what therefore does the personality consist? His answer is in terms of 'dispositions'. These are the qualities that make me what I am; the propensity to behave in a particular way in a particular situation; the sort of beliefs and knowledge that habitually inform my actions and words. If I say that someone is 'irritable', I do not mean that I have some privileged access to an 'irritability factor' in their mind, I just mean that, given a situation that is not to his or her liking, he or she is likely to start complaining, sulking, etc. In other words, irritability is simply a way of describing that disposition.

Thus, for Ryle, the ascription of mental predicates (clever, etc.) does not require the existence of a separate, invisible thing called a mind. The description 'clever' indeed refers to the way in which something is done, but, equally, cleverness cannot be **defined** simply in terms of that action.

Comment

A child is 'clever' if it learns to stagger to its feet and totter a few paces forward before collapsing down on the ground again. The same is not claimed for the drunk who performs a similar set of movements. If Ryle wishes to dismiss the 'ghost in the machine' he must equally dismiss the 'ghost in the action', for mental predicates refer to, but are not defined by, individual actions.

Actors create problems for behaviourists. I may shout, cry, hold the afflicted part of my body; I may scream and roll on the ground, curl up, look ashen: people will say I am in pain. But none of these things is actually the pain I am experiencing. I may watch an actor performing all these things, but, because he or she is acting, I do not imagine that there is any actual pain. We know there is a difference between being in pain and simply appearing to be in pain. The problem for a logical behaviourist is knowing how that difference can be articulated.

Idealism

The other possibility – although it seems rather an unlikely one at first glance – is that reality is fundamentally mental, and that it is the physical world that is problematic. This view is particularly associated with Bishop Berkeley (1685–1753) who famously argued that to be is to be perceived. To use his own example, he suggested that to say that a tree exists is to say that it can be perceived. This pre-dated the Logical Positivists of the early twentieth century (see above p. 39) – the meaning of the statement 'the tree exists' is 'go and look and you will see the tree'. But how do we know that the tree continues to exist if nobody is there to observe it. Berkeley's answer is that the tree exists because it is being observed by God!

At the heart of idealism is the recognition that we experience the world through our senses – so all we know are those sensations and what the mind does with them. Kant argued that the mind can only deal with **phenomena** (things as we experience them), not **noumena** (things as they are in themselves) which remain unknowable. And remember, Descartes came to the conclusion that the only thing he could know for certain was himself as a thinking being, since his senses could always be deceived.

To the materialist, physical bodies are obvious; minds are problematic. To the idealist, physical bodies are problematic, because all we know is filtered through the mind.

Idealism may sound crazy, because we know that bodies exist. The difficulty (given the parameters of the debate set out by Descartes and Kant) is to know how to **prove** that it is crazy.

A shifting identity?

A new sense of oneself is a feature of much religious experience; a religious conversion is about a life transformed. Whether through their moral rules, or in the process of confessing faults and receiving forgiveness, the rituals of organized religion look for the free choice of individuals to respond to 'God' or the spiritual path, and thus to enable their lives to be transformed.

A religion that claimed to make no difference would not survive for long. People want to understand what life is about, and to change their lives for the better – that is the impetus of much religious life, and it is this aspect of religion that requires us to consider the nature of the individual and his or her freedom to make and act on choices. Without the idea of a free self, morality makes no sense. Equally, the religious response makes no sense if we are mere puppets with fixed natures.

In the earlier part of this chapter we set out some of the options for looking at 'selves' in terms of minds and bodies. Before assessing these for their implications for freedom we shall look briefly at two other approaches to the 'self'.

A postmodern self

We saw above (p. 67) that, according to the 'postmodern' movement in philosophy, you cannot get beyond the language and signs by which people communicate: there are no hidden meanings – everything is as it is perceived to be. We live and express ourselves within a world of words and images, and we cannot get beyond them. This has implications for our understanding of the 'self'. Don Cupitt, a radical Christian theologian, explores the nature of the self from a religious perspective but within this overall postmodern view of the world.

> People are what they look like and what they say; they are the text of their own lives.

> (*The Time Being*, Don Cupitt, 1992, p. 35)

In other words, you live on the surface of your life and you are the communicative signs that link you with the rest of the world.

In this case, can there be any view of the self other than what a person actually reveals? Is there any sort of continuity holding together all the various things a person says and does throughout his or her life? What makes me me? Cupitt's view is that the distinctive thing is the network of communication within which a person lives and acts. What counts in the end is not found in some analysis of the self (of the sort that we have described above) but rather in the way that the person has related to the rest of the world.

> The question about the self, then, is going to come out like this: your life will have been worth living if one day a decently plausible story can be told about how you gave it for a cause.

(p. 145)

Now although this sounds unlikely at first glance, in practice it is exactly the way people are presented. Take the example of a cinema film. A character appears and one can identify with him or her – one can get involved, and be moved emotionally by what happens on the screen. Yet all that is known of the person acting are the words and images portrayed. There is no other way to get to know the character. Yet our knowledge of a character in a film does not seem to be radically different from our knowledge of other people. Soap opera actors become part of viewers' daily lives, they seem to be as 'real' as anyone else.

The same could be said of the way of summarising a person's life. Funeral orations speak of the person's links with the rest of the world – relatives and friends, organizations, causes supported. Qualities are described in terms of typical actions – he or she was always someone you could trust, or someone who would help generously where there was a situation of need.

This presentation of the self – and it is the stuff of which all biographies are made – does not require any privileged information. It is merely an examination and presentation of the surface of things; of the empirical evidence. 'He was a kind person' does not mean that there is some mysterious other ghost of a person who is seen to have the quality 'kind', it just means that the observation of the actions merit that description. The person is not first 'kind' and then, as a result, decides to do certain acts of kindness – they do those acts of kindness, and that is what causes them to be called 'kind'.

This view is not too far removed from Ryle's criticism of the 'ghost in the machine'. But the essential difference between Ryle and, say, Cupitt, is that whereas Ryle comes from a tradition which is basically reductionist, seeing the physical as the only reality, Cupitt and others of the postmodern viewpoint see language and communication as the basis of reality. A person is therefore a series of events, of communications, given coherence only by being presented together. But of course, such a presentation is always open to question, for it could have been told otherwise:

> A person is only a story, and stories are inherently ambiguous.

(Cupitt, p. 146)

The self, for postmodernism, is therefore a temporal procession of events, it is not an external fixed entity of any sort. This is not new. Hume's view of the self (coming from an empirical standpoint, is much the same. According to Hume we are:

> ... a bundle or collection of different perceptions, which succeed one another with an inconceivable rapidity, and are in perpetual flux and movement. The mind is a kind of theatre, where several perceptions successively make their appearance; pass, repass, glide away, and mingle in an infinite variety of postures and situations.

(*A Treatise of Human Nature* Book I, Part IV, Section VI)

Non-self

In Buddhism, all things are interconnected and you are therefore totally dependent upon things other than yourself, and as they change so will you. The Buddha therefore taught that that the idea of a separate, permanent self was a dangerous illusion, and that what we call the self is actually no more that an ever-changing procession of temporary events.

This is not a negative view of the self. In fact, Buddhism claims that the false notion of a fixed self is the cause of much of the world's suffering. Rather, it recognizes that we, and all experience, are in a constant process of change, and that we have a choice – either to recognize and adapt to that flow of changes, using every situation creatively, or to fight a losing battle to keep ourselves fixed and intact, a battle which will certainly be lost when we die.

In terms of spirituality, by concentrating in meditation on the present moment and present experience, Buddhists consider that they engage with a level of reality that is 'eternal' – beyond the changes of the ordinary phenomenal world (called *samsara*) – and therefore touch on a level of stillness, non-grasping and happiness which is termed *nirvana*.

Comment

There is, of course, far more that one could say about the Buddhist idea of the self. It is mentioned here in order to put the 'postmodern' self into perspective. Although it raises many problems for Western religion, the postmodern approach is neither totally new, nor incompatible with fundamental religious experience.

Freedom?

What makes us do what we do, and how does this relate to bodies and minds? We know two things:

- At any moment, the various parts of my body (including my brain) work according to the laws of nature. I can trace back a theoretically infinite succession of causes of any bodily activity. I do what I do, physically, because of what the whole of the rest of the universe does and has done.
- At any moment, I am aware of making choices, of moving my limbs, or speaking words that will influence the actions of others. As a thinking, living, acting self I set up chains of causes that theoretically extend to infinity in all directions. The rest of the world will be as it will be partly (even if that part is infinitely small) because of my action.

Neither of these things can be denied: the first because it is the basis of all science and all common sense; the second because it is the basis of all human experience. Any view of the world that does not take these into account is going to be rather limited.

The issue of freedom and **determinism** occurs at many points in the philosophy of religion: personal freedom and the nature of the self; miracles; science and religion. We need to examine in what ways the self is determined.

The first thing to be clear about is that science, in considering causal connections, will always seek (but never actually achieve) an exhaustive explanation for every event. In other words, science will always give a reason why something happens, or, if it does not know the reason, it will still assume that it would theoretically be possible to find one.

Hence, from a scientific and materialist point of view, freedom is always an illusion. It represents a point of indeterminacy, which it is science's task to whittle down by successively accurate explanations.

In terms of the self, there are two areas of science that attempt to give explanations of human activity: psychology and sociology. Psychology seeks to formulate the principles that lie behind human attitudes and actions. Faced with the freely chosen action of an individual, it seeks to show psychological causes (perhaps in terms of early experience, or established patterns of relationships) to 'explain' the choice. Although it is not generally set out in this way, the ultimate goal of psychology is therefore a total explanation – people would be shown to be acting in conformity with their deep psychological motives.

Following the same line of reasoning, many features of religion, including the free choice of individuals to take part in it, may be related by sociology to the needs of society, and therefore to the conscious or unconscious pressure to conform to religious social norms. The crucial thing to consider here is whether psychology and sociology, in giving an explanation for human dispositions and behaviour, have thereby removed freedom from the individual.

Of course, if the identity hypothesis is correct (the 'double aspect theory', see above p. 129) there is no freedom. Brain activity, like all physical processes, is limited by physical laws and is in theory predictable. But if mental events are simply another aspect of these physical events, they must also be limited by physical laws. If all my action is theoretically predictable, how can I be free?

Kant, on the other hand, held that we could be both phenomenally conditioned and noumenally free: as we are in ourselves, we experience freedom, but from the point of view of an observer (for whom our actions are 'phenomena') everything we do is causally conditioned and therefore predictable.

In other words

I know I'm free; you perceive I'm not. I can choose anything I like: the better you know me, the more likely you are to predict my choice correctly.

Freedom: West and East

For Western religions, human freedom is important, since it is necessary for moral responsibility. Although God is described as omnipotent and omniscient, he is said to allow human freedom, even though he could overrule it, if he chose. Of course, if God *did* overrule freedom, people would become little more that puppets, and the whole idea of religion in terms of personal choice, insight and response to God would be meaningless.

In Eastern thought, the issue is presented rather differently. The concept of *karma* in Indian philosophy refers to the results of morally significant action. One's actions today will have an effect on what happens tomorrow. In this sense, freedom is limited by past karma, and, for this reason, karma is sometimes presented as fatalistic. On the other hand there has to be a measure of freedom in order for there to be any present action that can generate karma. Particularly in Buddhist thought, this leads to a creative awareness of freedom working within the conditions present at any given moment – and a factor in those conditions (and also in one's ability to respond to them) will be the result of one's past action.

Life beyond death?

In *Phaedo*, Plato argued for the immortality of the soul on two grounds:

- That the body was composite, and was therefore perishable, whereas the mind was simple, and therefore imperishable.
- That the mind had knowledge of the universals, the eternal forms (such as 'beauty or goodness itself'), whereas in this world it could only experience individual events and objects. Such knowledge therefore suggests life in an eternal realm before birth into this one.

Few people today would wish to take up these arguments in the form that Plato presented them. But they persist in two widely accepted features of the mind/body question:

- That the mind is not within space/time and not material – and thus that it should not be identified with its material base in the brain.
- That the mind functions through communication and is not simply limited to the operations of a single particular body, i.e. the mind is not subject to physical limitations, and is related to transpersonal communication.

For a materialist, it is difficult to see how there could be life after death. The most that could happen is that the same material that composed the first person could be brought together again to form another person. And in that case, how could you establish an identity between the two?

Clearly, the various forms of dualism are more compatible with the concept of life after death, although there is the general problem of what continuity there could be. What would it be like to be a mind without a body?

In considering these things, we need to take into account two important distinctions: the first is between 'eternal' and 'everlasting' when applied to the self; the second concerns the difference between immortality and resurrection. By way of comparison, we will then also look briefly at Eastern concepts.

Eternal and everlasting

In considering concepts of God we considered the two senses of 'eternal'. On the one hand it could refer to that which was **beyond time,** and on the other it could be used in the sense of 'everlasting', in other words, existing in time but of **endless duration.**

When considering the possibility of life after death, we come up against the same issue:

- Is 'eternal life' timeless? If so, it implies that there is an aspect of ourselves that is outside time and space. Schleiermacher (see p. 8) took this view when he described the immortality offered by religion as being at one with the infinite. In this sense, eternal life is not something that you get later on, but something that you have **now.** The difference between that and everything else you may have now is that it is not subject to change.

- Or, does 'eternal life' refer to a life of endless duration? If so, did we have that life before our birth into this one? The Hindu concept of reincarnation implies that the self is neither born nor dies, so that, for example, in killing the body the warrior does not kill the true self.

- If endless duration is thought of as an endless continuation of something which has had a starting point in time (at our birth), the self is a very unusual concept – it is something that can come into existence, but cannot go out of existence again; subject to change (at least as far as this present life is concerned) but not to the point that it ceases to be itself.

Attached to this last option are questions about the nature of personal identity and eternal life. Is the self that can move on into an endless life after this one, an expression of the last state that the earthly self achieved? If so, eternal life (or heaven?) is going to be rather a sad place, populated by the elderly and dying. Or is there some point in life which is the definitive self that will inherit eternal life? If so, how can such a point be determined, since there is no point between birth and death when we stop changing?

Traditionally, eternal life has been associated with relationships, in the sense that people might be reunited with those they love in heaven. The small, innocent child my grandfather knew (and might conceivably want to meet again) is the same person that a grandchild of mine would know only as an elderly bore! What can identity and relationships mean in a situation of eternal life?

The ever-changing self takes a theoretically infinite number of forms. Each person with whom, in this life, it has a relationship, also has a theoretically infinite number of forms, and so on. We know, recognize and relate to one another in a situation of constant change. How could we relate, and with whom, if there were no changes?

And this brings us back to questions about the nature of the self, and that fact that everything we know as 'self' now depends upon our physical body and environment.

A personal comment

As a child, I had a recurrent nightmare in which I died and found myself flying forward over the surface of an absolutely flat, featureless world. On and on I flew, with that same drab world rushing past on either side. Then I suddenly realized that this movement was everlasting: it would never come to an end. I used to awake rigid with fear. (Clearly, part of my problem was the naive idea that my 'self', a self of flesh and bones and definite features, could be projected into a timeless and directionless environment.)

The nightmares only lifted when, pondering the nature of time and eternity, I realized that the same featureless world must logically have been there for me before my birth. I tried to imagine myself as a baby moving backwards through such an emptiness – but somehow the fear had gone, for this was something that must **already** have happened. How then could I fear it?

Clearly, I should fear a timelessness after my death as little as the timelessness before my birth. We have come into being and will pass out of being. What you go to is what you have already known.

At the age of 11 or so, I had enough to fear at school, without coping with eternity – but at least, the attempt to reduce eternity to a quasi-extension of present experience, with all its attendant feelings of being lost and isolated, was over. If there is such a thing as the experience of eternity, it is bound to be familiar.

Resurrection?

One problem raised by the idea of life after death is that of personal identity in the absence of a body. After all, what does it mean to be a person? If by 'person' you mean someone with whom you can have a relationship, who acts and speaks, then it is difficult to see what it could mean to say that a person exists after the death of his or her body, since the body is required for most of what passes as human personality.

This problem may be addressed by the idea of resurrection – that there can be another life at some point after death, in which one's body is restored, or one is given a new body. Here, of course there is no problem with having some kind of identity, because there is a body through which to express it. Or is there? Hick, in his book *Death and Eternal Life*, raises this point by way of a story about a man who dies suddenly in London but who then, at the moment of death, appears in New York with an identical body, complete with all the memories that the London man had up to the point of death. He then asks: Is it the same person?

Perhaps you might extend this question in terms of cloning. Imagine it were possible to create (before or after death) a body identical to your own. This body, with its brain identical and living, would have your characteristics and memory. Would it therefore be you? Could there be two of you? If so, then the idea of receiving an identical replacement in the future for the body that has died (as in the idea of resurrection) makes logical sense. If not, then what might be resurrected would not be yourself.

Reviewing these issues in *An Introduction to the Philosophy of Religion*, Brian Davies concludes that death followed by resurrection is a logical possibility. This is an important step in the philosophy of religion, for if something is logically impossible there is no point in continuing to ask if it can actually be the case. On the other hand, just because something is logically possible, that does not imply that it is in fact the case. One might argue, for example, that it would not be sufficient to reconstruct an identical body, but that (in order to be truly oneself in this future resurrected life) one would need to have an identical world in which to express oneself.

But what is this saying? Something along the lines of: 'If there were an identical world to this one, in which I had an identical body and memory, then I would be the same person I am now.' Surely, this is simply a long-winded way of saying 'I am the person I am now.' In an identical world, I would be an identical person. That may be true, for the idea of an identical world and an identical body implies an identical me, but it really asserts nothing about what may or may not happen after death.

Logical v. actual

If I had a twin brother or sister, I would be one of a pair of twins. In examining me, there is no reason why I could not be one of a pair of twins. Therefore it is logically possible that I am a twin. In fact, I'm not. Logical possibility has a purely negative function. It can show what cannot be the case, but it can't say what is in fact the case.

There remains a fundamental problem with resurrection, raised above in connection with eternal life; since the physical body is constantly changing, it is far from clear at what age I might be considered the definitive 'me' for the purposes of physical resurrection. Might we all end up like film stars after excessive cosmetic surgery, with old voices speaking out of ridiculously young faces?

Reincarnation

If the soul is everlasting and separable from the body, there seems no logical reason why it should not become embodied more than once, with a complete memory loss between one incarnation and the next.

In Hindu thought, the *atman* (or self) is eternal and also everlasting, so it may be embodied many times. In the Gita, the most popular of all Hindu scriptures, Krishna says to Prince

Arjuna, as he prepares for battle, that he can neither kill nor be killed. All he can do is slay the body.

Taken literally, one might imagine a simple succession of bodies, each becoming the vehicle for the soul. On the other hand, in the more philosophical tradition of Hindu thought, the eternal nature of the self implies that it can also be identified with all that exists.

> He who sees all beings in the self, and his self in all beings, he loses all fear.
>
> (*Isa Upanishad* 6)

It is important to get a balance between the literal sense of a soul taking successive incarnations, and the overall sense in the Upanishads (the more philosophical tradition within Hindu literature) of the self (Atman) being at one with the whole of reality (Brahman). The recognition of this oneness suggests that, with the dissolution of this body, the self is still 'at home' in a world teeming with life. Whether thought of literally, or in terms of a spiritual and emotional perspective, reincarnation expands the potential of the self, whilst recognizing that it is always liked to a physical body.

Re-becoming

The Buddhist concept of 're-becoming' is different from Hindu reincarnation in that there is no fixed, eternal *atman*. There is no 'thing' that can pass from life to life. This is simply an extension of the Buddhist view of the self within this life – a person does not have a fixed identity, but is constantly changing in response to conditions. Personal qualities and identity are ascribed in conventional language and may appear to be permanent, but ultimately all is subject to conditions and therefore to change. The idea that a self can be detached from its surroundings and continue an independent existence makes no sense within the overall Buddhist view.

In Buddhism, the process of influence that one life might have on another is based on the idea of *karma* – the working out of the effects of one's ethically significant actions, if necessary beyond this life. An image used to describe this is that of one flame lighting another. Nothing passes over from the first flame, but its presence ignites the second.

Some Buddhists take the idea of re-becoming in quite a literal sense – continuing the process of *karma* and change beyond death into successive lives in a way that is similar to Hindu reincarnation. The Buddha himself refused to say what happens to an enlightened person after death, so Buddhists may choose to remain agnostic about the details of any such process.

Notice that, unlike Hindu thought, Buddhism does **not** require – and is in fact largely incompatible with – dualism. The self is no more than a conventional notion, and its qualities are (rather as Ryle argued) a matter of dispositions to act in particular ways, rather than permanent features. The process of change and causation – assumed by materialism and by the scientific approach – is also fundamental to Buddhist philosophy.

Near death experiences

There is considerable evidence for the sort of experiences that people have after they lose consciousness and come close to death. Those who have survived such situations may describe moving down a darkish tunnel towards light at the end. There is often a feeling that all will be well once they move out into that light. They may feel emotionally positive, may encounter people they have known, or religious figures, like Jesus or Krishna. They may also experience themselves floating above their body, looking down on it as it lies on the field of battle or in the hospital operating theatre – recognizing what is happening, but quite calm and detached.

A person who believes that there is life after death, and that the mind is separable from the body, will see these 'out of body' experiences as evidence for that belief. In terms of the emotions, it is interesting that the response to having recovered from a situation in which one has come close to death and had just such an experience is a loss of fear. Death is no longer seen as a threat.

There are medical theories to account for some of these experiences. A shortage of oxygen to the brain may explain the situation where the centre of the visual field is an expanding disc of light – giving the experience of moving down a tunnel. Similarly, it is argued that, when someone is unconscious, the brain, starved of normal stimuli, is likely to create its own setting – something that does not correspond to any external state, but which feels as real as any other to the person experiencing it.

How you interpret near death experiences will depend largely upon your own presuppositions. For someone who believes in life after death, they may be seen as direct confirmation of that belief. For others, they may be comforting and calming, but are otherwise no more than curious phenomena caused by a brain starved of oxygen. In any case, they do not have the form of a logical proof one way or the other, fascinating though they may be.

For reflection

It is curious to reflect that many of the problems that concern the meaning of 'God' recur here in terms of the meaning of the 'self'. They function as a pair of concepts, and how you see one will influence how you see the other.

A dualism of body and mind is parallel with a dualism of world and God. From a materialist perspective, what we call 'self' is a particular interpretation of features of the physical body; similarly, 'God' is a word used in interpreting our relationship with the physical world, not something with an existence separate from it.

07

psychology and religion

In this chapter you will:

- examine psychological explanations of religion
- consider whether religion is healthy or unhealthy from a psychological perspective
- explore the idea of spiritual development.

Psychology, as a discipline, can examine the nature and effects of people's beliefs, attitudes and actions. It can devise theories to explain their origins and can comment on whether or not they are helpful to that person's life. It may show why, because of the psychological or emotional needs of a particular person, a belief may be welcomed or rejected, but **it does not thereby show whether that belief is true or false.**

So psychologists are likely to ask how beliefs come about and what they do. If the answers to these questions give a sufficient explanation for the belief, it suggests why that belief would be held even if it were shown to be untrue. But that, of course, still begs the question whether or not it *is* true.

Religion appears to offer a sense of significance to human life, a sense of its value in spite of its fragility. It offers values by which to live and therefore a basis for morality. As such, it is clear why religion has an appeal, and why it continues to flourish in spite of its many problems and criticisms. People may find it a comfort in time of difficulty and loss, and look to it for guidance in times of indecision.

But is that a positive or negative thing? Is religion a necessary feature of a thoughtful and sensitive life, or an invented prop for those who cannot accept life as it is? In this chapter we shall look briefly at some psychological perspectives on religion.

There are three aspects to the relationship between psychology and religion:

- The first is that psychology offers an explanation of religion in terms of human needs and responses. It shows why people might want to be religious, even if there were no objective basis for that religion.
- The second is that psychology challenges the value of religion for personal integrity and growth.
- The third is that the therapeutic applications of psychology – in psychiatry, psychoanalysis and counselling, for example – are alternatives to religion for those who seek personal healing and growth.

Is religion healthy?

If religious beliefs can be justified rationally and are based on a realistic understanding of life, then most people would conclude that religion is healthy. On the other hand, if we find that things are believed without any basis in reason or evidence, there is a chance that they are simply delusions – things we would like to believe to be true, but for which we have no good reason to believe that they are actually true – and holding such beliefs makes people vulnerable, since their view of life does not fit reality, and that may be regarded as unhealthy.

Sigmund Freud (1856–1939) famously described religion as a 'universal obsessional neurosis' and did so because he saw parallels between the compulsive washing and tidying routines of his obsessive neurotic patients and religious rituals designed to assure people that their sins were forgiven. Like the compulsive who constantly returns to wash his or her hands, but never feels clean, religious people are continually forgiven their sins, but need to return to hear that forgiveness proclaimed over and over again.

In this, Freud identifies religious activity with the symptoms of illness, rather than with its cure. The logic of this is that if attending a religious ceremony actually removed a sense of guilt and set that person right, then he or she would need to do it only once. The fact that religion becomes a routine activity suggests that it maintains a sense of need and dependency, rather than eliminating it.

There are two very different aspects to Freud's work on religion. The first, set out in his *Totem and Taboo* (1913), looks at the origins of religion in early tribal society. It develops his ideas about the origin of the idea of God and of social taboos that are given moral and religious authority. It also considers magic as the mistaken attempt to control the physical world through the mind. The second, in *The Future of an Illusion* (1927), looks at religion and evaluates what it does, taking the view that it is an illusion, and that people would be better served by addressing the reality of their lives. It is the second aspect that has continuing relevance for the philosophy of religion, since it argues that religion is an 'illusion' – a systematic attempt to shield people from the threatening aspects of the world. It raises fundamental questions about why religion continues to appeal, and whether what it offers is true or helpful.

Just as, in an ideal world, a small child can look to their physical father for protection and reassurance, so an adult, facing the hazards of life and recognizing his or her frailty, is tempted to use the idea of God as a father substitute. God controls the world and looks after you to make sure that, in spite of evidence to the contrary (which we shall consider under 'the problem of evil') everything is going to plan and you will be okay. Freud saw such religious belief as a human construct and therefore as an illusion.

Many aspects of Freud's work are open to challenge, including his understanding of the development of early society mirroring the development of the individual, the universal application of his idea of the Oedipus complex, and the way he relates individual behaviour to social behaviour among religious groups. There is no scope to discuss these here, but the fundamental issue he raises for the philosophy of religion concerns **whether religion is devalued if it can be shown to be a human construct.** Thus, if God is a projection (as, for example, in Feuerbach) the idea of 'God' may be judged not according to whether he exists or not, but what function he performs within religion and within the lives of believers.

Key question:

- Is it healthy to create an illusion in order to deal with the threat posed by life's hazards, or is it better to face reality as it is?
- Freud would argue that facing reality is better than depending on an illusion. But that, of course, is based on the assumption that God is an illusion, in the sense of being a human construct.

It is common, in books on the philosophy of religion, to contrast Freud's work with that of **Karl Jung (1875–1961)**, simply because Jung gave a more positive evaluation of the place of religion, and his idea of the collective unconscious enables an exploration of key features of religious belief and iconography across a range of religions. Indeed, moving from Freud to Jung involves a very different approach to religion, and one that follows this present book's emphasis on the phenomenon of religious experience. Jung looks at a wide variety of religious beliefs and practices and teases out the self-understanding they generate, in terms of **archetypes**, abstract entities that reflect different elements in human development and which are encountered through the collective unconscious. Religions are built up from these archetypes – which accounts for their appeal and the fact that they are found in such a variety of societies. For Jung, the archetypes have a positive role in guiding individuals towards maturity, and in so far as those archetypes are embedded in religious myths and rituals, religion can also have a positive function.

An essential difference between Freud and Jung, as far as we are concerned here, relates to the role played by the unconscious, particularly in religion. Through psychoanalysis, Freud sought to release individuals from the power of the unconscious – so that, once they were aware of the origin of their problems, they would be free from them. Jung, by contrast, examines the positive role of the unconscious (particularly through the collective unconscious) for shaping the self-understanding of individuals and allowing them to grow to maturity.

Although over-simplified, the fundamental choice might be put like this:

- Either God is a projection, an illusion, and needs to be shown to be such and replaced by a direct encounter with reality.
- Or God is an element in the unconscious mind, part of an web of myths and images, awareness of which may help individuals and society to move towards maturity.

The first sees religion as fundamentally **unhealthy**, since it blocks the direct encounter with reality; the second sees it as potentially **healthy**, since it provides a vehicle for understanding essential elements of human experience, encountered through the unconscious.

Religion as therapy

The aim of psychiatry and psychoanalysis is to enable an individual to be autonomous – in other words, to be able to function in society with a set of predictable values, and a sense of his or her own integrity. It seeks to free that person from whatever inhibits normal, rational and social behaviour. In other words, it works on the assumption that a person should be able to choose how to live and relate to others, freed from unhealthy (and thus inhibiting) unconscious motivations. It is not there to tell people **how** to live, but merely to enable them to live as their rational mind dictates, given the constraints of society.

Some aspects of religion may appear to offer the same thing. Thus, for example, a person plagued with a sense of guilt may find release through a religious ritual such as formal confession and absolution.

However, a possible objection to the therapeutic value of religion would be that a disturbed person may accept a religious ritual in a superficial way, and believe that he or she has been helped, without having fully examined and gone through the reasons for the problem in the first place. Was the guilt, for example, rational or irrational? The danger is that a person may think that they have been cured of their problem, because that is what they want to hear. However, without proper help and monitoring, it may be difficult to know whether any cure has been effective. In other words, from the perspective of a therapeutic discipline like psychiatry, religious 'cures' for mental conditions may appear to be dangerously unsupervised.

But there is a more fundamental difference between psychiatry, psychoanalysis and counselling on the one hand and religion on the other – namely that religion does not see the autonomy of the individual as the ultimate goal, but rather the setting of that individual in a new relationship with God and with the religious community. From a secular perspective that may or may not be a good thing, and will only be judged by the individual's subsequent behaviour.

So:

- Without doubt, religion can have a profound effect on people's lives, and it is reasonable to assume that this can sometimes be therapeutic.
- As with complementary medicine, it can be argued that it is dangerous to rely on religion as an exclusive alternative to conventional therapy.
- Whereas secular therapies aim at enabling the individual to be autonomous, religion aims to set the individual in a new set of relationships, which may suggest dependence on God, rather than autonomy.
- There is no objective way of deciding whether individual autonomy or dependence upon God should be the goal of therapy – since the secular therapist will argue for one and the religious person for the other, each reflecting a clear but different set of values.

Trained to be religious?

Although bypassed by the rise of modern cognitive science, behaviourism approached beliefs and attitudes through a process of stimulus and response. In the work of Pavlov in Russia and Skinner in America, it was shown that animals could be trained to respond to anticipated stimuli. Pavlov's dogs salivated at the signal that told them they would soon receive food, rats in cages were trained to press a lever when they wanted food.

A behaviourist might therefore argue that a person could, by means of rewards and punishments, be trained to be religious. Thus childhood experiences connected with religion and imposed by parents, might train the child in a religion that would continue through adult life.

Presented in such a crude form, such a process might be seen as unhealthy, since it would suggest that the adult believer was not free and autonomous in his or her beliefs. However, in many ways (and far beyond what the behaviourists were able to show) it is clearly the case that human society, and therefore the ability to pass on life skills from one generation to the next, depends on training. Children are taught to be clean, without having to know about hygiene. If religious beliefs are factually true (in the way that washing is necessary for hygiene) then training a child to be religious would be seen as a necessary and healthy thing to do. If not, then the process is unhealthy.

The problem is that any such training will be seen as healthy by a religious adult (who may have been trained in religion in his or her own childhood) and unhealthy by a non-religious one. The only 'objective' way to decide between those two points of view would be to determine whether religious beliefs were factually true or false, or – if false – whether they nevertheless contributed to an agreed measure of human integrity.

Religion as spiritual development

A common criticism of religion is that it offers pre-digested answers to fundamental questions. In other words, through creeds and set beliefs, it imposes ideas on individuals, encouraging them to accept them uncritically. This brings with it the additional hazard that people may define themselves as belonging to the group who accept one set of beliefs, and therefore oppose all whose beliefs are different. There are many examples throughout history of such differences of religious belief either directly causing hostilities, or being used to reinforce already existing divisions in society and making them worse.

We shall need to consider this phenomenon again, in looking at religion and society. For now we need to step back and ask what is involved with spiritual development, and whether conventional religion is an effective vehicle for this.

If spiritual development is defined in terms of the exploration and integration of all elements with someone's personality, then

– given that human beings are rational – it is important that everything that is integrated into a person's self-understanding should be scrutinized and accepted rationally.

Hence, the value of an image, myth or archetype for the individual requires that person both to enter into the experience of it, and to be satisfied intellectually that it is right to do so. Thus it is possible to argue that it is okay to accept a myth that works on the emotional rather than the intellectual level. It is rational to accept that some things are emotionally significant – even if they are not explained rationally.

Hence, spiritual development is not the same thing as intellectual development. It includes the intellect, but also embraces the emotions, the unconscious and such things as social skills. Just as the 'self' is seen as including but more than the physical body, so spiritual development includes but is more than the development of the mind.

Key questions

- Are the emotional and social aspects of religion such as can enhance the spiritual development of the individual? This is a real, not a rhetorical, question; the answer to it will depend on the religion and also on the individual. But it is a question worth asking, quite apart from the truth or otherwise of the creed of that religion.

- Does the religion in question allow sufficient flexibility of interpretation to enable the individual to be satisfied intellectually with its system of beliefs? In other words, can a person engage with this religion while retaining his or her intellectual integrity?

This book started by looking at religious experience and language, because religion is a phenomenon like any other, and deserves to be examined and understood, quite apart from the truth or otherwise of its beliefs. Looking at the self and then at psychology, we encounter the same issue. It is not sufficient simply to debate the truth or otherwise of religious propositions – for something can be fictional but deeply moving and culturally significant (as is the case with plays, stories or novels). Literal truth is certainly not the only level of human significance.

By raising the question of psychology and religion, this brief chapter has sought to highlight this crucial broadening of the task of the philosophy of religion. It is not enough to consider a belief and then dismiss it as a projection. Far more significant is the examination of what part it plays in religion and what part it plays in the life of the individual believer. In other words, we need to consider not just *what* is believed, but *why* it is believed.

08
suffering and evil

In this chapter you will:
- explore the problem posed for belief in God by the fact of suffering
- examine two classical approaches to this problem
- consider the way world religions have responded to the problem of suffering.

Human beings are fragile and short-lived. They are liable to accidents and diseases, and those who escape these still have to face the inevitable prospect of old age and death. The world is not a safe place in which to live, but it is the only place in which to live.

Human beings add to this suffering by their treatment of one another. From world wars to domestic unhappiness, people cause one another pain, whether deliberately or accidentally.

These two features of life are generally referred to as natural evil and moral evil respectively. All religions have to face and interpret these facts of suffering and evil, since they are an inescapable feature of life, and no attempt to give an overall view of the meaning and purpose of life can be credible if it overlooks them.

Suffering and evil create for religions both a challenge to which they can respond, and also a problem about their beliefs.

The challenge and the response

A frequently described feature of religious experience is a sense of oneness with the rest of the world and an awareness of its suffering and fragility. This generally gives rise to feelings of compassion towards all who suffer. Some articulate this in terms of a God of love, or a God who is all merciful and all compassionate. Even Buddhism, which does not tend to make statements about God or gods, responds to this basic awareness in terms of the four 'divine dwellings' – loving kindness, compassion, sympathetic joy and equanimity. These are said to the qualities through which one is joined with Brahma, or the divine.

The challenge for religion is how to respond to suffering and evil in a way that can express this basic sense of love and compassion. Generally speaking, religions do so in two ways:

- To counter natural suffering, they may promote compassion towards those who are in need. All the major religions have, in various ways, created organizations, structures and rules to help develop this concern for those who suffer – rules about giving to those in need, for example, or organizations to deliver relief to those who suffer. In other words, religion recognizes, but aims to reduce, the natural consequences of human frailty.

- To counter human cruelty, they promote moral principles. This may take the form of rules to deter followers from doing those things that are likely to inflict pain on others, or spiritual exercises (like prayer or meditation) which seek to promote a view of life in which deliberate cruelty has no part. In other words, religion recognizes the potential for human cruelty and sets about attempting to minimize it.

Examples

- the Sikh *langar*: a place for different people to share food together as equals
- the Hindu principle of *ahimsa*: non-violence towards all living things
- the Muslim practice of *Zakat* and *Ummah*: charity, and the principle of unity and equality within the Muslim community
- the Jewish *Torah:* commandments to prevent human exploitation and cruelty
- the Christian concept of love: sharing together in the life of Christ, the idea of self-giving for the benefit of others, and the setting up of charities to aid those who suffer
- the Buddhist principle of *karuna*: compassion towards all living things.

These are all ways in which the religions respond to the challenge of suffering and cruelty. They provide the background against which we shall examine the specific 'problem of evil'.

Why consider these responses?

As we shall see, within the philosophy of religion, evil and suffering are usually considered primarily as a *problem* for those who believe in God. But if there is any truth at all in the later Wittgenstein's argument that meaning is found in the context within which words are used, then to understand the meaning that suffering and evil have within the religious language game, we should examine their context, and that will include the responses that have been presented above, for religious people often see themselves as engaged in the task of overcoming suffering and evil. (Whether or not they succeed in doing so is another matter, but not one that is relevant for the purpose of this discussion.)

In the major theistic religions, the task of overcoming evil is something in which God is seen as active, mostly using humankind as his agent, but occasionally acting directly (as we shall see when we examine the ideas of providence and miracles).

In general, it would appear that the 'problem of evil' only emerges when the degree of evil is such it threatens to overwhelm the whole concept of a loving God. At this point there is a switch in the overall structure of thinking – from engaged and unquestioning co-operation with God to overcome suffering, to one in which belief in a loving God is questioned.

But what is implied in such a switch? Clearly, while God is seen as aiding and inspiring the challenge of overcoming suffering, the implication is that God is *not* the deliberate author of that suffering. Rather, given that the world is such that there is suffering, he works to alleviate it. The switch occurs at the point at which God does not seem to be taking his fair share in the task – the point at which is he seen as an agent separate from human agents, a potentially victorious agent (if he is believed to be omnipotent), and yet an agent who seems content to allow suffering to continue. Once that point is reached, there would seem to be only two options:

- to abandon the concept of God as a separate or external agent
- to try to understand why an omnipotent God should choose not to use his power to eliminate suffering and evil, and why (if he is the creator) he should allow it to exist in the first place.

If the first option is taken, 'God' simply becomes a word that describes a source of inspiration for those who seek to overcome suffering – valuable, but not omnipotent. If the second option is taken, you have the classic 'problem of evil'.

The problem

Can an all-powerful and all-knowing God also be all-loving? In its simplest form, the problem can be stated like this:

- **If** God is all-loving (omniscient), he would want to do away with suffering and evil.
- **If** God is all-powerful (omnipotent), there is nothing he cannot do. He is therefore able to overcome suffering and evil.
- **But** there is evil and suffering in the world.

The philosopher David Hume can generally be relied upon to state a problem directly. Here is what he says in Book XI of his *Dialogues*. It is the point at which he turns the argument from design on its head, and presents a world that is far from a comfortable, reassuringly designed machine:

> Look round this universe. What an immense profusion of beings animated and organized, sensible and active! You admire this prodigious variety and fecundity. But inspect a little more narrowly these living existences, the only beings worth regarding. How hostile and destructive to each other! How insufficient all of them for their own happiness! How contemptible or odious to the spectator! The whole presents nothing but the idea of a blind nature, impregnated by a great vivifying principle, and pouring forth from her lap, without discernment or parental care, her maimed and abortive children!

The conclusions to be drawn from this problem would seem to be:

- **either** God is not all-powerful
- **or** God is not all-loving
- **or** suffering and evil are either unreal, necessary, or a means to a greater good
- **or** the whole idea of an all-loving and all-powerful creator God was a mistake in the first place.

Note

It could be argued that suffering and moral evil are caused entirely by natural processes and therefore there is no need to implicate God. But that will not do, for the fact is that God did not **intervene** to prevent evil from happening (whatever its immediate cause) which (if omnipotent) he might reasonably be expected to do. Also, a God who creates *ex nihilo* is presumed to be absolutely responsible for creating and sustaining the laws of nature, and with them the limitations that give rise to suffering.

Therefore, for the purposes of this argument, it does not matter exactly **how** evil has come about, it is enough **that** it has come about.

Let us start with the last option. The whole 'problem of evil' is based on some basic religious assumptions:

- that the world is capable of being understood rationally
- that there is an overall meaning and purpose in everything that happens
- that there is a single underlying reality (God) rather than two or more basic realities in conflict
- that the underlying reality can be described (even if not literally) as in some way 'good' and 'loving'
- that this underlying reality is such that it has a direct and absolute control over events.

Now, the problem only really applies to *theism* – the belief in one God who is the creator of the world, infinite, perfect, omnipotent and omniscient. Let us therefore look first at the possibility of side-stepping the problem by limiting God's power.

It is possible to argue (through the cosmological or design arguments) that the world is created by God, but that he is not active within the world, and thus not able to change events (this position is generally known as *Deism*, and it was a popular feature of natural religion in the eighteenth century). Equally, it is possible to take the view that God's power is limited, either by the matter out of which he has created the world, or by being opposed by an active force of evil. Clearly, if God is limited in this sort of way, then suffering and evil are at least partially out of his control.

In other words

If you insist that there is a God who is both free and able to do anything, and is the sole cause of all that happens, then the problem remains. On the other hand, any limitation imposed on him by independent forces or matter will serve as his excuse.

If we stay with the idea of a loving, omnipotent God, then suffering and evil need to be explained as part of his intention for the world. Such an attempt to show that God is right and just is called a *theodicy*.

Throughout this chapter we need to distinguish between two things:

- Suffering that results from the nature of the universe in which we live and the effect this has upon fragile human life. This would include diseases, earthquakes and all other forms of 'natural evil'. This is sometimes called 'metaphysical evil' since it is a form of evil that is built into our whole understanding of the world.
- Moral evil, which results from the free choice of individuals to inflict suffering. Warfare, torture, inequalities that lead to suffering, emotional pain – all these come under the general heading of moral evil.

But we need to keep in mind that these two forms of evil are not equally balanced, for the following reasons:

- **If** everyone behaved perfectly, there would still be natural evil. Disease and death do not depend upon moral wickedness, but are the result of the way the world is made.
- **But if** there were no natural evil – that is, if everything were created perfect – then it could be argued that there would be no moral evil either, since moral evil results from an inadequate or defective understanding of self and world. The murderer is not a perfect being who just happens to choose to kill an innocent person, but a human being who, because of his or her imperfections and/or the imperfections of at least one other person, chooses to kill.

Therefore 'natural' evil is the greater problem for theism. If suffering results from an act of deliberate wickedness by a human individual, it is logical to blame that individual for the suffering, but there is a more fundamental question to be asked: **Why is the world such that people can choose to perform deliberate acts of wickedness?**

There have been the two traditional lines of approach to the problem of evil – the Augustinian and the Irenaean. They were set out by John Hick in *Evil and the God of Love*, and they have been taken up by many other writers, including Peter Vardy in *The Puzzle of Evil*. These books deal with this important subject in greater depth than is possible here.

The Augustinian approach

The Augustinian approach is named after St Augustine of Hippo (354–430) and reflects the influence of Plato on his thought. Plato had argued that the world we experience is made up of imperfect and limited copies of the ideal, eternal 'forms'. Augustine argued that evil is not a separate force opposing the good, but is a *lack of goodness*, a deprivation (his term for which is *privatio boni*). Like Plato, he sees the world as a limited, imperfect place, and suffering and evil reflect this. His theory does not imply that evil is a *separate reality*, it is merely an indication that the world has *fallen short of its intended perfection*. The Augustinian approach has been particularly influential because it was taken up by Aquinas, and through him has dominated Catholic thinking on this topic.

For reflection

Is the balance between good and evil a matter of perception? We may believe that the colours of autumn are beautiful, inspiring and therefore good. But those colours are simply the result of the dying of leaves. If a leaf were conscious, would it welcome the beauty of autumn? Would autumn not be an evil to be avoided, an inexplicable denial of all the rising of sap and nourishing that the leaf had known since the spring? You might say: 'But that's what a leaf is, that's what it does. It grows in the spring and dies in the autumn – it ends up as leaf mould.'

There is a further problem here, as pointed out by Peter Vardy. It runs rather like this:

- **If** goodness is the same thing as completion (or perfection), then, in order to know if something is good or evil, you have to know what its true nature is.

- **But** do we, for example, know what perfect or complete human nature is like? Is it a matter of being natural? If it is, then there may be many things (like rape or violence) which may seem 'natural', in the sense that it arises out of deep seated natural urges that are not restrained by reason. Does this therefore make them 'good'? Clearly not; so the final judge of what is good or evil is reason, applied to our observation of the world.

- **But that is the problem:** when reason assesses what it sees, it is confronted with both good and evil, happiness and suffering. It cannot see perfection, so how can it judge?

But even if we do not know what perfection is like, we certainly know that this world is – from a human perspective – far from perfect. Need it have been so? If it is believed that this is the only world that God **could** have created, then he is limited. If, on the other hand, it would have been possible for God to create different worlds, then he could have created one that did not have the imperfections of this one.

The key question:

Evil may be a lack of goodness, but why is there a lack of goodness? If God is all-powerful, could he not have organized the world differently?

Augustine answers this in terms of the origin of evil and suffering. He argued that evil first came into the world through the 'fall' of the angels. In books XI and XII of his *City of God*, he says that all angels were created perfect, but that some received less grace than others, and were able to 'fall'. This fall is then repeated by Adam and Eve in the Garden of Eden. As a result of their disobedience, they are cast out and face a world that involves both hard work and physical suffering. He therefore saw natural evil as a consequence of the 'fall' of humankind. *It is both a result of sin and also a punishment for sin.* His argument is an uneasy mixture of philosophy and a literal interpretation of the biblical story in Genesis. In the end, if Augustine is not to hold God ultimately responsible for this present state of affairs (even if brought about as a result of human disobedience), he still has to show that evil is merely a lack of goodness – a falling short of the goodness that a good God intended for his creation. Any other possibility suggests that God is responsible for creating something that is inherently evil.

Aquinas (in *Summa Theologiae*) presents the issue in another rather stark way. His argument starts with the fact that God and evil are incompatible:

- God is believed to be both good and without limit, so there is nowhere that God is not present
- in that case, evil cannot exist; there is no room for it, since it cannot arise where God is present, if God is good
- but we know that evil exists
- therefore there cannot be an infinite and good God.

Clearly, for Augustine and then Aquinas, the way out of this dilemma is to say that evil exists only as an limitation of good. But does this Augustinian approach actually solve that problem? Can, for example, the torture of an innocent child be regarded simply as a *lack of goodness* in the torturer? Is there not a very definite act of evil in such situations?

Comment

If evil is defined as a lack of goodness, it is equally possible to define goodness as a lack of evil. In an impersonal world, or one created by a psychopath, where nature deliberately forced its way forward only by means of suffering and death, there would be a 'problem of goodness'.

If there is a God, and if he chose to create a less than perfect world, then it is logical to seek a reason for his doing so. That brings us to the second of the traditional ways of answering the problem of evil – that set out by Irenaeus.

The Irenaean approach

The Irenaean approach is named after Irenaeus, Bishop of Lyons (*c*.130–*c*.202). It does not deny that suffering and evil exist, nor that they are permitted to exist by God. Rather, it argues that God chose to allow these things to exist in the world **in order to bring about a greater good** – human freedom and the ability of human beings to have a relationship with God.

This approach admits that human life is imperfect but, having been made in the image of God, men and women should have the opportunity to grow and develop into what God intended them to be. As they encounter the sufferings of life, people have an opportunity to grow and to learn.

He asks: 'How, if we had no knowledge of the contrary, could we have had instruction in that which is good?' (Irenaeus *Against Heresies* iv. xxxix.1 quoted in Hick p. 220) In other words, evil is a necessary feature of any world in which people could make moral choices and strive to be good.

This approach is followed by John Hick in *Evil and the God of Love* (1968). He sees evil as something to be tackled and overcome, but with the hope that, ultimately, it will be seen as part of an overall divine plan. He sees the world as 'a vale of soul making' – an environment within which people can grow. In this sense, evil is a necessary evil, without which there can be no spiritual growth:

> A world without problems, difficulties, perils, and hardships would be morally static. For moral and spiritual growth comes through response to challenges; and in a paradise there would be no challenges.
>
> (p. 372)

Comment

Notice that belief in some sort of life beyond death is important for this approach. The world may give people an opportunity to grow – but why should they bother to do so? Clearly, they will be motivated only if present hardships can be justified in terms of something better for which this life is a preparation.

If belief in God and life beyond death are removed, it might still be possible to say something like this:

- When we consider life, we cannot avoid acknowledging that human beings are fragile and fallible, liable to practise cruelty as well as kindness, liable also to seek goals that are limited and which may cause them suffering. People may seek excitement through driving dangerously fast or taking drugs; some will die as a result. Relationships may fail, and hatred between people may fester. That is the sort of world we live in.

- The fact that we call some things good and others evil shows that we are able to stand back from these realities and interpret them in terms of an overall view of human life and its place in the universe.

- Whether we like it or not, we therefore find ourselves in the sort of world in which we are forced to be creative in personal terms – we have to make choices and live with the results.

- A person who acknowledges personal responsibility and reflects on the consequences of the choices that he or she makes, is already using the world as 'a vale of self making' (to remove the rather loaded term 'soul'). That is what intelligent life is about.

- We don't get a choice in the matter; we cannot take our world back and exchange it for another! We either live creatively, or we complain at the fundamental injustice of a world that we naively had assumed was fashioned solely for our benefit.

The free will defence

Might it not have been possible for God to have created a world in which there was no moral evil, because everyone freely chose to do what was right? If such a world were a logical possibility, then God would stand accused of having chosen not to have made it.

God's position is defended by what is generally called 'the free will defence'. It runs like this:

- if you are to be free to choose to do good, then it must be possible for you to choose to do evil
- if the world were to be such that moral evil were made impossible, then it makes no sense to speak of having a free moral choice
- **but** having free will is an essential condition of a moral life
- **therefore** there needs to be the possibility of moral evil in order for people to have free will and to live morally.

This argument has been presented very starkly by Swinburne. He points out that, for a moral choice to be real, you need depravity, in other words, you need to *want* what is wrong and then decide to reject it. But he then makes an important distinction between the *possibility* of evil and the *fact* of evil. He argues that, as a condition of the greater good, there has to be the possibility of moral evil, but not the actual evil itself. In other words, if we are free, then it is up to us whether we choose to do evil, but for us to be moral there has to be that possibility.

One way to counter this would be to argue that God, if he is all-powerful, should be able to make people freely choose what is good. Both alternatives are there, but the evil one will never be taken. But is that freedom?

A greater good?

The implication of the 'free will defence' (and, indeed, the Irenaean approach that lies behind it) is that it is better to have a world in which people are free to choose evil, rather than a world in which they are not free at all. Human freedom is the greater good, for the sake of which we have to cope with mass murder, abuse of children, torture and the like.

The implication is that an all-knowing God weighed the evil of all these horrendous things against the benefit of human freedom, and chose freedom. Can that be justified?

A classic example of the argument against such a choice is given in Dostoyevsky's *The Brothers Karamazov* (Book 5, Chapter 4). There is a gruesome story of a child who, for a minor misdemeanour, is punished by being torn apart by hounds in front of his parents. Dostoyevsky presents the case for saying that no end can ever justify such means. Whatever benefits might come from it, nothing could ever justify the torture of an innocent child. Ivan Karamazov says to Alyosha:

> … if the sufferings of children go to swell the sum of sufferings which was necessary to pay for truth, then I protest that the truth is not worth such a price.

In other words, Dostoyevsky is challenging the morality of a God who would allow evil, no matter how good the end result of allowing it might be.

For reflection

Generally speaking, the problem of evil has focused on the impact of suffering and evil on human life, but other species also suffer 'natural evil' and in some cases (like that of a cat playing with a mouse) they appear to choose to inflict unnecessary pain – which would be the equivalent of moral evil, if animals were rational and able to choose how to act.

Humankind has only emerged very recently on Earth. What of all the suffering experienced by non-human species that came before us? How can human development be its justification?

The Irenaean approach in general, points to human experience and the possibility of human development (the 'vale of soul making') as justification for all the suffering of all the species since life first appeared on planet Earth. That raises a comment and a question:

- It is arrogantly anthropocentric – making humankind the reason for the sufferings of all other species.
- **Was such a divine sledgehammer really necessary to crack the human nut?**

Revealing the nature of God or good?

Notice that the problem of evil, as it has been explored so far, assumes that we have a knowledge of good and evil that is independent of any knowledge of God. If that were not the case, then we would have no reason to challenge the goodness of God.

Let us put this in philosophical terms. As we saw earlier (see p. 43) an analytic statement is one in which its truth can be known simply by defining the terms. 'A triangle has three sides' is analytic; you don't have to examine triangles to show that it is true. A synthetic statement is one that can be shown to be true or false on the basis of evidence. 'The cat is sitting on the mat,' can be affirmed or denied only after looking.

Now the question to be considered is this: is the statement 'God is good' analytic or synthetic?

- If it is analytic, anything God does is good by definition (that is what 'good' means). If he allows the torture of children, then – within the whole scheme of things – that must be good.

Note

This issue arises also in connection with the Euthyphro Dilemma, see below p. 238.

- If, on the other hand, the statement 'God is good' is synthetic, the implication is that we have some idea of goodness that is over and above our idea of God, and by which we can assess whether it is right to call God 'good'.

But, in the ontological argument, God is described as 'that than which a greater cannot be thought'. Yet here, in the 'problem of evil', the clear implication is that there is, over and above the idea of God, a prior sense of what it means to say that something is 'good'.

And that suggests that the image of God in this debate is inadequate. It is of a god who is external to events, who permits but is not within the suffering. But if God is thought of as being fully immanent as well as transcendent (see Chapter 03) then he might well be thought of as active within suffering, and as actually suffering alongside the individuals in and through whom he lives.

A suffering God, working through particular situations to bring about healing and good, is an idea that may find echoes in the day-to-day experience of religious people, but it seems at odds with the external creator who chooses to permit suffering as part of his greater scheme.

And this, of course, was one of the great stumbling blocks in developing and presenting the Christian concept of God – since the idea that God could suffer in and through the person of Jesus went against the more absolute transcendence of the Jewish idea of God. Equally, for Islam, the absolute transcendence of Allah means that he can be seen as merciful and compassionate, but not as actually becoming immanent in the person who is suffering. For Muslims, Jesus is hailed as a prophet, but he cannot be divine.

This highlights the dilemma of believing in a god who is both transcendent and immanent. Take the example of a child dying of disease. If it happens just because that is the natural fragility of human life, then it is sad, but must be accepted. People may be helped by the idea that God, through Christ, understands and shares in the suffering of this child, giving courage and strength to all who are involved.

But how does this square with the idea that the suffering of the child, far from being an accident of human frailty, is actually part of a divine plan – that the Creator decided in his inscrutable wisdom that this particular child should die? It is particularly difficult to square the idea of an overall designer with that of the immanent, suffering God. The problem is not one that can be solved by some form of logic, for it concerns the clash of fundamental ideas of God that are being employed.

If God remains literally the designer for whom everything has its chosen place, then the price of his design is too high. However good his intention, his method of bringing it about seems disastrously bad – such a God appears like an army commander who, having freely allowed the enemy to take up positions, sends wave after wave of unarmed troops towards their lines!

Three thoughts

- If God is the omnipotent creator of the world, shaping the whole creative process but deliberately permitting suffering and evil, how can he be called 'good'?
- But if God is immanent within the suffering, sharing and helping, and identifying with those who suffer (as in the image of Jesus on the cross), then how can he be an omnipotent creator?
- And in any case, we seem to have an intuition about what is good that does not depend upon our concept of God. Within this argument, 'good' becomes a god beyond God.

Modern science, and in particular the recognition of the contribution of genetic mutation to natural selection, has brought a new factor into this discussion. The very process of mutation that leads to examples of natural or metaphysical evil, is fundamentally necessary for the development of life. This is how Arthur Peacocke describes the issue:

> The chance disorganization of the growing human embryo that leads to the birth of a defective human being and the chance loss of control of cellular multiplication that appears as a cancerous tumour are individual and particular results of that same interplay of 'chance' and 'law' that enabled and enables life to exist at all.

(Theology for a Scientific Age, p. 126)

Comment

It is one thing to strive to overcome the problems caused by harmful mutations, seeing them as an unfortunate by-product of a process that is central to all life; but quite another to justify that process in terms of the intentions of a loving God. Can a believer really be committed to helping overcome cancer, for example, and at the same time see the cancer as a necessary side-effect of the purposes of God?

God as moral agent

Brian Davies (in *An Introduction to the Philosophy of Religion*, p. 22) points out that much of the argument presented by John Hick and others depends on the idea that God is a moral agent – that the things he does (or permits individuals to do) can be labelled good and bad, just as if he were a human agent. Now, for classical theism (see above p. 59) God creates *ex nihilo* and is therefore involved with everything that comes into being. God cannot be one being among others (see above p. 14 for Tillich's description of God as 'Being Itself'). But to describe something as a moral agent implies that it is an individual being, for it must be able to act and have effects external to itself, which can be called good or bad. But nothing is external to God – so how can he have effects, and without them how can he be called a moral agent?

The second point that Davies makes is that to be a moral agent one must have duties and obligations. But how can one describe God in this way? If God is changeless, it makes no sense to speak of him choosing to do one thing or declining to do another.

> The notion of God's changelessness means that God just does what he does, or, as some would prefer to say, that he just is what he is.
>
> (Davies, p. 24)

Now Davies makes another important point. Moral agents can either succeed or fail, and which of these is judged to be the case depends on comparing their actions with those of others. There has to be some external standard against which action can be judged. But there is no external standard in the case of God; no alternative God creating alternative worlds with which our own may be compared. Davies concludes:

> But what is the background for judging the Creator *ex nihilo*? There cannot be any, in which case the God of classical theism cannot be said to be even capable of succeeding or failing. And in that case he cannot be a moral agent, for such an agent must be able either to succeed or to fail.
>
> (p. 24)

An issue to ponder

- Classical theism may take the idea of God beyond the world of beings and therefore beyond the possibility of individual good or evil actions or intentions. But if that is the case, then as far as morality and suffering are concerned, God becomes irrelevant.

- That which is everywhere, is perceived nowhere. That which has no boundaries cannot be seen and compared with others. That which does everything equally, takes responsibility for nothing in particular.

- In which case, what has this sort of God to do with the deepest intuitions of people, who, in the face of life's fragility and cruelty, still want to say that life is fundamentally good and that compassion is a natural human response to suffering?

The devil and hell

The idea of a force that opposes God, personified in the figure of the devil, is one way in which religion can express the origin of evil without compromising God as a moral agent.

However, that involves either diluting the idea of God's omnipotence – since omnipotence is incompatible with any opposing force – or making the devil part of an overall divine plan. The latter, of course, is the approach taken by Augustine, in presenting the origin of evil in the fall, first of the angels led by Satan, and then of humankind. Thus, there seems to be no way that the idea of a devil lessens the fundamental 'problem of evil'.

If God has established a moral order, that might suggest that certain actions deserve punishment, and where that punishment is not obviously forthcoming in this life, a natural sense of justice suggests that (if the world is controlled by God, and he wishes to act justly towards it) then there should be some punishment for those who do wrong – hence the idea of hell as a place of post-death punishment.

During part of its history, particularly in the medieval period, Christianity used images of hellfire to warn people of the consequences of evil actions. Islam too has a concept of hell, in contrast to the joys of heaven, and Buddhism has a whole variety of hells, both hot and cold. In Buddhism it is generally emphasized that the hells describe a self-created state of unhappiness to be experienced within life, rather than seeing them literally as places to enter after death. The same is generally true of Christianity – although whether the devil and hell exist in any real sense is a matter of debate between those of a more literal and those of a more liberal interpretation of Christian doctrines.

At its crudest, the threat of hell is an incentive to do good rather than evil. At a more subtle level, it is a reminder that evil actions can have painful consequences. However, if a person behaves correctly simply in order to avoid hell, is that behaviour genuinely moral?

For further reflection

• If the world is believed to be ordered by a just God, then a place or state such as 'hell' might well be thought to exist. If by a loving God, he might in fact decide to spare everyone from actually having to experience it.

This is highlighted by the contrast between the Augustinian and Irenaean approaches to theodicy. Whereas Augustine allowed for punishment in hell, Irenaeus – in putting forward a theory in which people would gradually learn to grow into God's likeness – emphasized the compassionate aspect of God, allowing all eventually to work their way towards salvation.

Suffering and the major religions

We have already noted that the world religions offer moral guidelines in order to attempt to curb the tendency for people to inflict suffering on one another, along with spiritual practices in order to help people to cope with suffering and loss, and organizations to promote sharing and compassion. But each religion has its own distinctive approach to this, along with its own view on the nature of and reasons for suffering.

Judaism

The event which now dominates the Jewish way of thinking about suffering is the holocaust – the murder of six million Jews under the Nazis. The fundamental question, in the face of such extreme evil is 'Where was God?' and all subsequent Jewish theology has had to take this into account.

In the Book of Job, Job is struck down by all kinds of suffering, and this is presented as being allowed by God as a test of his faith. His complaint that he does not deserve to suffer is finally silenced by witnessing the power and wonder of nature. Faced with that, he concludes that it is impossible for humankind to understand the purposes of God. In Judaism, one holds on to faith and tradition, in spite of suffering, and without expecting a rational explanation.

Islam

Here a dominant theme is 'the will of Allah' – since it is paramount in Islam that God has absolute control over everything. There is no doubt here but that suffering is allowed by God, even though his purpose in doing so is beyond human understanding. In terms of moral evil, however, there is a recognition that people are free to either accept or reject the teachings of Allah, and Islam has never been soft on the punishment of what it sees as human wickedness in deliberately turning away from the path set by Allah.

As with Judaism, an absolute and transcendent God cannot be questioned. On the other hand, Allah is always described as merciful and compassionate, so he is certainly not seen as indifferent to human suffering.

Christianity

The central image of the Christian religion is the figure of Jesus on the cross. Although most Christians would say that we cannot know the purposes of God, the arguments presented earlier in this chapter have largely come from within the Christian tradition and show a serious concern to present a theodicy (the general term for an attempt to justify belief in God in the face of suffering and evil) that is logical and coherent.

On the other hand, there is the general recognition in theology and also in the practical and pastoral concerns of the Church, that God in some way suffers with people and works to alleviate that suffering. The image of Jesus on the cross represents the immanent aspect of God, suffering alongside human beings, and also – through the person of Jesus – forgiving those whose moral evil has inflicted suffering.

The tension within Christianity on this issue is between this image of God in Jesus, healing, suffering and forgiving, and the

God of 'natural theology' presented as the uncaused cause etc. – a tension between saying something **particular** about God (that he acts in a particular way and through a particular person) and saying that God must be everywhere and in everything.

Notice that the belief that a suffering and forgiving Jesus is God incarnate is the point at which Christian thought parts company with the more strictly monotheistic systems of Judaism and Islam. Christianity deliberately sets this image of the suffering Jesus, which reflects the tensions of 'the problem of evil', at the very heart of its creed. Its answer – the 'resurrection', of good triumphing over evil – presents an image of hope, rather than a logical answer to the problem.

Hinduism

It is difficult to ascribe a single theory of evil to Hindu thought, simply because Indian religious traditions are so diverse. In general, the fact that (at the popular level, at least) there are a diversity of gods and goddesses means that no single deity is required to account for everything that happens, so the typical 'problem of evil' faced by Western monotheism does not really apply.

A key concept to understand the Indian approach to suffering is *karma*. At its simplest level, karma is the result of action. Good deeds bring favourable results, either in this lifetime or in future lives (since Indian thought includes the idea of reincarnation). This has the effect of giving a balance to moral evil (since the person who does evil will have to bear the consequences in terms of the bad karma that it generates). It also serves as an explanation of natural evil, for moral and natural evil are linked through the idea of *karma*: those who suffer natural evil are experiencing the result of *karma* generated in former lives.

Buddhism

Buddhism claims to offer a path to overcome suffering, a path than includes morality, spiritual development through meditation, and the wisdom to take a radical look at the world as it is, with all its imperfections.

Unlike the other religions, it does not work on the basis of a creator God, whose existence needs to be defended, or whose creativity is thought to be revealed in the way the world is organized.

Buddhists believe that natural suffering occurs because everything is in a constant state of change, and individual things do not exist independently of the conditions that bring them about. We are fragile, limited and very vulnerable things. Why should we expect to be free from natural suffering, old age, sickness and death? That is simply what life is like. The task of the Buddhist path is to help to find happiness even in a world which is recognized as fragile and fleeting.

When it comes to moral evil, Buddhism teaches that actions have results (*karma*). Any action which Buddhism sees as morally wrong (for example, the deliberate taking of life) has immediate harmful consequences to the victim of the act, but also, in the longer term it diminishes the person who performs it. Some Buddhists present this in terms of reincarnation – so that the good or bad *karma* accumulated in one life determines how one will be born in the next. Others speak in more psychological terms: that it is a person's intentional actions that shape and reshape his or her life, with one's present state determined to a large extent by one's earlier choices.

In terms of the challenge of suffering, compassion (along with wisdom) is seen as a key feature of the Buddhist path. Helping those who suffer both improves their situation, and also generates more good *karma* for the helper.

Sikhism

Sikhism is a monotheistic religion, and therefore faces the 'problem of evil' as do other monotheisms. Where it differs from the three Western religions, however, is that it is devotional rather than intellectual in its approach.

From its earliest days, the Sikh community suffered persecution, generally at the hands of Muslim rulers. Its response was to seek justice for all, to celebrate martyrdom as a triumph of truth and justice over oppression, and to emphasize self-respect, both for individuals and the community.

In terms of a response to physical suffering, Sikhs place great importance on service to the community and the relief of suffering and want. This is symbolized particularly in the *langar*, the free kitchen which is attached to every Sikh place of worship (*gurdwara*). All are welcomed, and all sit together as equals to share food.

Without entering into the philosophical debate, Sikhism, in its symbols of carrying a *kirpan* (a small sword or dagger) and sharing food in the *langar*, proclaims a struggle for justice and right and also a homely compassion for all in need.

Comment

All too often, the philosophy of religion has been too narrow in its focus, considering the logic and coherence of religious propositions in a kind of vacuum, and seeking logical answers without taking into account the various ways in which religions actually respond to the problem. But the task of the philosophy of religion, if it is to understand what religion is about, needs to take a broader view.

By introducing these brief comments on how the world's major religions have responded to the fact of suffering and evil, the intention has been to show the narrowness of presenting an answer based only on logic. This is particularly clear in the cases of Christianity and Buddhism:

- Christianity, without achieving a logical answer to the problem of evil, nevertheless explores it in the person of Jesus, and in what it understands by 'dying and rising to life again'. Within that religion, the idea of resurrection is a symbol of hope, affirmed in the face of suffering. It is less an answer to a logical problem, more a way of affirming a religious experience.

- Buddhism, again focusing centrally on the problem of suffering, considers how it may be overcome, rather than speculating on its cause. In the well-known Buddhist image, a man who has been shot should be concerned with having the arrow removed from his body, rather than with the details of how the arrow was made. In Buddhist terms, the Western 'problem of evil' is merely an exercise in arrow analysis, it does nothing to remove the dart or bind the wound.

Coming to terms with suffering

Funeral rites and the process of mourning show how many religious believers come to terms with suffering and loss. It would therefore be instructive to look at the language used at a traditional funeral in order to see how it relates to the problem of evil.

Let us, by way of example, consider the implications of the Church of England's *Book of Common Prayer* service for the Burial of the Dead.

Arriving at the graveside, the priest is instructed to say:

> Man that is born of woman hath but a short time to live, and is full of misery. He cometh up, and is cut down, like a flower; he fleeth as it were a shadow, and never continueth in one stay.

> In the midst of life we are in death: of whom may we seek for succour, but of thee, O Lord, who for our sins art justly displeased?

In the first statement, there is a recognition of the fragility of life, and in the second there seems to be a shift towards the idea of a God who is displeased, and rightly so. But does that imply that sin is the cause of death?

> Yet, O Lord most holy, O Lord most mighty, O holy and most merciful Saviour, deliver us not into the bitter pains of eternal death.

> Thou knowest, Lord, the secrets of our hearts; shut not thy merciful ears to our prayer; but spare us, Lord most holy, O God most mighty, O holy and merciful Saviour, though most worthy Judge eternal, suffer us not, at our last hour, for any pains of death, to fall from thee.

Here there is to be a contrast between the eternal life or death of the soul and the natural death of the body – with all the implication for an understanding of the self that were explored in Chapter 05. God is still seen as Judge and as one to whom one should plead, as though he were totally in charge. And if so, might he not have decided that, in the overall scheme of things, this death was beneficial? That, of course is what follows ...

> Forasmuch as it hath pleased Almighty God of his great mercy to take unto himself the soul of our dear brother here departed ...

Here again there is the contrast between the temporal with the eternal. The point remains, however, that God is believed to have designed this world in which a person does well to escape from this body into something better, as is then reinforced ...

> We give thee hearty thanks, for that it hath pleased thee to deliver this our brother out of the miseries of this sinful world ...

Again, notice the Augustinian approach here. The world of suffering is also the world of sin, and the implication here is that the two are inextricably linked. Through sin came death and all that goes with it.

Of course, few people now choose to use the traditional forms of the *Book of Common Prayer*, but it does throw into stark relief the various approaches to the problem of suffering. At one and the same time, it affirms God as sovereign and almighty, and also absolves him from any accusation of evil, by saying that his decision to cause this death is simply in order to allow the person to pass from this world to something better.

Furthermore – and this relates to the whole idea of God, creation, and a sense of value – the implication of the Prayer Book service is that the world, through the fall of Adam, is judged negatively. There is more evil in it than good, and people would do well to escape.

For reflection

The Prayer Book service presents a world of suffering from which the person who has died has escaped to something better. This might provoke the question: is religion escapist?

Marx saw religion as the cry of the oppressed, the voice of the voiceless and the opium of the people, at a time when opium was widely used to alleviate suffering of many kinds. He saw in religion's promise that one might be released out of this world into an eternal one, a form of escapism, to be contrasted with his own demand that people take responsibility for the improvement of their situation here and now.

Was Marx right? Is religion an opiate that people administer to themselves rather than face the harsh reality of the world in which they live, and the death that they must one day face?

Was he fundamentally Buddhist in the demand that people face reality?

Was Marx taking a kind of self-help Irenaean approach – that the suffering of people here and now is the spur they need to develop themselves and improve their material conditions?

Conclusions

The problem of evil remains the major obstacle to traditional Christian theism. Any understanding of the world which includes evil will be at odds with the literal acceptance of the concept of an all-loving God who has the power to order everything according to his will.

This is shown very starkly in terms of the belief that God creates the world *ex nihilo* – in other words that he does not merely shape and influence something that exists outside himself, but is the sole ground and origin of everything. He is thus absolutely responsible for everything, hindered neither by external matter nor external agency. If he permits human freedom, knowing that evil will result, he is in some measure responsible for allowing that evil to come about.

The only way out, it would seem, is in terms of the value that we place on that freedom and on the possibility of human growth through the challenge of evil and suffering. But even Swinburne, who presents the Irenaean approach to this problem in a very positive way, has to admit that prolonged suffering must count against belief in a good God.

Various attempts to find a place for evil within an overall positive view of the world include:

- evil as a necessary contrast to good
- evil as merely the absence of good, not a reality in itself
- evil as a just punishment (and Augustinian approaches)
- that, on balance (according to Leibniz) this is the best of all possible worlds, and that, for example, compassion is made possible by suffering, thus balancing good against evil
- that all is (or will be) well from God's perspective (including Irenaean approaches in terms of the world, including suffering and evil being the only environment within which humans can grow).

And yet all of these together still have to face the challenge of Dostoyevsky – that no final result can be worth the price of the suffering of even one innocent child.

Comment

All three Western monotheistic religions (Judaism, Christianity and Islam) accept that, to some extent, God's purpose in allowing suffering and evil is a mystery. It is something that is deemed to be beyond the power of human understanding.

But from a rational point of view, assessing all the arguments, it would seem most unlikely that there can be a god who is literally both omnipotent and loving.

09

religion and science

In this chapter you will:
- consider the impact of science on our view of the world and of religion
- contrast scientific method with the source of religious beliefs
- look at key issues: the origin of the universe, evolution and miracles.

Science is the systematic attempt to understand the world through observation, analysis and deduction. **Science is a process based on observation and reason.** It seeks to formulate theories by which observations may be understood, and which may then be used to predict events and their consequences.

An important feature of science is that it is always changing and throwing up new ideas. Its theories are provisional; they represent what scientists see as the best way of making sense of observations. They are constantly being tested out and modified. For a time they may become established and normative for understanding the world, and some scientists may seem reluctant to discard them, but eventually – if science is to make progress – they are likely to be discarded as new theories, which may be more comprehensive, or more successful in predicting what will happen, emerge to take their place.

Science seeks two things:

- **Understanding** – In this it reflects the natural curiosity that has always led human beings to wonder about the nature of the world in which they live.
- **Control** – As a result of increased understanding, it is possible to develop technology which may seek to improve the quality of life.

Technology illustrates the effectiveness of science. If something works in practice, you may generally assume that the theory upon which it is based is correct. We know that modern science has transformed many aspects of life, and are therefore predisposed to say that the scientific method of understanding the world is 'correct'; if it were not, none of this technology would have been possible.

For reflection

The achievement of science, and therefore the justification of the scientific method, is seen in every aspect of life in the developed world – medicine, transport, computing, banking, communications, entertainment and so on. Where it has negative consequences (for example, weapons of mass destruction, computer viruses, unsightly electricity pylons in an area of natural beauty), these are generally attributed to human misuse of the potential that science offers, or (as with the side-effects of otherwise beneficial medical treatment) with a failure to check everything adequately, or a limitation of our present state of knowledge.

Science in itself, as a method of understanding the world, is therefore seldom blamed for the failures of technology to deliver human happiness. It generally only comes into conflict with ethical and religious principles when its experimental methods are seen as requiring actions that are themselves seen as immoral (for example, the use of human embryos in genetic research).

This broad acceptance of the benign impact of science is so widespread that those religious groups who reject technology (for example, the Amish in the United States) are regarded as eccentric, even by those who see the benefits of a less technologically dominated lifestyle.

However, science and technology are tools in the hands of fallible human beings – and we should not be blind to the destructiveness with which they have sometimes been used, not least in their impact on the natural environment. To agree with the scientific method of gaining knowledge does not require an uncritical acceptance of all that science and technology have done.

The problem science poses for religion

Most forms of religion have teachings which claim to give knowledge about the nature of the world and the place of humankind within it. But religion is to do with commitment as well as discernment. The view of the world offered by religion is not simply a passing hypothesis waiting to be replaced; it is held as an eternal truth.

This is where science causes difficulties for the religious believer. The scientist examines the evidence and may find an existing hypothesis inadequate. If that is a scientific hypothesis, there is (relatively speaking) no problem: if the evidence for the adoption of the new theory is established, then it replaces the old. But if it is a religious belief (for example, that a miracle has taken place) then, in the face of much evidence to the contrary, the religious person may seek to continue in his or her belief, and will (if necessary) change the meaning of 'miracle' or 'God' in order to accommodate the inescapable evidence provided by science.

The scientific world-view therefore challenges the literal understanding of many traditional religious doctrines, which were formulated in a pre-scientific age, couched in non-scientific language, and make assumptions about the world that science cannot endorse (for example, the literal notion of the world being made in six days).

There are some 'quick' ways out of the science and religion issue:

- Science is concerned with facts, religion with values.
- Science looks at life in an impersonal way, religion in a personal.
- Religion is a left-over from a pre-scientific age. It will diminish as science reveals more and more about our world.
- Religion does not depend on reason, but on faith. What science has to say about the world is therefore irrelevant to religion.

None of these does justice to either religion or science; the situation is far more complex than that.

Science may also suggest explanations for the phenomenon of religion. Psychology and sociology both do so, but they tend to ask 'What does it do?' rather than 'Are its teachings true?' Just because they come up with an answer to the first question, does not mean that the answer to the second is negative. Just because a society maintains the structures of an established religion in order to hold itself together, or an individual prays fervently in order to cope with a problem of deep-seated guilt, does not mean that the religion is *nothing but* a means of solving those problems. Its teachings *may* also be true – but that is quite another matter.

The interaction between science and religion is a vast subject, and much of it relates to topics covered within the philosophy of religion. However, for the purposes of this book, we need to limit ourselves to a number of key issues:

- the changing world-view in Western thought
- the contrasting methods of science and religion
- the idea of providence and miracles
- the origin of the universe
- the nature of humankind and its place within the universe.

The first two of these provide the background to any discussion of science and religion. The other three show how the science impinges on religious belief.

Science and Buddhist thought

In general this chapter will deal with the science and religion issues that occur within Western religion. This is because it is within Western culture that the rise of modern science has created a 'problem' for the literal acceptance of some religious beliefs. By contrast, Buddhism, with its undogmatic and open exploration of reality, its emphasis on the interconnectedness of all things, and its recognition of impermanence, has no problem whatever with modern science. The view of the world presented in its teaching is very similar to that of modern physics, and where it uses traditional images (for example, heavens and hells), it has little problem interpreting these in symbolic or psychological terms.

What is even more crucial is the fact that clinging on to a fixed doctrine or a set form of words is, for Buddhists, a hindrance rather than a help on the spiritual path. Teachings are like a raft used for crossing a river – you leave it on the far bank and walk on; you do not carry it with you as a burden. This attitude has parallels with modern science's willingness to let previously useful hypotheses go when a new situation presents itself.

The changing world-view

In order to understand the religion and science debate, it is important to appreciate something of the historical context within which it has taken place.

In Western thought, there have been two major shifts in the overall way in which people have viewed the world. (These are sometimes referred to as 'paradigm shifts'. A paradigm is the overall model of reality, around which various theories are clustered – an important idea of the philosophy of science, set out by Thomas Kuhn, in *The Structure of Scientific Revolutions* 1996). Without becoming involved with the history of science, we should at least note the impact of these shifts, for each has had a profound effect on the interpretation of religious beliefs.

From the medieval world to Newton

The first paradigm shift gained momentum during the sixteenth and seventeenth centuries, causing the medieval world-view to give way to one based on Newtonian physics. This is the period to which is generally ascribed the rise of modern science. Although some features of later science are found before this time (for example, the attitude to evidence and experiment taken by Roger Bacon at the end of the thirteenth century), it was this period leading up to Newton that saw a decisive shift in thinking.

Medieval Christianity had a view of the world that was based partly on biblical imagery, and partly on a mixture of Aristotle (384–22BCE) and the cosmology of Ptolemy of Alexandria (second century CE).

As we saw earlier, Aristotle argued that everything we know about the world comes from experience interpreted by reason. In this, Aristotle was at one with modern science. But Aristotle also considered that everything had both an **efficient cause** (which we would normally think of as a cause: that which produces an external effect) and also a **final cause**, which is the intended result. That suggested that everything happened for a purpose, rather than simply because of antecedent causes.

Example

If a baby grows, the **efficient** cause of that growth is the food and drink and oxygen that it takes in, but the **final** cause is the adult human being into which it is growing. If the growth were not controlled and shaped in this way, individual tissues would grow wild, and not fit the overall system of the body.

For Aristotle, there was an unmoved mover who constituted the final cause of everything (see above Chapter 04). In the medieval world-view, this was linked to Ptolemy's view of the Earth at the centre of the world, surrounded by ten glassy spheres. Seven of these spheres were thought to carry the seven heavenly bodies, the eighth carried the stars, a ninth was invisible, but turned all the others, and a tenth was the abode of God. Everything that happened on Earth was thought to be controlled by the movement of these spheres, and they, in turn, were controlled by God.

It is important to realize that this way of thinking was **deductive**. A person would consider the ideas of perfection, or of biblical revelation, and come to a conclusion about what the world should be like. Observations of the actual world were intended to confirm this idea, but not to challenge it.

Example

Everything above the sphere of the Moon was considered to be perfect. The circle is a perfect shape, therefore the motion of the planets must be circular. If observation suggests otherwise, it must be accounted for in terms of a planet moving round one circle, whose centre was simultaneously moving round another (an epicycle), hence an elaborate system of such epicycles was devised in order to account for planetary motion and at the same time remain true to the tradition of circular perfection.

It is unlikely that there was ever a single, universally accepted view of the universe. What was believed religiously was a combination of some ancient near-Eastern views with Greek philosophy. The idea of the heavenly perfections, or the uncaused cause, so vigorously defended at a later date by the Church, would have been quite meaningless to the characters described in the scriptures.

In practice, different people accepted different views. For the uneducated majority, the more primitive view of a three-decker universe, centred on the Earth, with hell below and heaven above, was portrayed in Church murals and probably accepted with varying degrees of literalness. Depicting the joys of heaven and miseries of hell was regarded as beneficial for promoting morality.

Natural philosophy (as science would have been known at that time), in spite of more than a thousand years of respect for the authority of Aristotle, reinforced by the work of Aquinas in the thirteenth century, who interpreted and integrated Aristotle into Christian thinking, gradually moved towards the examination of evidence. This is illustrated by the work of Copernicus (1473–1543), a Polish priest. He wrote *De Revolutionibus Orbium Coelestium* (On the Movement of the Heavenly Bodies) in which he appeared to claim:

- that the Sun (rather than the Earth) was at the centre of the universe
- that the Earth rotated once every day and circled the Sun once every year
- that the stars were further away from the Earth than was the Sun, since there was no shift in their relative positions from different viewpoints on Earth.

Although unremarkable claims by modern standards, they broke new ground because:

- they were based on observation rather than on an interpretation of authoritative texts, scriptural or otherwise
- they therefore challenged the authority of Aristotle
- they displaced the Earth from its central position.

On its publication, the book was prefaced by the Lutheran theologian Osiander, who argued that it was no more than a hypothesis and did not challenge the factual correctness of the traditional view. Later, his work was brought very publicly into the religion and science debate by Galileo (1564–1642) who, in 1632, published a book comparing Copernicus' system with the traditional one, and concluding that Copernicus was correct. Galileo was put on trial and forced to recant his views. Thus we see a growing desire to look at evidence and formulate theories – in other words, to develop a new body of knowledge – in the face of opposition from religious authority.

The full flowering of this new approach to natural philosophy, based on reason and observation, came with the work of Isaac Newton (1642–1727) and particularly in his *Philosophiae Naturalis Principia Mathematica* (1687). He devised a system of physical laws, using concepts of mass, force, velocity and acceleration. To put it crudely, Newton saw the universe as a huge machine, the operation of each part of which was controlled by fixed laws. These laws could be discovered by observation, there was no need to seek either authority or supernatural revelation. God might be the creator, but he had devised a creation which was capable of being understood on the basis of rational observation.

A monolithic system of ideas does not crumble overnight. The medieval world-view was shaken by the scientific discoveries of the sixteenth and seventeenth centuries, but its authority base was also weakened by the Reformation.

The implications of this shift for religion were:

- Authority was challenged by reason and observation. Sadly, the Church found itself largely on the side of authority, and fighting a losing battle.
- Newton, and many others who contributed to the rise of science, were themselves religious, and certainly did not see their work as undermining religion. God was seen to have written two books – scripture and nature – both of which could be studied profitably, and both offered a reflection of his glory.
- The very regularity of the universe, as set out by Newtonian physics, became an argument for the creative and providential work of God – in the Teleological Argument (see above p. 90).

A religious basis for the scientific quest?

Four Christian beliefs encouraged the rise of science:

- that the world had been created good, and therefore was worthy of examination
- that God had created a world capable of being understood rationally
- that nature itself should not be worshipped, but be examined critically
- that humankind had been given authority over the earth, encouraging technology.

Many of the great scientists of the past were religious, and saw the attempt to understand the world rationally as a valid expression of their religious convictions. However, it would probably be fair to say that their approach to religion was mostly rational and/or intuitive rather than **fundamentalist** and literal. Among their number one might include Copernicus, Galileo, Newton, Darwin, Mendel and Einstein.

Into the twentieth century

Two major scientific theories – relativity and quantum theory – formulated early in the twentieth century, brought about another fundamental change in the understanding of the universe, and the old world of Newton suddenly seemed rather parochial, covering the physical laws that operated only within a limited set of conditions.

For Newton, space, time, matter and energy had been discrete, *a priori* concepts. They formed the framework of his whole view of the world. And of course, within the range of observations and experiments within which Newton worked, they served well enough.

With the formulation early in the twentieth century of Einstein's theories of relativity, Newton's concepts proved inadequate. Central to the change in perspective was the recognition of the interplay between concepts which, for Newton, had been separate:

- The theory of Special Relativity (1905) stated that matter and energy were linked, such that – using the famous formula $e = mc^2$ (where e represents energy, m mass and c the speed of light) – the destruction of a small amount of matter could release a large amount of energy. Matter is no longer 'solid'; it is energy locked into a physical form.
- In the theory of General Relativity, published in 1916, time, space, mass and energy are all related to one another. Time and space are no longer fixed, but relative to one another, and both are influenced by gravity.

For reflection

As I look out through space, I am also looking back through time. I do not see what is now, but what has been. I observe a galaxy as it was millions of years ago, and an observer within that galaxy now, observing the Earth, might well see a planet upon which human life had not yet developed.

How does a universe on this scale relate to traditional arguments for the existence of God? Creation, for example, is not something limited to the past, but a continuing feature of the present, with its unfolding design linked to its early features.

The other dramatic area of change is at the atomic and sub-atomic level. In Newtonian physics, bodies obey fixed laws, and their behaviour can be measured and predicted. But with the discovery of the electron and the subsequent development of particle physics and quantum theory it came to be recognized that, at a fundamental level, the component parts of matter could be predicted only with degrees of probability.

So we have a universe in which space and time, energy and matter are all bound up with one another, and one of the aims of physics is to find a theory which will link the basic forces of gravity, electromagnetism, and the strong and weak nuclear forces to one another (a Grand Unified Theory or GUT) and eventually to see how this would relate to relativity and particle theory, thus providing a Theory of Everything or TOE.

The universe also reveals many different levels of complexity. We see it most obviously all around us in the physical, chemical, biological and social levels. Complex wholes tend to behave in a way that is different from their component parts.

In other words

Nothing is 100 per cent certain – that is the implication of much of this new view of the universe. The very act of making observations will influence what is being observed. Equally, it is unrealistic to isolate one thing from everything else in the universe. Everything influences everything else, but you cannot take everything into account. You have to settle for an approximation, based on a reasoned limitation of evidence.

The implications of this shift for religion

In a world controlled by predictable mechanical processes, God may be relegated to the realm of 'before' or 'outside' (deism); he is no longer required within the machine, even if its original design and creation is ascribed to him. But the more complex and integrated view of the world that came in with relativity and quantum theory rendered a simplistic deism incredible (which was no bad thing, since from a religious perspective eighteenth-century deism is quite inadequate).

The original tendency was for religion to regard all science as reductionist – in other words, to accuse it of reducing every complex thing to its physical component parts and then claiming that, since those parts obeyed fixed laws, that constituted a sufficient explanation of the activity of the more complex whole. That view remains true only to a certain extent, for modern science is rather more holistic in its approach and recognizes the significance of different levels of complexity, without automatically wanting to reduce each to the simplest. It is therefore unwise to attempt to argue that all science remains crudely mechanistic or reductionist.

Summary

- Most Christian doctrines and arguments were formulated at a time before the rise of modern science. They can best be understood against the background of biblical imagery and the Greek philosophy.
- The rise of science was the result of knowledge gained through evidence and rational thought. This approach challenged authority, and was seen by some (but not all) religious people as a threat to traditional beliefs.
- The world revealed by twentieth-century science suggests that both the Newtonian world-view, and the religious arguments that developed alongside it, are limited.

The methods of science and religion

Both science and religion claim to be exploring and making claims about what is 'true'. But what counts as truth depends on the way in which it is arrived at. In his *History of Western Philosophy*, Bertrand Russell makes the following comment:

> … it is not *what* a man of science believes that distinguishes him, but *how* and *why* he believes it. His beliefs are tentative, not dogmatic; they are based on evidence, not on intuition.

This, of course, does not prevent intuition from playing a part in the scientific method, but no theory would remain scientific if it depended solely on intuition, for it would need to be confirmed by testing out evidence. But, in general, Russell has highlighted the central feature of all assertions that claim to be scientific, namely that they are scientific by virtue of method used to establish them.

But what about religious claims? If someone says 'God is within my heart' or 'Everyone has a Buddha nature', can such statements could be shown to be true or false? If so, what sort of evidence would count for or against them?

If a scientist and a religious believer (even if they are one and the same person) believe the same thing, they do so on different grounds. So, in order to appreciate the different sorts of claim to truth that religion and science may put forward, it is necessary to see the sort of methods they use at arriving at the things they claim.

The scientific method

Science works through *rational empiricism* – in other words, it is based on the rational examination of evidence. The process may involve the following:

- **Observing and collecting data**
  Scientists try to make sure that the information they collect is influenced as little as possible by their own particular assumptions, and they eliminate those factors that are not relevant to their enquiry. Thus, for example, drug trials involve the use of a 'control group' of patients suffering from the same condition, who are not given the drug, but whose progress is monitored. Without such a group, it would be impossible to know if the patients receiving the drug would have recovered anyway.

- **Forming and testing out a hypothesis based on that data**
  This is where imagination and even intuition may come in, since there may be many possible hypotheses suggested by the same data. But each of these will be tested rationally to see if it conforms to whatever data is available.

- **Devising experiments and assessing their results**
  A theory generally depends on the experimental testing of an initial hypothesis. In other words, the scientist judges what results might follow from an experiment if the hypothesis is true, and then checks the actual results against this.

- **Making predictions based on the theory**
  If a theory is correct, then certain things should follow from it. Checking out these secondary results is an important confirmation of the truth of the original theory.

- **Verification – testing out the theory by devising further experiments**

  This is often a long-term process of checking a theory against new experiments and perhaps new evidence, as a result of which it may eventually need to be modified, or may be discarded in favour of a new one.

Nothing is claimed with absolute certainty. The more a theory is confirmed, the greater the statistical likelihood of it being correct, but it is anticipated that every theory will eventually be superseded, or will be shown to apply only within a limited range of circumstances.

Induction

Induction is the term used for the process by which a theory is derived from evidence.

It might be tempting to argue that you can simply gather facts and establish with certainty a theory to explain them. But David Hume pointed out (in his *Enquiry concerning Human Understanding* Section 4) that induction can never in itself be adequate to establish truth. His reasoning is very straightforward: however many examples of something you check, there will always be the possibility that the next example will prove you wrong. Thus, having checked a considerable number of pieces of evidence, a person has to *presuppose a basic orderliness in nature*, and frame a hypothesis accordingly. But that orderliness remains a presupposition, it is not something that can be proved.

With typical humour, Bertrand Russell gives an example of this in his *Problems of Philosophy*:

> Domestic animals expect food when they see the person who usually feeds them. We know that these rather crude expectations of uniformity are liable to be misleading. The man who has fed the chicken every day throughout its life at last wrings its neck instead, showing that more refined views as to the uniformity of nature would have been useful to the chicken.

Uniform evidence increases the probability that we will find more of the same, but does not guarantee it. After all, the gambler who finds that red comes up on the wheel a number of times in succession might argue that a black number must be expected soon – and the more reds come up, the greater likelihood that the next one will be black. The problem is that, on the roulette wheel of life, we do not know the proportion of blacks to reds, or indeed whether there are any blacks at all.

Interpreting data

In the early part of the twentieth century, the Vienna Circle of philosophers (see above p. 44) argued that the only meaningful language was that which pictured reality. All meaningful statements (other than statements of logic, mathematics or definition, which are analytic) needed to verified with reference to evidence. They took that view because they were impressed by the success of the scientific method, and regarded scientific statements as ideal for describing the world.

However, this view worked largely on the assumption that there was a simple, literal way of perceiving and describing reality, and that the information gathered by scientists was free from their particular interpretations and prejudices. This view has been challenged by some modern philosophers, including Quine and Popper. Popper argued, for example, that all observation was impregnated with theories, and that there are no uninterpreted facts. Even the basic selecting of data involves interpretation.

Karl Popper (in *The Logic of Scientific Discovery*, 1934) pointed out that science does not progress by concentrating on indubitable facts (i.e. not by induction) but by constantly putting forward theories and testing them against the facts to see if they work. Progress is made when a theory fails and is replaced by a better one.

Two very basic features of traditional empiricism are challenged by the idea that all data is interpreted:

- Locke's view that the mind starts as a *tabula rasa*, and gradually gets filled with information. Instead, the mind is constantly creating images in order to enable it to interpret information brought by the senses. To experience something is therefore to interpret it.
- Wittgenstein's early view (in *Tractatus*) of language as providing a straightforward image of the external world. Instead, language is already shaped by the way we perceive things. In other words, our use of language is creative, and part of the interpretive process.

Neither experience nor language therefore works in the simplistic way that the earlier positivists had thought – both are creative activities.

Note

The creative role played by the mind in shaping and testing out theories reflects a philosophical view that goes back to Kant. Kant pointed out that concepts like space, time and causality were a necessary part of the way in which we experience the world, since we impose them on our experience.

So, whether we are looking at the creative use of 'language games' in the work of the later Wittgenstein, or Popper's recognition of the imaginative and creative use of theories, there is a general movement away from a simple gathering of indubitable facts or literal picturing of the world.

Understanding the world is a complex and creative activity, and that applies as much to science as it does to religion.

As part of the process of interpretation, scientists use models – analogies drawn from something familiar. These models are simply convenient ways of conceptualizing things, and are always subject to change. We should not think of scientific language as uniform and totally empirical. It can be as rich as any other, full of imagery and interpretation.

Example

- Originally, an atom was thought of as a very small but solid piece of matter.
- Later the model used for the atom was that of a solar system, with the nucleus as a sun and the electrons circling it like planets.
- Now even that model breaks down, since sub-atomic particles are not locatable objects.
- A quantum entity can be considered either as a wave or as a particle, but it cannot be both things at once.

Religious method

Religion does not have a systematic method of arriving at its beliefs. In general, however, it draws upon three sources:

- Revelation: the belief that God has revealed truths direct to humankind. These may be embodied in scriptures, or learned directly from inspired teachers.

- Personal experience: we saw in Chapter 01 that there are a whole range of religious experiences, many of which lead a person to make claims to special knowledge.
- Natural theology: beliefs based on reason and an observation of the world.

The third of these comes closest to the scientific method. The key difference, however, is that (for most religious people) their religious tradition provides the concepts and words through which everything is experienced anyway. Also, because those beliefs are held on grounds that are not simply rational, religious people may be less willing than scientists to see them replaced.

Faced with the challenge of the scientific method, religious thinkers tend to respond in one of two ways:

- to minimize the factual content of belief claims
- to claim the religion is a matter of faith, to which human reason and empirical facts have little to contribute.

The second of these is sometimes argued in Christian terms by referring to the 'fall' in Genesis, with the implication that human reason is also fallen and therefore incapable of knowing God. This approach was taken by Protestant thinkers (typified in the nineteenth century by Kierkegaard and in the twentieth by Karl Barth), whilst natural theology – as expounded by Aquinas – was officially approved by the Catholic Church and allowed that reason could give an understanding of God.

In other words

The degree to which religion accepts the findings of human reason alongside its commitment to divine revelation, suggests a key distinction:

- For religion, trust is placed in **a particular view of the world**, whether or not that is endorsed by reason, whereas for science, trust is placed in **the rational process by which views of the world are formed, evaluated and modified**.

Reductionism

A complaint regularly made by religious philosophers about the scientific method is that it tends to be reductionist.

Reductionism is a term used for a process which analyses complex entities into their component parts and then claims that it is the component parts that are 'real' rather than the original complex whole. It is commonly characterized by the tendency to say that the complex wholes are 'nothing but'.

> **Examples**
> - A symphony is 'nothing but' sets of vibrations in the air.
> - A painting is 'nothing but' arrangements of particles of pigment on canvass.
> - You are 'nothing but' the sum total of all the cells in your body.

This is less true today than it was during the period dominated by Newtonian physics, since there is now a wider examination of the operations of complex structures and chaos theory.

In terms of human evolution, however, the issue has been raised again by the publication of Dawkins' book *The Selfish Gene*. To put it crudely, the argument is that genes struggle to survive and propagate, and that – from their perspective – people are really just their survival suits. Dawkins was not arguing that individuals should be selfish, indeed there are many reasons to think that positive social co-operation can benefit a species. His point was that selfishness operates at the genetic, rather than the human level.

The key question then is the extent to which a complex entity, like a human being, can realistically be 'reduced' to its component parts. Complexity brings with it different levels of operation and significance. The reductionist issue is about which level of activity you consider to be primary and which secondary. Are we here for our genes? Or, are our genes here for us? Or, do genes and human beings work at entirely different levels, so that the one cannot be understood in terms of the other?

The problem is to strike a balance between looking at those things that take place at a simple level (for example, cell reproduction) and those that involve the whole complex organism (for example, learning to play a physical game). The complex entity makes no sense apart from its constituent parts, but neither does it make sense to explain a game in terms of particular neurones firing in the brain and muscles contracting in the arms and legs!

In terms of evolution, the limitations of a reductionist approach are clear from the work of Karl Popper (*The Open Universe*, 1982). He argues that evolution is indeterminate and unpredictable, since at a higher level there are developments that could not be predicted at a lower one.

Comment

There has been a tendency for both philosophers and scientists to analyse things into their component parts. For Locke, Hume and the whole empirical tradition in philosophy, the real is known through the basic building blocks of sense experiences. For a nuclear physicist, atoms give way to sub-atomic particles and then quarks – everything is 'really' a collection of tiny quanta of energy.

Both Plato and Aristotle recognized that reality comprised both matter and form. Going beyond the earlier Atomists, they tried to express what it meant for physical matter to take on character, to have a shape, to 'become' something. For Plato, the eternal 'forms' defined the reality of individual things. For Aristotle, a 'final cause' gave shape and essence to otherwise unformed matter. In other words, reality did not just lie with atoms, but with what atoms had gathered together to become.

Reductionism is a process by which form gradually gives way to formless substance. Its logical end is a vision of a single universal reality – perhaps such as existed in the first milliseconds of the 'big bang', before our universe expanded, cooled, differentiated out its components and took on character. As such, it is a valid quest, but it is not the only way to view reality. The universe has been moving away from that simplicity for 13.7 billion years. As we encounter it now, it is shaped and known only through its differentiated structures and forms.

In a world of constant change, the reductionist asks, 'What has made this come about?', always looking to the past for a sufficient explanation of the present. The more interesting questions are 'What may this become?' and 'In which direction is this going?' and these require an appreciation of present complexity.

Providence and miracles

In order to appreciate the issues raised by the religious ideas of providence and miracles, it is necessary to reflect for a moment on the nature of causality.

Kant argued that space, time and causality were three things that our minds imposed on experience. In other words, we are predisposed to think that everything that happens is brought about by one or more causes. We do not entertain the idea that something may or may not be caused, we simply try to find out what caused it. The problem is that a single event may be brought about by many separate causes, and those causes have causes of their own. Hence, for practical purposes, we may never know the **whole** story about what caused something to happen. All we look for is a sufficient explanation for whatever purposes we have in mind. If my car breaks down, I need only find the broken part, I do not need to understand the fundamental properties of steel or nature of gravity.

Thus when we talk about causation, we are really addressing the issue of sufficient explanation for something happening. As time goes on and science progresses, we may revise our understanding of those causes, but that does not challenge the basic assumption that everything has a cause or causes.

Science is, among other things, a process for discovering causes.

Causes and necessity

Once something has happened, the rational mind analyses the factors that have brought it about and then declares that it was necessary. It does not matter that it was not predicted, the point is that (with the benefit of hindsight) it is possible to see its causes and thus to see that no other outcome was possible. In this sense, everything is seen as necessary, or determined.

On the other hand, we are never in practice able to know all the causal factors at work at any one time. We cannot say, therefore, that we have evidence for the necessity of everything. We also experience ourselves as free to make choices, even though we know that an observer who knew us well might predict our choice.

For reflection

I play a game of chess. Strategies are planned, choices are made, both players are free to work out how best to guess and inhibit the choices that the opponent is likely to make. We are free to play the game, to win or lose, and it is that freedom (and the ability to manipulate it) that constitutes the skilled player.

On the other hand, every move on the board is carefully defined. I am not allowed to move my bishop sideways, but only diagonally. I may move only my own pieces, not those of my opponent. My pawns move forward, but cannot retreat.

Now it is possible that an observer, noting every move of the game, will conclude that there is no personal skill or freedom of choice involved, for every move has followed very carefully defined rules. There has been no breaking of rules, and therefore no freedom.

It may be argued that no two games are exactly the same, but our rule-bound observer will rightly comment that the differences do not depend upon flouting the rules, but simply in the sequence of movements that are made within those rules.

Am I free to win, or is the game determined?

In the case of the game of chess, the rules are fairly straightforward. When it comes to the ordinary events of life, the matter is more complex because (unlike the game) we do not know the extent of the rules under which we are playing. We are often surprised to find that there is something which we can or cannot do, because some other factor has come into play.

Example

I decide to go for a stroll. It pours with rain. I am determined that the changed circumstances will not inhibit my freedom to walk, and stride off through the rain. A moment later, I am knocked over and killed by a car, which is being driven too fast in restricted visibility because the driver wanted ... And so on.

I always act within a network of circumstances that are brought about by factors about which I have no prior knowledge.

Modern science reveals that the apparent orderliness of nature is (at least in part) the product of randomness at the sub-atomic level. Complexity and order emerge at a higher level out of a sequence of random events at a lower level. This suggests that we do not need to posit a single law-giver to account for order, nor are we entitled to examine occasions when the law has been set aside for some higher purpose. Orderliness and disorderliness occur simultaneously, and complex entities come into being whenever apparently chance events create the right conditions.

Of course, just because something has a causal explanation does not mean that God could not be active within it. The idea that divine causality *excludes* ordinary physical causality would imply that God operates as one cause alongside others in the space-time structure of the universe. On the other hand, if God's activity is thought to be present everywhere, then its absence or presence would not be noticed, for it would have no characteristics of its own. **In which case, to say that God caused it would be no different from saying that it took place.**

Providence

Science shows relationships between phenomena; one thing may be caused by another; one set of conditions is necessary for something else to come about. It may even show how a particular phenomenon relates to the universe as a whole. What it *cannot* show, however, is that any of these relationships are deliberately brought about for some *purpose*. Religion, on the other hand, seeks to find purpose in the design of the world, and in particular seeks to express a purpose for humankind.

In religious terms, 'providence' is the idea that God takes special care to provide for humankind's needs. If God is omnipotent and loving he might well be expected to provide for his creation. But a major problem with such 'providence' was set out by Hume in his *Dialogues Concerning Natural Religion*:

Health and sickness, calm and tempest, with an infinite number of other accidents whose causes are unknown and variable, have a great influence both on the fortunes of particular persons and on the prosperity of public societies; and indeed all human life, in a manner, depends on such accidents. A being, therefore, who knows the secret springs of the universe might easily, by particular volitions, turn all these accidents to the good of mankind and render the whole world happy, without discovering himself in any operation. A fleet whose purposes were salutary to society might always meet with a fair wind. Good princes enjoy sound health and long life. ... One wave, a little higher than the rest, by burying Caesar and his fortune in the bottom of the ocean, might have restored liberty to a considerable part of mankind. There may, for aught we know, be good reasons why Providence interposes not in this manner, but they are unknown to us; and, though the mere supposition that such reasons exist may be sufficient to *save* the conclusion concerning the Divine attributes, yet surely it can never be sufficient to *establish* that conclusion.

(Book XI, p. 74)

In other words, we do not have evidence to suggest that God (via nature) benefits the good and frustrates the evil, since in reality the world appears to offer a mixture of good and evil. 'If God acts providentially, why does he not ...?' is a question we have already considered under 'the problem of evil'.

But if particular events are ambiguous in terms of providence, what about the design of the universe as a whole? This possibility is explored in what is termed the **Anthropic Principle**, a widely-discussed theory, presented in detail by J. D. Barrow and J. A. Tippler in *The Anthropic Cosmological Principle* (1986).

If the fundamental features of the early universe had been different, things would not have evolved in the way that they have. If the size of planet Earth, or its distance from the Sun, or its atmosphere, or the prevalence of carbon and water, or any of a multitude of other conditions were other than they in fact were, then humankind would not have evolved.

So much is obvious. But this argument is sometimes given a twist – and one which may seem useful to someone who is looking for evidence of God's design and purpose in the universe. The Anthropic Principle claims that all the fundamental features **had** to be as they were, in order for human life to have appeared. Since intelligent life **has** appeared, the universe must have been fine tuned to make this possible.

The believer in God may then take this Anthropic Principle and use it to show that, without God's guiding hand, it would have been highly unlikely that – with all the billions of possible worlds that could have emerged – the world did actually evolve in exactly the right way for humankind to develop.

There is an additional problem here, however. It is highlighted by the two forms of the Anthropic Principle: the 'weak' one and the 'strong' one. The 'weak' form claims no more than we have discussed above: that we are as we are because the whole universe is as it is; in a different universe, we would not be here. However, the 'strong' form argues that the universe started off with the potential for human life, such that **it was impossible for us not to have appeared.** This implies that there was some sort of inevitability about the way the universe was put together. But that is something for which there can never be any evidence; we may know that the universe is the way it is, but not that it **has to be so.**

From a religious perspective, the Anthropic Principle is a mixed blessing. On the one hand, it allows the possibility that God may have fine tuned the universe for our benefit. On the other, it shows that the universe is fine tuned for our benefit anyway and therefore no God is needed to achieve this providential result.

So the key question becomes:

- Do the structures of the world **reveal** divine providence? Or is it the providential structures of the world that give us the **illusion** that there is (beyond them) a divine providence?

We are left with the old choice: God or nature. There seems to be no way of proving that we are entitled by the evidence to say more than that, since the universe is such that we have evolved, its laws facilitate that evolution. But that, in effect, says nothing!

> **For reflection**
>
> If the world did not favour our evolution, we would not be here to think any such providential thoughts! Those not favoured are not here, and their perspective (that the universe did not 'provide' for them) is not taken into account.

For a detailed account of the Anthropic Principle and the issues it raises, see *The Goldilocks Enigma: Why Is the Universe Just Right for Life?* by Paul Davies (2006).

But for someone who believes in a personal God, such general providence is unlikely to be enough. There need to be moments when providence becomes quite specific – moments when, contrary to the way the world usually works, things seem to act together in a uniquely purposeful way. They are generally termed 'miracles'.

Miracles

Knowing whether something has happened or not depends on the gathering and validation of evidence. If you are told that something highly implausible has happened, the most you can say to express your doubt is 'I believe you may have been mistaken.' The grounds on which you say this is that the event described does not fit into your existing view of the world.

The more unlikely the event, the more evidence you would need if you were to accept it as true. Also, the more unreliable you judge the person who gives the account of the unusual event, the more likely you are to believe that he or she was mistaken.

This is the basis of the famous argument about miracles put forward by David Hume in the tenth book of his *Enquiry Concerning Human Understanding*.

He starts by making the point that a wise man, in assessing the truth of a report, weighs the evidence with which he is presented. So, if all the evidence points in one direction, that is what he will be inclined to believe. If, on the other hand, the evidence for and against something is almost equal, he will consider his judgement on the matter to be tentative. He will also take into account the reliability of any witnesses. Thus Hume sets up the issue rather like assessing evidence in a court of law.

He defines a miracle as an event which goes against the laws of nature – on the grounds that an event which conforms to the laws of nature is unlikely to be called a miracle, since an alternative explanation for it can be given. But the difficulty with any evidence for a miracle is that it will always be outweighed by the evidence on the basis of which the laws of nature have been framed. He therefore argues:

> A miracle is a violation of the laws of nature; and as a firm and unalterable experience has established these laws, the proof against a miracle, from the very nature of the fact, is as entire as any argument from experience can possibly be imagined. Why is it more probable that all men must die; that lead cannot, of itself, remain suspended in the air; that fire consumes wood, and is extinguished by water; unless it be, that these events are found agreeable to the laws of nature, and there is required a violation of these laws, or in other words, a miracle to prevent them? Nothing is esteemed a miracle if it ever happen in the common course of nature. ... The plain consequence is ... That no testimony is sufficient to establish a miracle, unless the testimony be of such a kind, that its falsehood would be more miraculous, than the fact, which it endeavours to establish.

In other words

It will always be more likely that the report of a miracle is mistaken, than that a law of nature has actually been broken. For the evidence against the miracle will always be greater than the evidence for it.

For Hume, a miracle could be accepted as such only if it would be a greater miracle for all the evidence for it to be shown to be mistaken. Notice that Hume does not say that, on principle, a miracle **cannot** take place, only that there can never be sufficient evidence to **prove** that it has taken place.

In his *Natural History of Religion*, having come to the conclusion that there was no way to establish religious belief rationally, Hume commented:

We may conclude that the Christian religion not only was at first attended by miracles, but even at this day cannot be believed by any reasonable person without one. Mere reason is insufficient to convince us of its veracity; And whoever is moved by faith to assent to it, is conscious of a continued miracle in his own person, which subverts all the principles of his understanding, and gives him a determination to believe what is most contrary to custom and experience.

In other words, he concludes (with the hint of a smile, I sense) that it really is quite miraculous how people are willing to suspend their rationality in order to continue to embrace religion.

In this, too, Hume may be right. But we then need to ask about why people do indeed continue to be religious, and what that says about the limited place of rationality in the whole scheme of human experience.

Regularity and miracles

Hume assumes that the world is reliable and regular, and that its regularity may be expressed in terms of 'laws of nature'. Such laws are not apodictic (in other words, they are not commands issued to nature) but are simply descriptions of what has been observed. Science is based on this regularity. Without it, the idea of conducting experiments would be nonsense – because you would never know whether the world would decide to operate in the same way on any two different occasions. **But to accept a miracle, in the sense of a violation of a law of nature, is to believe that the world is selectively unreliable.**

The religious believer may want to accept the reliability and regularity of the world, but wants to do so in a way that allows a broader view of causality – a view that allows spiritual agents (God, the devil, angels, spirits) to play a part. But there is a fundamental problem here for the philosophy of religion. The idea of special providence or 'miracle' seems to go against the cosmological and design arguments for the existence of God. Those arguments present the world as structured in a way that displays an overall purpose. They work on the basis of regularity, for only in regularity does the sense of design and purpose appear. Yet the idea of some miraculous event, not available to all, introduces a sense of arbitrariness and unpredictability into an understanding of the world.

Religious requirements?

In examining miracles Brian Davies (see the Taking it Further section) asks if the account of a miracle is logical and coherent. In many cases he would argue that it can be. But the point is that a person who does not wish to accept that something is a miracle is just affirming that there can be a non-miraculous explanation of that event, even if that explanation is not available to us at the moment. So we need to get beyond Hume's argument, to see why a religious person would want to interpret the unexpected as a miracle.

The essential point to recognize here is that to call something a miracle is to make an *interpretation*. A person who believes in God will only call something a miracle if the apparent purpose achieved by that event is in keeping with his or her understanding of God's character.

Let us take a situation which might or not be called miraculous:

- A plane crashes. Three hundred and ninety-nine people die and the four hundredth is brought out alive from the wreckage. For that one person, his or her survival may be described as a miracle by friends and relatives. But the event overall is a tragedy.

- But, how do you know what that person will go on to do? Suppose the person who survives becomes a mass murderer. Is his or her survival in the plane crash then to be considered a miracle or a further disaster? If he or she had died then, the victims of the later crimes would be alive and well.

- But what of those victims? Suppose … and so it goes on.

This is a popular argument to make the point that we can never get a final assessment of results. The point we need to establish here is that **to speak of anything as a miracle implies an interpretation and a value judgement.** And that, in turn, requires **a selective consideration of facts** (we can never know the whole story).

Someone who believes in God and providence may well say that, if we knew the whole story, we would see that this unexpected event is 'miraculous' because it has significance beyond what we can see here and now.

'The Miracle of Stairway B'

A programme with this title – screened to coincide with the fifth anniversary of the 9/11 attacks on the World Trade Center – featured the 13 men and one woman who survived the collapse of the North Tower. As the floors crashed down around them, their stairwell remained exposed as a stump sticking up in the pile of rubble, and they were able to walk out alive.

It was a remarkable escape from what otherwise seemed certain death; there were no survivors from the fall of the South Tower. But does the survival of 14 people, when all the others were killed, constitute a 'miracle'? If so – if, in other words, God had intervened to allow those few to survive – what does that say about why he decided to let all the others die?

This alone suggests that the word 'miracle' needs to be rethought.

Appropriately special?

Miracles are generally only seen to be such because they are *appropriate*. Nothing would be deemed a miracle unless some good came of it. Just as we saw that an experience was deemed 'religious' if it had certain qualities in terms of giving insight or integrity, so an event may be deemed a miracle on the same basis. And just as the experience could be religious even if there were some perfectly rational account of it, so also an event might be termed a miracle even if there were a full account of the events that caused it.

Religion is a way of interpreting the world; a miracle is a way of interpreting an event. However inspiring that interpretation may be, it is always optional.

There is a Buddhist story which tells of a Tibetan Buddhist who, about to leave on a pilgrimage to the holy sites in India, is asked by his mother to bring back with him a relic of the Buddha or one of his holy followers, so that she can use it as a devotional aid on her personal shrine. He is about to arrive back home when he suddenly realizes that he has forgotten about the relic.

Hoping that she will be fooled by it, he picks up a bone of a dog from the side of the road, wraps it up and delivers it to his mother, who believes it to be the genuine article. As a result of her devotions, many great healings and other wonders are performed by the holy/doggy relic.

The implication of this – and the purpose of the story – is to emphasize the point that (for Buddhists) there is no automatic magical force in operation, but that all benefits come from human attitudes and striving. The 'miracles' were performed by the dog's bone simply because it became a vehicle for devotion, and the positive feelings and energies that developed as a result of it were able to effect cures.

Clearly, the significant point here is that at the physical or mechanical level a relic is of no particular significance. The saint's bone and the bone of the dog are equally effective. What matters is the devotion of the person concerned. It is that devotion that is said to produce the fortunate *karma*.

Note

Both science and Buddhism accept universal causality. 'Whatever arises, does so in dependence upon conditions' is the basis of Buddhism, but also of science. The whole debate about miracles in the West has come about because the rationalist has said that every event (even the one claimed as a miracle) must have arisen in dependence on a particular set of causal conditions, even if the causes are not known. Buddhism would not argue with this, whereas theistic religions have feared that it would remove God from the action.

Hume and other religions

In his *Enquiry Concerning Human Understanding*, Hume sets out one argument that we are most unlikely to consider seriously today. He notes that all religions report miracles, and use those miracles to support their own beliefs. But he argues that if one religion is correct, then the others must be false. The miracles of each religion, if accepted, disprove the truth of the other religions, and therefore destroy the credibility of the miracles of those other religions. **In other words, miracles – taken as a basis for validating religious beliefs – are mutually destructive across religions.**

If you take the view that there can be only one absolute truth and one correct way of interpreting it, then you might try to show that the miracles of 'incorrect' religions could not have taken place, or, if the reported events did take place, the way of interpreting them offered by those religions must be wrong. Hume's view simply highlights the problem of trying to use miracles as the basis for validating religious beliefs. An event is termed a miracle because it is interpreted through religious beliefs. It cannot be used at the same time as independent evidence for those beliefs.

To sum up on miracles

- If a miracle is simply the violation of a law of nature, then (according to Hume) there can never be sufficient evidence to command its acceptance.
- A miracle is an interpretation of an event: if the event has no significance, it cannot be a miracle.
- The concept of 'miracle' may conflict with the cosmological and teleological arguments for the existence of God, since those arguments presuppose regularity, whereas miracles presuppose a suspension of the very laws that sum up that regularity.

The origin of the universe

Scientists seek theories that give the most comprehensive explanation possible; the wider the successful application of a theory, the greater its acceptability within the scientific community.

This assumes that there is a fundamental unity within the universe. In other words, laws which appear to work only in one part of the universe are regarded as special cases of a broader law operating throughout. Thus, Newtonian physics is valid for a limited range of conditions (those within which Newton worked, of course) but cannot be applied to the sub-atomic or the cosmic dimensions.

Hence the quest for a TOE (a Theory of Everything) and the drive for explanations that are simple and universally applicable. Any such theory will also address the issue of the origins of the known universe – since the present state of the universe is a guide to seeing the way in which it has developed.

The generally held view is that the world that we observe now began about 13.7 billion years ago, expanding, in what is termed the 'big bang', from a space-time singularity – in other words, from a point at which all known space was compressed into an infinitely small point.

It is impossible to ask what happened before the big bang, since time is related to space, and therefore time began in the same singularity out of which the world unfolded. Looking out through space and back in time, we probe the earliest phases of the universe, but beyond that is the singularity, the point beyond which our faculties can no longer probe.

Logically, that does not mean that there is nothing beyond a singularity, but that to say that something exists means that it exists in time and space. Everything that can be said to exist therefore exists within this universe. To describe anything existing 'outside' the universe is a rather crude image, for the whole concept of 'outside' implies existence in space and time. That does not prevent the idea of there being other possible universes like our own (the idea of a multiverse) but simply indicates that we are unable to detect them, so they remain only a theoretical possibility.

In other words

We cannot get **outside** or **beyond** or **before** the universe that has exploded outwards in that original hot big bang. Our faculties and our concepts work only within this universe. And even then, our knowledge is limited, for much of the universe comprises dark matter and dark energy, whose presence we infer rather than observe. *All* we see is an expanding universe of 200 billion galaxies, each containing billions of stars!

In terms of scientific cosmology, it therefore makes no sense to 'locate' a God literally outside the world. Creation is an ongoing event, the gradual unfolding of a process that started with the big bang. If God is described as 'Creator' then that is his sphere of operation.

We have already considered the idea of 'design' in the universe (through the Teleological Argument, see above p. 90) and also the Anthropic Principle which relates design to providence. Both of these have been used to link features of the observed universe with a religious sense of a purposeful and benevolent creator. And, of course, we are not in a position to get 'behind' the process of creative organization to see whether there is an external agent.

More often, however, the point at issue between science and religion in terms of the origin of the universe is the apparent clash between accounts of the creation of the world in scripture and the account given by science. And it does not matter that scientific accounts are qualified and open to revision, for the split is more fundamental than that. It comes down to a question of interpretation.

If it is held, as a matter of religious faith, that the words of scripture are to be taken literally and are factually correct, then any scientific account of origins will conflict with a biblical account of creation in six days. For those who hold the literal inerrancy of scripture, the anthropic argument will be irrelevant, since their belief in creation is not the result of logical investigation of facts.

On the other hand, there are two categories of religious people for whom the scientific account of origins will not cause significant problems:

- those who take the biblical accounts of creation as a poetic and religious reflection on the relationship between God and the world
- those whose religion (for example, Buddhism) regards speculation about origins as not profitable.

Summary comment

Features of the universe as it is now provide evidence for how it started, but **nothing in that evidence requires us to go beyond the fact that the world exists and that it is as it is.** Even if we imagine that other worlds might exist, this is the only one we can ever know. The idea of external agency in creation (i.e. the literal idea of a creator God) is outside the scope of the sort of evidence that science can provide.

From a religious point of view, for those not holding a literal view of scripture, questions about the creation of the universe link with the idea of design and providence, as seen in the Teleological Argument and the Anthropic Principle.

Evolution and humankind

Science describes the way life has evolved on this planet from the simplest of organisms about 3.5 billion years ago. But the very notion that humans have evolved from other species contradicts a literal interpretation of the Book of Genesis, in which God creates Adam and Eve as a separate and distinct species and gives them authority over the rest of creation. Hence the sometimes bitter debates between creationists – those who believe that the world was created by God exactly as described in Genesis – and those who present the theory of evolution to explain human origins.

In looking at this issue, however, we should keep in mind that most scholars see the Book of Genesis, like other stories in ancient literature, as poetic and symbolic, expressing intuitions about meaning and value. It does not pretend to be science. They therefore have no problem, in principle, in accepting the truth of a scientific theory about the evolutionary origin of species.

There seems little point here in rehearsing the history of these debates. Instead, we shall look at some of the ways in which evolution impinges on religious belief, and (to illustrate that religion is not always reactionary) at one religious philosophy that takes up the evolutionary theme.

Darwin

At its crudest level, the argument about Darwin's theory of natural selection, presented in *The Origin of Species* concerned whether humankind was a unique and special creation, or whether it was descended from apes. Opposition to all theories of evolution was fuelled by two things:

- the desire to give humankind a special position with respect to all other species
- a belief in the literal truth of the biblical account of creation.

But beneath this – and of greater interest from the perspective of the philosophy of religion – was a threat posed by Darwin's theory to beliefs about the action of God.

The teleological argument had presented God as the designer and creator of the world – the watchmaker, whose mechanisms far outstretched human mechanical abilities. Each creature, it was argued, had a unique and effective design, and even parts of creatures (for example, the human eye) seemed so perfectly adapted to their particular use, that there seemed no way to account for them other than as a special action of God.

The central feature of Darwin's argument was the mechanism by which evolution worked – **natural selection**. There are small variations within the characteristics of every species, some beneficial, some not. Those individuals whose beneficial characteristics make them better adapted to their environment than others are more likely to survive to adulthood and breed. In the next generation, there will therefore be more members of that species with the particular characteristics of those breeding survivors. As time goes on, this self-selecting of beneficial characteristics will cause the species to 'evolve'.

The theological problem posed was that this theory, if correct, could account for exactly those features in creatures that had previously been ascribed to the designing agency of God. Over time, according to natural selection, things would design themselves. In other words, natural selection did not remove the element of design from the world, but gave a purely natural explanation for how it had come about; an explanation which rendered God redundant.

Note

Darwin himself was modestly religious, and he certainly did not put forward his theory with the intention of undermining belief in God. Indeed, he was reluctant to publish, and did so only after years of painstaking analysis of the evidence.

Equally, Christian folk at that time were divided in their views on evolution – so this debate should not be seen as one with scientists on one side and religious people on the other. It was simply a matter of whether or not the discovery of a mechanism by which species would self-design over long periods of time, would in itself threaten the idea of a creator God.

It is increasingly difficult to justify the claim that the human species is radically different from others. In part, this comes from a recognition of the closeness of the genetic make up between members of ape species, but also from the recognition that there were a whole range of hominids, of which others died out to leave homo sapiens dominant on the planet.

> ### 'Skull of "hobbit" proves it was a different species, say scientists'
>
> Under this title, an article in The Independent (30 January 2007) confirmed the separate identity of Homo floresiensis. This followed the discovery on the island of Flores in Indonesia of a small skull and partial skeleton. At first thought to be of a human suffering from microcephaly (having a small head), it was discovered that, although small, the brain was sufficiently developed to have allowed this species to create and use small tools. It probably lived alongside Homo sapiens, and died out due to a volcanic eruption about 13,000 years ago.

The 'hobbit' illustrates the way in which nature evolves in particular directions. Here, although having a small head and brain (about one third of the size of a modern human brain), the Homo floresiensis brain had become complex enough to give the species an unexpected level of sophistication.

But does that change anything in terms of humankind's place in the universe? As a close relative, Homo floresiensis lived, developed, and then died out. Homo sapiens is equally likely to die out at some point. What implications does this have for belief in God, and the associated idea of God's providence? Is belief in God only viable for those with an anthropocentric view of the world?

Neo-Darwinian approaches

Genetic theory has clarified the way in which the random variations, which form the basis for Darwin's natural selection, come about. Random damage to genetic material leads to these variations which are either to the advantage or disadvantage of the individual members of the species.

Richard Dawkins (in *Climbing Mount Improbable*, 1996, but see also his earlier book *The Blind Watchmaker*, 1986) examines the apparent improbability that scattered atoms and molecules (at the foot of the mountain) could ever, by themselves, come together to form complex entities like an eye (representing the peak of this mountain of ascending complexity).

His argument is that, because natural selection preserves advantageous gene mutations and discards disadvantageous ones, there is a gradual path up the back of that mountain. In the end, one comes to the conclusion that – far from being improbable – it is perfectly reasonable that complex forms will arise that are particularly well adapted to their environments. Using computer simulations, Dawkins shows that it is possible, using just a few variables, to produce a wide range of complex shapes.

Thus, aided by genetic theory and by computer simulation, the modern exponents of natural selection can show the mechanisms by which all those phenomena, which previously had been ascribed to God's design, can be brought about.

By contrast, John Polkinghorne (see *Science and Creation*, 1988) argued that the likelihood of any individual thing happening is so remote that he cannot see how the universe can be controlled by 'bland chance', and therefore postulates an overall intelligence to account for it.

The problem with this argument is in the relationship between 'chance and necessity' (itself the title of a famous book on the subject by Jacques Monod, published in 1972 in which he said 'pure chance, absolutely free but blind, is at the very root of the stupendous edifice of evolution'). The need to posit an external intelligence to account for each individual improbability arises only once individual things are removed from their setting:

- In a complex world where everything is interconnected, each thing comes about because of an almost infinite number of chances.
- If any one thing were to be different, then everything would be different.
- In retrospect, everything seems very improbable, but equally, everything seems absolutely necessary and predictable.

The mistake is in trying to extricate something from its causal connections, and then trying to find out how it came to be as it is, and – failing to find a path through the infinite number of chances in life – positing an external influence. What Dawkins has shown in that chance is 'tamed' by a succession of small changes.

Comment

There seems no doubt that Richard Dawkins is correct. Life can develop and organize itself into more and more complex forms. It is therefore logical to reject any idea of an external designer God.

Fine – the external watchmaker bows out. But what has gone? Consider the discussion in Chapters 03 and 04. Is an external watchmaker really an adequate concept to account for what religious people mean by God?

The implication of Mount Improbable is that life is creative. The world is not a heap of dull matter waiting for an external spark. That spark is within it – taking up every opportunity afforded by genetic mutations. Life is opportunist, pushing forward to develop and adapt as best it may. And we, as human beings, both take part in that process, and are also capable of recognizing that process all around us.

But that is what creation *ex nihilo* is all about! There has been a long tradition of seeing God as the creative power within matter, not as some external mechanic. Surely, what Dawkins has demolished is the case for deism – a concept that was never religiously adequate. **Life is essentially a creative process. Stripped of its imagery, is that not what belief in a creator God is really about?**

Teilhard de Chardin

Teilhard de Chardin argued in a number of books (the best known being *The Phenomenon of Man*) for a religious vision which not only included the idea of evolution, but which made it a key feature. In describing the process leading from atoms up through cells to simple life forms and finally to humankind, he noted that it was one of increasing complexity and rising consciousness – the more complex a being, the more conscious it became. In terms of simple observation, this was hardly controversial, since a very basic creature has little scope for perception, thought and action, whereas more developed life forms are increasingly observed to take on character and to show signs of emotion and thought.

Looking to the future, Teilhard saw humankind converging, with a growing network of communications spreading and deepening over the limited surface of planet Earth. Where could such a process of increasing complexity/consciousness lead?

Having the Christian conviction that all things would find their fulfilment in Christ, he claimed that all things would eventually converge on a single point in the future – a point Omega. That point, the culmination of the whole process of evolution, he identified with the Cosmic Christ.

His whole scheme can therefore be expressed in terms of a cone, with simple atoms at the base, rising up to Christ Omega at the apex. This scheme enabled him to integrate his religion and his science. Previously, he had felt torn between development of the Earth and a religious aspiration that had nothing to say about the terrestrial future of mankind. Now, since all that helped the further evolution and convergence of humankind would be a step in the direction of the fulfilment of all things in Christ, he could incorporate his science in an overall religious vision.

In such a scheme, the whole movement of evolution is 'pulled' from above – from the final goal of Omega (rather like the 'final' cause of Aristotle). For Darwin and neo-Darwinians, the process is more like Aristotle's 'efficient' causality, evolution is pushed from the present into the future, not pulled from that future.

Teilhard de Chardin effectively took a scientific hypothesis (the rise of complexity/consciousness towards a single point in the future) and overlaid it with Christian imagery. In a way, he 'baptized' an evolutionary structure, much as earlier Christian theologians had 'baptized' the philosophy of Plato and Aristotle. The problem is that, if one adopts a particular hypothesis and makes it a vehicle of religious convictions, it subsequently tends to be defended on religious grounds. For Teilhard, the future Omega is not merely a provisional deduction from present observations, but an act of faith.

Such an approach is vulnerable on two counts:

- Science may show its factual basis to be flawed, and religion would then be fighting a losing battle if it felt obliged to defend an indefensible hypothesis.
- The scientific theory may have religiously undesirable consequences. Teilhard de Chardin found himself arguing in favour of the racial and cultural superiority of Europe, and even welcoming the atomic bomb as a sign of humankind's triumph over nature! In short, having identified his religious vision too closely with a particular evolutionary theory, he finds that the theory rather than the religious tradition determines what he can believe.

But however flawed the attempt at integrating a scientific hypothesis and a religious vision may be, it does have the advantage of integrating the religious impulse with an overall structure for understanding the world. The main religious disadvantage is that it redefines religious ideas which work well symbolically but not literally (for example, the return of Christ at the end of time) and attempts to set them in a literal, scientific context (for example, the inevitability of Christ–Omega at the end of the process of evolution). This may give the appearance of reconciling religion and science, but in practice it does justice to neither – claiming certainty for a particular hypothesis in a way that is unacceptable to science, and attempting to give religious concepts a literal interpretation that does not do justice to their rich, symbolic origins.

Comment

One of the great problems for religion, particularly since the time of Newton, has been the separation (either by externalizing God through 'deism', or by making religions exclusively concerned with emotions and values) of the religious vision from an overall scientific and philosophical grasp of reality. At least Teilhard de Chardin attempted to overcome the effect of that separation, even though his views are vulnerable to criticism from both science and religion.

Some conclusions

If we look back to the time before the rise of modern science, we find a world in which the claims of religious intellectuals (for example, Aquinas) and those of natural philosophy fitted together reasonably well. Both had been influenced to a great extent by Greek thought, both used the same language. Particular views may have been wrong in terms of what we understand now – but at least they were consistent with the generally accepted understanding of the world at that time. (The same could not be said about popular views of religion, but that would apply equally to the thirteenth century and the twenty-first!)

With the rise and success of science and technology in providing an effective and useful view of the world, the tendency has been for religion to retreat from making statements about the world that might conflict with science. It has emphasized meanings and values rather than facts.

Now, although nobody can deny that religion does deal the affective side of life – exploring the moral and spiritual responses of individuals to their experience of the world – that does not mean that religious people have ceased making claims about the nature of the world, claims based upon their own religious experience. Such claims can be examined in the same way as those of science, to see if they give a reasonable account of what is experienced, whether they are widely applicable, and whether they are fruitful in helping people to interpret other aspects of life.

Arthur Peacocke, in *Theology for a Scientific Age*, took a critical realist view of science. That is, he saw it as depicting, as well as it can, actual structures and entities in the world. He then sought to apply this same critical realist position to theological claims. He pointed out that both science and religion use models in order to interpret reality, both are able to use metaphors and both accept that there is a limit to what literal language can express. In other words, he accepts that both science and religion make cognitive claims, and both should therefore be judged in terms of their reasonableness. Both, equally, should always be open to examining and modifying the concepts they use.

Hence there is a fundamental choice to be made. Either, following Peacocke, one seeks to balance the claims of religion and science and examine them in terms of their reasonableness, or one makes the division between fact and value – with science trusted to provide facts, and religion concerned with values.

If this second option is taken, religious claims are not treated as quasi-scientific, but are interpreted existentially, as expressing intuitions about the self and its relationship to the world. That may resolve many disputes between religion and science, but it is not likely to satisfy all religious believers, who will want to claim a factual and objective basis for their faith, even if those claims conflict with science.

In the 1996 Richard Dimbleby lecture, Richard Dawkins attacked what he saw as an epidemic of interest in the paranormal, and argued that science, if properly taught, could satisfy the 'appetite for wonder'.

He pleads for reason in the face of superstition:

> Let's not go back to a dark age of superstition and unreason, a world in which every time you lose your keys you suspect poltergeists, demons or alien abduction.

His argument against such superstition is the economy of explanation – if there is a straightforward reason why something happens, why should one chose to believe something elaborately improbable instead?

Clearly, Dawkins is not suggesting anything radically new. The principle of taking the most likely and simple explanation has a long history, and can be found in different forms in Ockham's razor and Hume's critical evaluation of evidence. Nor would the traditional proponents of the cosmological or teleological arguments have necessarily thought that they were doing anything other than finding the most reasonable and straightforward explanation for fundamental features of the universe. What Dawkins does point to, however, is a fundamental choice; a choice between informed reason and superstition. But is a religious belief necessarily superstitious?

Most of this book has been concerned with rational argument; with the grounds on which it is reasonable to believe various things to be true. Many religious people would claim that their faith is a reasonable one, in that their beliefs do not require them to deny what a majority of people hold to be true, nor do they require a personal loss of integrity.

However, there is a fundamental difference between religion and philosophy. Religion, in addition to its reasoned arguments, offers many people an emotionally satisfying and personal way of engaging with life. It goes beyond reason.

Now this, in itself, should not set it at odds with Dawkins or other scientists. A sense of wonder is at the very heart of serious scientific enquiry. So wonder and emotional engagement does not separate the scientist from the person who holds religious views. That division centres on the willingness to allow all beliefs to be examined in a rational way, tested out and set in the context of the whole raft of beliefs and ideas that are available to us. When Dawkins attacks superstition, his target – quite correctly – is the tendency that some people have (and it is not limited to those who are religious) to dodge rational consideration and retreat into giving glib explanations that lack evidence.

It is a valid complaint against some religious beliefs, that they are not only incapable of being justified rationally, but that they are shielded against rational examination on the grounds that they are religious. But that is not the approach taken within the philosophy of religion as an academic branch of study. Religion, like everything else, can be examined and evaluated, and its claims can be related to other things that people hold to be true. In this sense, the philosophy of religion and science have a common cause against superstition.

Comment

It is crucially important, in assessing the relationship between science and religion, not to allow religion to be identified with superstition. When Aquinas or Newton spoke of God, they were not setting aside their rational faculties, but attempting to integrate their knowledge into a single vision of reality. Nor is it valid to claim that eccentric and supernatural beliefs are more genuinely religious than those of a more subtle variety. Religion embraces a whole spectrum of ideas and views of reality, only some of which are superstitious. It is unfortunate that some who challenge religion from a scientific perspective – as does Richard Dawkins in *The God Delusion* (2006) – tend to focus on only the most obvious target of crude, supernatural beliefs.

10 religion and society

In this chapter you will:
- examine the relationship between ethical theories and religion
- look at the political and social impact of religion
- consider how religion impinges on personal lifestyle.

In looking at the various philosophical issues that are raised by religious beliefs, we have seen that religion offers both a way of understanding the world and also a way of evaluating it. It does not give an objective, detached view of how things are, but a view that embodies both value and commitment.

That being the case, it is clear that a person's religious beliefs will influence his or her moral choices, and that the moral values held by a society are likely to reflect those of its dominant religion, even if these are not made explicit in each and every individual moral choice, or in each piece of social legislation. So in this chapter we shall take an overview of how religion relates to moral, social, political and lifestyle issues.

Moral issues

There are two kinds of ethics:

- **Descriptive ethics** simply describes what is done in a particular society at a particular time: this or that tribe is cannibalistic, this or that religion insists on monogamy. There is no attempt to make any evaluation of what is described. You can give a descriptive study of the moral attitudes taken by the world religions; some general principles (for example, not taking innocent life, or not stealing) are held by all the major religions; on other issues (for example, on sexuality or wealth generation) there will be a variety of views. Descriptive ethics is uncontroversial – it doesn't say that a particular view is right, merely that it is held.
- By contrast, **normative ethics** examines the principles upon which moral choices are made. In other words, it does not just describe what is done, but asks whether it is right or wrong.

In terms of the philosophy of religion, we are therefore particularly interested in normative ethics. Nobody doubts that religion can often influence what people do; the question is whether it is right to do so, and on what basis it does so.

It is also important to be clear about the grounds upon which people make moral judgements:

- An **autonomous** morality is one in which a person's ethical principles are justified by reason and evidence. They do not depend on any external source of authority.

- By contrast, morality may be described as **heteronomous** if it is based externally – in the teachings of one of the world religions, for example, or imposed by cultural tradition.

It is possible, of course, that two people may take the same moral view on an issue, but for one it is based on reason, while for the other it is a matter of obedience to a tradition. So the relation between religious ethics and autonomous ethics is not one of *content*, but of *method and justification*.

> **Example**
>
> One person will say it is wrong to steal, because it is against one of the Ten Commandments. Another will agree that it is wrong, but will justify that in terms of the effect on society if everyone felt free to steal whatever they wanted.

So let us briefly consider the major ethical theories to see to what extent they are autonomous, and where they overlap with religious views.

Natural Law

Aristotle distinguished between efficient causes and final causes. Efficient causes were those things which existed prior to something happening and which were perceived as agents in bringing it about (for example, the sculptor and his chisel are the efficient causes of a piece of marble becoming shaped into a bust). Final causes are those things which lie in the future but which give direction to what happens in the present (for example, the idea of the bust is the final cause of the work of the sculptor). The final cause of a thing defines its true or ultimate character.

This theory was taken up by Aquinas, and became the basis of the **Natural Law** theory of ethics, which has dominated Roman Catholic ethical thinking. According to Natural Law, everything has a purpose (or 'final cause') for which it has come about – and in a Christian context, of course, that is seen as the purpose given by God, its creator. An action is morally right if it is in line with that purpose, wrong if it frustrates it.

Take the example of self-preservation. It is both reasonable and natural that one should seek to preserve one's own life when it is threatened, for in most cases that is the best way to fulfil one's purpose as a human being. Therefore a 'natural law' argument would say that everyone has a right to life, and that it is therefore wrong deliberately to take life. However, once that is established, there will be debates about the circumstances when taking life is permitted – to prevent further loss of life, for example – or when we are considering the life of other species that we wish to eat.

Example

A clear example of the application of the Natural Law theory is the Roman Catholic opposition to contraception. It is argued that the conception of a child is the natural purpose of the sexual act. That act may also be enjoyable and strengthen the relationship between the partners, but – however positive these things may be – they arise in the context of an act which has as an essential purpose: the conception of children. Therefore, anything which deliberately frustrates that outcome must be morally wrong, and every sexual act should at least be **open to the possibility** of the conception of a child.

The conception of a child remains, of course, a possibility rather than a certainty. Nature itself certainly does frustrate that outcome, since the vast majority of sperm never make it to the egg, fertilized eggs do not always implant successfully, and miscarriages can end the process at a later stage. But such things are outside moral control, and since they are part of the natural order it might be argued that God had used them for some particular purpose.

By contrast, anal intercourse, oral intercourse, homosexuality and masturbation cannot lead to the conception of children, and are on that basis considered to be against nature and therefore morally wrong.

From the above example, it is clear that something can be considered morally wrong, and yet be perfectly 'natural' in the usual sense of that word. Masturbation, oral sex, homosexual acts and so on are the result of 'natural' desires, but the nature considered by Natural Law is nature **as interpreted by reason**. More specifically, it is nature as seen as having a sense of purpose, in which each event looks for its justification to its 'final cause'.

The Natural Law approach to morality is the attempt to understand and evaluate each action in the light of some universal purpose and direction.

Since it is based on Aristotle, it is perfectly possible to take a Natural Law approach to ethics without being religious – all that is required is the belief that life is purposeful and that reason can reveal the essence and 'final cause' in each thing or act and how it should be expressed.

However, having been taken up by Aquinas, that same philosophy becomes religious by being linked to the idea of God as creator, and his will as expressing the purpose of everything. Therefore, as a theory, Natural Law may be autonomous, but generally is not.

Utilitarianism

Utilitarianism is the attempt to justify a moral action in terms of its expected results, and is associated particularly with the work of Jeremy Bentham (1748–1832) and John Stuart Mill (1806–73).

In its simplest form, this argues that the right thing to do in any situation is that which is judged to give the greatest benefit or happiness to the greatest number of people involved.

There are various forms of utilitarianism: act utilitarianism (which concentrates on looking at the results of individual acts), rule utilitarianism (which accepts the need for rules, but only on the grounds that those rules could be justified by the anticipated benefits to society as a whole), and preference utilitarianism (in which the preferences of all those involved are to be taken into account, so that morality is not just decided upon results, but on the sort of results that people choose).

All of them, however, are based on the general principle that people seek happiness for themselves, and therefore need to take into account that others will seek it too. But clearly, the attempt to maximize one's own happiness at the expense of others is likely to be frustrated by the desire of other people to do the same. Utilitarianism, in seeking the maximum happiness for the maximum number, aims at a compromise in which everyone ultimately benefits.

In other words

Utilitarianism is enlightened self-interest. It is broadly based on **hedonism** – the theory that everyone seeks happiness – but recognizes that, in a competitive world, happiness is most likely to be achieved by fostering a co-operative spirit.

Utilitarianism is a very practical and commonsense approach to ethics, and the most widely argued today. It is the moral equivalent of democracy, recognizing that every individual has the right for their own benefit to be taken into account. In itself, utilitarianism does not prescribe particular actions, it merely gives the framework within which people can determine what is the right thing to do.

Clearly, utilitarianism is an autonomous moral system, in that it does not depend on any external authority. It assumes only two things: the agreement to seek the well-being of others, and a willingness to examine the evidence of a situation and to think through its implications for those involved.

One criticism of utilitarianism, particularly from a religious point of view, is that it works on the assumption that people are in fact willing to take the well-being or benefit of others into account – and that, so some would claim, does not recognize the basic selfishness of 'fallen' human nature.

Note

Nietzsche contrasted the morality of slaves with that of masters. The former were likely to promote a morality which gave them a more equitable share of life's good things, and Nietzsche saw that exemplified particularly in the Christian morality of love and compassion towards those who suffer. By contrast, masters are more likely to seek what is noble and to develop themselves to the limit. His fear was that the Christian slave morality would weaken society, depriving it of its nobility and striving. He did not want to see the strong held back on account of the weak.

Nietzsche therefore presents us with fundamental questions: Why be utilitarian? Why seek a fairer sharing of happiness? Why not seek for a higher goal for yourself even if it is at the expense of others?

As a personal mission statement, 'the greatest happiness to the greatest number' might seem, from a Nietzchian perspective, to offer a goal of comfortable inertia!

However utilitarian it might be in practice, a religious morality is therefore likely to want to underpin the utilitarian theory either with a Natural Law argument of some kind, or with other statements about the meaning and purpose of life. Without such underpinning, utilitarianism may be seen to offer a formula for sharing equitably, without also providing a good reason to do so.

Kantian ethics

Immanuel Kant (1724–1804) famously carried out a 'Copernican revolution' in the theory of knowledge, in which he argued that features that had previously been thought of as being 'out there' in the world – like space, time and causality – were in fact contributed to experience by the mind. A similar revolution took place in his ethics, in that he started with the experience of an unconditional moral 'ought' and argued that morality should depend entirely on the pure practical reason, rather than on external facts.

He considered the nature of duty and of the 'good will', and eliminated from his consideration of morality all those actions from which one expects to gain personally, or those which flow from a natural interest (since he saw both as essentially selfish) and those where one simply acts under orders.

A 'categorical imperative' refers to an absolute moral obligation – an 'ought' that does not depend on any expected results (as opposed to a 'hypothetical imperative' which says 'if you want to achieve this, you need to do that'). Kant set out the criteria by which such categorical imperatives should be assessed. There are three of these (although different variations of them are found in his work):

- So act that the maxim of your action could always hold at the same time as a principle establishing universal law.

A 'maxim' is a principle of action, and it takes the form 'whenever A happens, I think it right to do B'. So this first criterion is that something is right if, and only if, you are prepared that everyone else should act on that same principle in those same circumstances.

Example

Kant argues that it is always wrong to break a promise, because if everyone were free to break any promises they made, then the whole idea of making a promise in the first place would become nonsense. Keeping promises is therefore justified on the grounds of pure, practical reason.

- Act in such a way that you always treat humanity, whether in your own person or in the person of any other, never simply as a means, but always at the same time as an end.

In other words, everyone should be considered as an autonomous moral agent, with the respect and rights that involves – never as simply a means to my own end.

- Act as if a legislating member in the universal kingdom of ends.

In deciding whether something is right, you should imagine that you are responsible for legislating in a society where everyone is a free, autonomous moral agent.

There are many issues connected with Kantian ethics, which we cannot explore here. For now, however, we should note that this theory is genuinely autonomous. It does not require any external legislator or source of moral values, but is entirely the product of the pure practical reason.

Although Kant himself was religious – a Protestant Christian – his theory of ethics can stand independently of his own (or any other) religion. The only essential presupposition it makes is that human beings are rational, and able to consider and act on that basis. If you regard human reason as 'fallen' (as many from his own religious tradition have argued) then it is difficult to see how human reason can be trusted to provide a basis for morality.

Virtue ethics

Virtue ethics, like Natural Law, originated in the philosophy of Aristotle. It is based on an assessment of those qualities that enable a human being to live the 'good life' in the broadest sense of that word. Rather than starting with various actions and assessing whether they are right or wrong, virtue ethics considers qualities (for example, kindness, courage, moderation) that can be cultivated, and considers how each of these can contribute to human flourishing.

In some ways, Natural Law and Virtue ethics can be seen as two sides of the same coin. Natural Law looks at the essence of what it is to be human, and the final aim of everything in life. Virtue ethics does much the same, considering the exercise of the virtues in order to bring about the 'final' end of humankind, for 'human flourishing' is really a way of describing a situation in which human beings express their human nature to the full.

And religious morality?

Clearly, all the above theories are basically autonomous; they do not require any prior religious belief in order to make their case. Religious people may, of course, use one or more of them to justify moral claims that come through their religious authorities or from their scriptures, but that is another matter.

Where religious moral principles are based on rules found in doctrine or scripture, there are two options. Either the rule is taken literally and as expressing a truth valid for all time, or it is set in the context in which it was first formulated.

Thus, for example, within the Hebrew scriptures, there are rules about not killing or stealing, and these have been generally adopted as of universal application. Others concern the prohibition of particular foods or regulations for personal hygiene, and these may more easily be seen as relevant to the particular time in which they were originally devised.

Most religions therefore examine moral rules from their scriptures and reinterpret them in the light of the changed circumstances that prevail in today's world. This happens very clearly in Judaism, for example, where layers of interpretation build up to provide an encyclopaedic set of rules for living, based on original scriptural injunctions. In Buddhism, there is the principle of 'skilful means' which requires that all teachings must be shaped to address and meet the needs of those being taught.

Debate within any one religion may therefore depend on the particular approach to scripture, and on the degree to which scholars within that religion allow the reinterpretation of moral rules. At the same time, debates between religious and secular thinkers occur when the moral principles established within a religion come into conflict with one or more of the autonomous moral theories outlined above.

Example

In January 2007, an appeal was made to the UK government to allow Catholic adoption agencies an exemption from anti-discrimination legislation that made it illegal to exclude same-sex couples from applying to adopt a child. The grounds on which that appeal was made was that the Catholic Church has strict principles about the nature of marriage and family life, which would preclude a Catholic from placing a child with a same-sex couple. And, beneath this, of course, there was the more general issue of the attitude of the Catholic Church to homosexuality. It was argued that to comply with the law would go against the conscience of practising Catholics in the adoption agencies.

'The rights of conscience cannot be made subject to legislation, however well meaning.' (From a letter to the British Prime Minister from the Anglican Archbishop of Canterbury, supporting the Catholic position, January 2007.)

The outcome was something of a compromise, with Catholic agencies being required to conform to the law, but having an extended period in which to adapt their procedures to achieve this. Nevertheless, the point was made that there should not be a religious 'opt out' of a moral principle (of not discriminating against same-sex partnerships) established by law in a democracy.

Responsible moral choice depends on freedom and the ability to choose rationally; it is difficult to see how someone is acting morally if they are forced to do something. If you are made to do something against your will, responsibility for that action should lie with the person who forces you to do it. But religions have sometimes inculcated rules that should be obeyed out of fear of punishment. Rewards and punishments may be offered after this life – either in terms of heaven or hell, or in terms of rebirth into higher or lower forms of life. With such religious pressure to conform, can a person be truly free or responsible? This would suggest that it is safer to stay with one of the autonomous moral theories, rather than accept externally imposed rules.

However, things are not that simple. People cannot escape from the influence of religious values and attitudes. They have an unconscious effect, even for those who reject religion. As soon as you try to define moral terms (such as 'goodness' or 'justice') you are using language which has been shaped within a culture, and cultures are generally influenced by the prevailing religions. Religion has largely supplied the language of ethical debate.

We have already seen that metaphysics – the study of questions about the nature of reality as a whole – can be used as a basis for morality (as in Greek thought, in the Natural Law tradition, and as explored recently by, for example, Iris Murdoch in

Metaphysics as a Guide to Morals). But metaphysics may also be used to justify religious beliefs, so it may be difficult to disentangle the religious and moral implications of these fundamental ideas about reality.

The areas where religion and morality come together most often are those concerned with sexuality, marriage and family life, and also with the issues of life and death. These are spheres of human experience where ultimate values come closest to the surface of conscious decisions. Euthanasia, suicide and abortion all raise fundamental questions about the inherent value of life. Equally, sexuality and family life raise fundamental questions about relationships and the overall purpose of human life for individuals and for society as a whole.

But notice here that the interplay between autonomous ethical thinking and religious rules needs to be considered in the broader context of society, for in reality religious views and language permeate and influence us on many levels. Hence the need to look more generally at the way in which religion relates to society.

The Euthyphro dilemma

If morality is based on divine commands, there is a philosophical problem – generally termed the 'Euthyphro dilemma', because it occurs in Plato's dialogue of that name. It may be presented in the form of a question:

- Are things good because God commands them, or does God command them because they are good?

If the former, we may want to question whether anything that purported to be a divine command would therefore be considered good. If God ordered you to kill an innocent person, would that be right, just because God ordered it? If the latter, it shows that we have an idea of good that is independent of God's commands – for otherwise we would not be able to judge them 'good'.

The social impact of religion

Religion can be examined purely as a social phenomenon. Like psychology, sociology is less concerned with whether religious beliefs are true, more with the part that religion plays in the lives of individuals and society.

Thus we can examine the relationship between religion and family life – the tendency of children to continue to practise the religion of their parents when they grow up. Equally, we can examine the different styles of religion that flourish in different social or ethnic communities – from the cool, meditative detachment of Zen or a Benedictine monastery, to the exuberance of a West Indian evangelical church or a Tibetan Buddhist festival. Each of these will be influenced by, and in turn influence, that society.

There are also general theories about the role of religion in society. Emile Durkeim (1858–1917) saw religion as having a positive role, allowing people to participate in the values and identity of their society. It allowed people to get together and affirm their common purpose and enabled them to think of themselves as a unified moral group.

When it simply analyses the effect of religion on society and vice versa, the sociology of religion simply observes, without necessarily contributing to the debate about whether religious beliefs are true or false. However, once a function is found for religion, it is tempting to say that religion is created in order to perform that function. In other words, that belief in God is created in order to give social cohesion.

A force for good?

In a poll in the UK, published in *The Guardian* (23 December 2006) 33 per cent of those questioned described themselves as 'religious' and 64 per cent, when asked which religion they belonged to, said they were Christian, yet only 13 per cent visited a place of worship once a week of more. This suggests a general social allegiance to religion, even if the practice of religion is diminishing in popularity.

When it comes to a general perception of the social implications of religion, the results seem ambiguous. While 82 per cent considered that religion caused divisions between people, 57 per cent thought that religion was a force for good.

And in terms of social identity and religious allegiance, 62 per cent considered that Britain was a country of many faiths, as opposed to 17 per cent who saw it as a 'Christian country'.

Once again, as with psychology, we are caught in a dilemma about the factual truth of beliefs:

- **If God exists,** and is loving and providential in providing for humankind, then belief in God is likely to give cohesion and other benefits to society.
- **But if God does not exist,** then belief in God is a social construct, produced for the benefit of society – or, more likely, for the benefit of those who control society (the view taken by Marx).

Sociology may therefore offer an explanation of religion, but it does not thereby automatically decide on the factual truth or otherwise of religious beliefs. On the other hand, if there is no rational or objective basis for religious belief, sociology is able to suggest reasons why religion may still continue and thrive.

However, there is another aspect of the sociology of religion, exemplified in the work of Weber (1864–1920). Weber pointed out that religion provides society with a range of attitudes and values. These go beyond the narrow confines of organized religion and permeate society as a whole. His own famous example of this is the 'Protestant work ethic' – the general view of the value of honest work and thrift that originated in Protestant Christianity, but became a defining social feature in much of northern Europe and the United States.

We therefore need to keep in mind two different but related features of religion:

- Religion as providing social identity and cohesion
- Religion as a transmitter of value and meaning.

These will be important as we look at political issues related to religion and also at social values and lifestyles.

If religion is a significant factor in shaping society, then – whether its beliefs are correct or not – it is something of which everyone should be thoughtfully aware, so should religion be taught in schools?

Religious education

This is another huge topic that we can only touch on here. If a religion, especially one established by the state, is a social construct whose purpose is to transmit social identity and values, then clearly any state education system is going to require religion to be taught in its schools. However, education is not simply a matter of feeding information, but of training young people to think and evaluate evidence for themselves.

Hence a dilemma for the teaching of religious education. Should the doctrines of religion be taught as true (with the intention that the next generation will accept them and thus maintain the social cohesion offered by religion), or should they be taught in a way that allows students to evaluate them and come to their own conclusions?

Educational theory requires the latter. The content of what should be taught in schools in Britain is set out in non-statutory 'Guidelines for RE' which are published by the Qualifications and Curriculum Authority, and this includes both the range of major world religions and also humanism. There is also local input, so that the content of RE can be influenced by the religious balance of a particular education authority.

But there is also a tendency towards the former, especially in schools that are aligned with an established religion or (even more) are set up by a particular religion or denomination. Hence, for example, an act of worship may be included in the school day, which most pupils will be expected to attend – unless their parents specifically require them to be excused it. The same proactive stance by parents is required for pupils to be exempt from Religious Education lessons, which are compulsory, while not being part of the National Curriculum.

With faith schools, there is the additional claim that education is not just about content but also about ethos – hence the desire on the part of some parents for a school that reflects, say, Muslim or Catholic values and teaching.

Are religious schools indoctrinating and divisive?

In an article for *The Guardian*, 14 April 2006, Polly Toynbee commented, in arguing against faith schools, 'There is all the difference in the world between teaching children about religion and handing them over to be taught by the religious.' She expressed concern, shared by others including the teachers' unions, about the teaching of 'intelligent design' as a valid alternative to evolution in science lessons, and argued that it was most inappropriate to hand over education to the world of faith, commenting, 'There is a clash of civilizations, not between Islam and Christendom but between reason and superstition.'

She also argued that faith schools are divisive, not just along religious lines, but also by class, race or tribe, threatening social cohesion. The question is also raised as to whether faith-based education is suitable to equip pupils for life in today's Britain.

So what is the 'ethos' of a faith school, and what is its educational value?

A further problem arises in a multi-faith society. How should education reflect individual religious traditions, but also keep in line with the main social and cultural traditions of society? Teaching all world religions equally and in as objective a manner as possible is one approach to this. But what of the traditional assembly? Should this reflect the membership of religious groups locally? What if a majority are not members of a religious faith? Should there be secular assemblies, devoid of specifically religious content, but presenting values deemed to be of benefit to society and compatible with religion?

There would seem to be two logical approaches:

- To make all education secular, but including within it information about religions as part of a general awareness of social phenomena. This may, of course, include religious traditions in literature, art and so on – which are valuable in order to understand culture.
- To allow religious groups to provide their own schooling, in which specific religious traditions are taught as true, even if they are not believed by the majority of society. This might include, for example, the teaching of creationism alongside modern cosmology and natural selection.

The crucial issue here is what constitutes good education, and how one balances the requirement to teach **about** religion, as opposed to teaching children **to be religious**. The former is a necessary part of understanding the world, whether the latter is appropriate or not depends on your view of the social value of religion. In either case, it is difficult to see how any uncritical presentation of religious ideas can be justified educationally.

Political issues

John Locke (1632–1704) writing at a time when England was torn by religious divisions between Catholics and Protestants, saw the chaos and bloodshed that resulted in the attempt to impose a religious settlement, and advocated toleration in his *Essay Concerning Toleration*, written in 1667.

He considered that the task of the state was to secure for the people life, liberty, health and private property. Politics should concern itself with these things, and not interfere with religious matters. By contrast, he saw religion as a voluntary gathering of individuals for the purpose of worshipping God and saving their own souls – and they should be free to do that in any way they choose. Remarkably, for his day, he was prepared to say that he considered it did not matter whether he worshipped on Friday as a Muslim, Saturday as a Jew or Sunday as a Christian, provided that he did so sincerely. He considered that such things made no difference to his loyalty as a subject, or his ability to be a good neighbour to his fellows.

That position of separation of religion and state, and toleration of all faiths, was influential both in Britain and in the founding principles of the United States. Problems arise, however, when religious views conflict with civil law. This is chiefly seen in moral issues – particularly concerning sexual orientation, and life and death (euthanasia and abortion).

Example

Under the headline 'Gay rights law attacked as "charter to sue Christians"', Ben Russell, reported (in *The Independent*, 10 January 2007) on protests by representatives of Christian denominations in Northern Ireland against new rules that outlaw discrimination against gay couples. They argued that Christians who were not prepared to accommodate gay couples in their boarding houses or stock gay titles in their bookshops might face prosecution. They argued that actions on the basis of religious faith should be immune from such prosecution.

What Locke opposed was the idea that the state should determine the practice of religion. This, of course, had been the situation following the Reformation, where Europe was divided along religious lines, with some states becoming Protestant and others remaining Catholic.

Where there is a single, state endorsed and imposed religion, it may be difficult to know whether the impetus for that comes from religion or from politics. Some states (for example, Saudi

Arabia, Iran) are clearly run on strictly Muslim principles; in others (for example, Ireland) Christianity has had a direct influence on civil law, for example, on the issue of abortion. In the fourth century, when the Roman Empire embraced Christianity, it is less clear whether it did so on religious grounds, or whether having a single popular religion was regarded as politically expedient, as a means of holding together a culturally diverse empire.

So does religion manipulate politics, or politics religion? The Marxist view is that religion is used by the ruling class in order to maintain a status quo that is to their benefit. In other words, he recognized the ability of society to use religion.

A diverse culture is inherently more difficult to rule than a monochrome one. Hence, looking at the history of 'religious' wars, it is often the case that the root cause of the warfare is not religion but the different states that have used religion as a means of reinforcing national identity. An example of this would be the wars of religion in Europe between Protestant and Catholic nation states.

Religion and social status

In India there have been mass conversions to Buddhism of *dalits* (previously known as 'untouchables') who are at the bottom of the caste hierarchy and therefore see little chance of improving themselves within Hindu society. Buddhism gives them a new status, separate from but equal to the upper castes within Hindu society.

In any society where different religious groups have different status, conversion will have a political and social aspect, as well as a religious one.

There is also the fear that a religious minority, holding views differing from the majority, will either seek to declare their independence, or will threaten the unity of purpose of the state by having a loyalty to that which is wider than the state – and therefore potentially seeing themselves as in alliance with other states or organizations that share their religion position, rather than with their country of residence.

The response of the majority of Muslims to acts of terrorism by Muslim extremists illustrates this. The Muslim community, whether in the UK or the US, have defended their political credentials, as loyal citizens of the states in which they live, while at the same time both acknowledging their fundamental identity as members of the worldwide community of Islam, and criticizing the extremists as not representing the true spirit of Islam.

Imposing secular rules?

Recently, France banned Muslim girls from wearing the hijab (a traditional head covering, seen as an expression of modesty) in school. This was intended to reaffirm the secular status of French society and to prevent any sense of separate identity for Muslim pupils. Presumably in the name of liberty, equality and fraternity it therefore imposed a restriction on a cultural and religious minority.

In Britain, individual cases of a conflict between what is expected in the workplace have hit the headlines. In one case, a teacher was suspended for wearing the full veil on the grounds that it inhibited her ability to teach. In another, British Airways agreed to change its rules about the wearing of religious symbols, after a dispute with an employee over the wearing of a small cross over her uniform.

The crucial question is how to balance the right of religious conscience in matters of dress with the needs of society – whether that be practical needs in the workplace, or the need to encourage social cohesion and therefore oppose visible signs of difference and separation.

Religion and terrorism

A most extreme form of deliberately inflicted human suffering is that brought about by acts of terror. Particularly since the events of 11 September 2001 and 7 July 2005, attention has been focused on the relationship between religion, **ideology** and terrorism. Recently the particular focus has been on Islam, but terrorism in the name of religion has a long history, including the persecution of minority groups within a religion (i.e. those branded as heretics), those belonging to different branches of a religion (for example, the mutual persecution of Catholics and Protestants following the Reformation) and those belonging to other religions. Religion does not have a good track record when it comes to the torture and execution of those whose beliefs it regards as suspect.

Generally speaking, no world religion approves of acts of violence that lead to innocent suffering. Indeed, showing compassion towards other people is a quality that all major religions share and promote.

It is therefore tempting to isolate terrorism from the religious background of those involved, and claim that it is always carried out for political reasons. However, this may not reflect the views of the terrorists themselves, who may have deeply held religious convictions and see themselves as martyrs. In the opening chapter of his book *The End of Faith*, Sam Harris points out that, when the reasons for someone carrying out a suicide bombing are considered, they are generally presented as personal, political or economic – faith tends to be exonerated, on the grounds that, even without it, desperate people would still carry out desperate acts. However, just because one acts in the name of a religion or a religious group, it does not follow that one's actions are either a necessary interpretation of its teachings, nor do they automatically show those teachings in their entirety to be either true or false.

We therefore have to make a distinction between what is done in the name of religion, and the fundamental beliefs of that religion. What cannot be avoided is the simple fact that, if religion is concerned with morality and the values by which people live, it will inevitably have a political dimension. It is illogical to claim that one follows a religion with a moral code, and then argue that it has nothing to say about wider political commitments. It was precisely the attempt to present religion as separate from politics that led Marx to accuse it of being the opium of the people, the other-worldly compensation for suffering in this life, and therefore to be deeply implicated in political control.

If someone claims that an act of terror is a religious duty, or leads to martyrdom, then it is reasonable to examine that claim, testing it out against the teachings of that religion (for example, it is perfectly right to ask any Muslim if his or her actions reflect submission to Allah, who is described in the Qur'an as 'merciful and compassionate'). Although it is far beyond the scope of this book, it is a valid function for the philosophy of religion to perform. It may lead to some uncomfortable conclusions, but it is more honest than dismissing all those who carry out terrorist attacks as 'fanatics', or as duped by those whose motivation is personal or political rather than religious.

Beneath the issue of terrorism is a broader one of extremism. It is a mark of maturity in an individual that they are able to reflect on their views and their inclinations, rather than simply being carried along by whatever impulse is uppermost in their life at a particular time. The same could be said of the following of a religion. A mature approach would be one of critical commitment. Without commitment a person is unlikely to engage at an appropriate level – the casual observer of religion is unlikely to appreciate its significance. But without critical reflection, the individual fails to engage at a level which allows personal integrity.

Comment

To believe something with conviction, believing it not just on authority but because one has reflected on it and been convinced of its truth, is a sign of maturity. To ignore doubts, setting aside one's personal integrity for the sake of identifying with a particular idea or cause, is to split off religious commitment from normal rational scrutiny. Extremism depends on being able to split off religious or political commitment from the natural human element of empathy with other people and even the most natural sense of self-protection.

Although in the early twenty-first century religious extremism and terrorism is seen as a particularly Muslim problem – highlighted by the bombings in New York and London – it is important to see it in a broader context. Both the idea of martyrdom and the willingness to kill in the name of religion have a significant place within the history of Christianity. That applies internally, as, for example, in the European wars of religion following the Reformation, and externally, as, for example, the Crusades against Islam. Hence it is important to see this as a general problem in terms of extreme or radical views, not one related to one particular religion or political ideology.

Social values and lifestyle

If we observe the spread of world religions as social phenomena, leaving aside for now any questions about the truth of their beliefs, they fall into two different camps:

- Hinduism, Islam, Judaism and Sikhism have tended to take their existing lifestyle and social values with them wherever they go.
- Christianity and Buddhism have tended to adapt their lifestyle to accommodate the prevailing traditions in the countries where they have become established.

Thus a devout Muslim living in Britain will wish to follow traditions of dress, food and attitudes to family and society that are shared with Muslims in the Middle East. This raises many issues about social conformity – should a Muslim woman wear traditional Muslim dress and head-covering, or adopt a Western lifestyle? Similarly, Orthodox Jewish communities worldwide follow similar traditions and dress.

By contrast, if you compare the lifestyle and devotional traditions of Buddhists in Thailand, Tibet, Japan and the USA, they may have relatively little in common. Indeed, the Buddhist idea of 'skilful means' suggests that teachings are adapted in order to fit the needs of hearers, and will therefore change over time and distance.

Similarly, in any cosmopolitan city you will find different Christian communities reflecting the culture and part of the world from which their members have come. Move from a Greek Orthodox church to an evangelical church filled with Christians of Caribbean origin, or to the more restrained style of English Anglicanism or Northern Protestantism, and you move from one culture to another within a single religion.

Examples

- There may be a direct clash between secular and religious lifestyles. Should Sikhs be allowed to wear turbans rather than crash helmets? Should Muslim women by allowed to have their faces covered in the workplace?
- There may be fundamental differences of values and importance of, say, the family or establishing a day of rest. Hence, disputes about the observance of Sunday for Christians, or the Sabbath for Jews.

The lifestyle of a mature person will include such things as his or her beliefs, values, morality, attitude towards others and the environment, economic and social circumstances. At a superficial level, it is about what people buy and how they choose to live. A lifestyle change implies not just a changed set of circumstances – work, home etc. – but also a change in the general attitude towards life.

Clearly, some lifestyles are secular, others are religious. The key question here is:

- What does religion add to a lifestyle?

In part, this depends on the level of religious involvement and commitment. A superficial approach to religion – taking part in religious ceremonies when required, as part of one's social life, but without engaging either emotionally or intellectually in the beliefs of that religion – is not going to make any significant contribution to one's lifestyle.

On the other hand, to belong to a religion, or minority sect within a religion, which is not the established religion within the society in which you live, may involve a radical lifestyle change. So, for example, someone who had previously been nominally Christian who then adopted the Jewish or Muslim faith, would thereby agree to adopt different traditions in food, dress, times of prayer and so on. This is because both religions have a distinctive culture as well as a distinctive set of beliefs and religious traditions. Hence a multi-faith society becomes, at least to some extent, a multicultural society.

Example

The Amish communities in the USA have deliberately turned their backs on what they see as the corrupting trimmings of modern life, and adopted a lifestyle that has changed little since the nineteenth century; horse-drawn vehicles rather than cars, no television or radio. This is a clear lifestyle choice as a way of implementing religious values – although those same Christian values are claimed by others who nevertheless seem satisfied to live them out within the prevailing secular lifestyle.

So the question is: how do you judge whether the Amish have a more authentic Christian lifestyle (in the sense of being true to Christian teachings) than that of other Christian denominations in the USA?

Following a secular lifestyle does not imply that one is not influenced by religion. In the West, much art, music, philosophy and so on has been influenced by the Christian religion.

A person may regard himself or herself as a humanist, and may be an atheist, but still find that part of their lifestyle involved, for example, enjoying music that has been created in a religious context, or visiting places of religious worship. That does not, in itself, either discredit or endorse the religion – it is simply a recognition that religion and culture are deeply interfused, and it is almost impossible to enjoy the prevailing culture without receiving influences from the prevailing religion.

We therefore need to recognize that there is no simple division between secular and religious in terms of lifestyle. There is something of a sliding scale here:

- Most secular people are influenced by religious ideas and culture (for example, humanists can still enjoy Bach's religious music!).
- A person may belong to a religious group, adopting some aspects of that religious lifestyle, whilst retaining most elements in the prevailing cultural and secular lifestyle (for example, you attend church, but do not take religious ideas into account particularly in matters of choice about how you live or what work you do).
- A person may adopt a religion that requires some changes of lifestyle, compared with that in the prevailing culture (for example, rules about food or dress, attitudes to work or wealth) whilst continuing also to think of themselves as part of a wider social community.
- A person may deliberately reject most of their previously held values and separate themselves off from the wider culture as far as possible (for example, if someone joins a monastic or closed religious community).

A key question here is the degree of intellectual autonomy that the person retains. Is it possible to belong to a religion and retain the ability to look critically at its teachings? This is equally significant when it comes to moral issues. Religions lay down moral principles that may conflict with those of secular society. Where an individual stands on the scale of involvement given above will then determine the degree of discomfort that such conflict causes.

Where a lifestyle change reflects fundamental beliefs and values, the results may be quite traumatic, leading to separation from friends and family, and even loss of life. Apostasy – the deliberate turning away from a religion – carries a heavy penalty in some societies.

Places of dispute

Buildings have a powerful significance in religion. A current dispute concerns Muslims who wish to pray in Cordoba's mosque. When the Muslims were expelled from Spain in 1492, a Christian cathedral was built inside the original mosque. Arguing that mosques are open to Christians, the President of Spain's Islamic Council wants Muslims, at least individually if not in an act of collective worship, to be allowed to pray in what is now also a cathedral. The Catholic bishops have, to date, refused to allow this.

The Dome of the Rock mosque is built on the site of Solomon's temple in Jerusalem, and many Christian churches are built over earlier Roman temples. This reusing of sacred sites is symbolic of the supplanting of one religion by another, hence the strong feelings that such buildings can generate in believers.

Sects and conversion

One issue concerning a radical change of lifestyle concerns those, particularly young people, who join a fundamentalist branch of a major religion or one of the smaller sects. They may be encouraged deliberately to cut themselves off from their families and former friends, and to reject secular life and values.

Studies of this phenomenon suggest, not surprisingly, that those seeking the comfort and security offered by religion have a greater than average tendency to social and emotional problems. In other words, a person may turn to religion because society as a whole has failed to meet their personal and emotional needs. Now that in itself need not be a bad thing; it shows that, for some people, religion may offer a genuinely therapeutic experience. However, a small religious group comprising mainly those who have arrived with social or psychological needs, may not be the most balanced of communities.

It is mainly the smaller sects that present such problems; mainstream religion tends to be rather more aligned to the prevailing culture and lifestyle, so that its members still function comfortably in a secular context. Indeed, religion is regarded by many as a purely private affair, and their lifestyle may be indistinguishable from their secular neighbours.

An outline of this and other issues, summing up scholarship in this area, may be found in *Psychology and Religion: an introduction* by Michael Argyle (2000).

Religion in a multicultural society

Multiculturalism is the view that different cultures can exist within a single society, each respected and each contributing to its overall set of values and traditions. It attempts to get over the 'us' and 'them' opposition of earlier historical periods, where for example:

- The Bible records clashes between Israelite and Canaanite tribes. There is no question of choosing which religion you might prefer – those who go after 'false' gods are to be put to the sword.
- Before the fourth century, Christians suffer intermittent persecution in the Roman Empire, on the grounds that they would not perform token worship of the Emperor – a form of nominal state religion set as a test of political loyalty.
- In Medieval Christendom heretics are persecuted, Jews are intermittently tolerated and Islam, expanding and imposing its social and religious norms by force, is regarded as heresy by Christians, who launch the Crusades.
- Hindus are forced to convert to Islam as Muslim rulers expand their empire into northern India.
- Following the Reformation, sixteenth- and seventeenth-century Europe is divided: each state has its form of religion, Protestant or Catholic. Following the 'wrong' religion is, at times, punishable by death.
- As European empires expand into Africa, the Far East and the Americas, Christianity is exported and imposed.
- In the Soviet Union under Stalin, and later in Tibet under Chinese rule, atheism is imposed and attempts are made to eliminate the existing religions – Orthodox Christianity and Buddhism.

All of these are, by necessity, gross over-simplifications – but the point is made that positive multiculturalist assumptions are a recent phenomenon.

If religion is a personal matter, without social, moral or political implications, then it might be assumed that all religions can co-exist in a single society with few problems. In practice, however, religion is not simply a personal matter, and it is easy to characterize different cultures and ethnic groups in ways which may then give offence.

One problem is the creation of crude and exaggerated stereotypes, particularly of Muslims. Films, from *Aladdin* to

Indiana Jones, have been criticized (for example, by the Islamic Human Rights Commission) for the way in which Muslims are depicted, on the grounds that stereotypes are portraying Muslims as dangerous or threatening, and may serve to deepen existing prejudices.

Separate treatment for Muslims?

In January 2007, David Cameron, the leader of the opposition in Britain, suggested that people who argued that Muslims should be treated separately, or who called for Sharia law to be imposed, were trying to make divisions in British society. He opposed any 'us' and 'them' division. He also launched a report into the position of Muslim women in British society, arguing that they did not enjoy the same rights and opportunities in terms of education and employment as Muslim men or non-Muslim women, and that community cohesion required the lowering of divisive barriers (as reported in *The Independent*, 30 January 2007, p. 17, in an article by Andrew Grice).

But the crucial question is this: how do you allow distinctive religious lifestyle choices, whist at the same time promoting equality? And how, if there are divisions, to you prevent them from being exploited by extremists, who seek to undermine secular society in the name of religion?

Madeleine Bunting, commenting in *The Independent* (25 January 2007, p. 32) on the issue of Catholic adoption agencies and the gay couples, posed three key questions:

> Do faith institutions have a legitimate role in public life in a largely secular country? Are faith institutions subject to the laws of the land even when those are contrary to their own beliefs and doctrine? Does the state recognize the 'rights of conscience' in the phrase used by the Archbishop of Canterbury in his letter to the prime minister?

All three get to the heart of the problem of living in a multi-faith, multicultural society. Underlying them is the broad issue of how accommodating a society can be, when there are a variety of beliefs, values and lifestyles among minority (or majority) groups. Clearly, until recently, religious groups could expect to have a dominant role in framing laws that touched on deeply held moral principles. However, in a secular and multicultural society that is far from being the case. It is different, of course, in those countries where a single religion frames the law; some Muslims argue that it is ideal to live in a state run according to Sharia law.

The word 'religion' is problematic here. In literal terms, it refers to following a rule or practice – so, for example, Catholics may use the term to refer to those who belong to monastic orders. But is that the right word to use for Islam, for example? Islam comprises a set of beliefs, a social tradition and a political framework – in other words, to be Muslim is not just to believe certain things, but to live in a certain way, preferably in a society that is organized on Muslim lines. The idea that someone can be entirely secular in their lifestyle and yet have a personal preference for the Muslim religion is a contradiction in terms.

Multiculturalism has arisen because of the post-Enlightenment, secular and democratic tradition of respecting everyone's views and allowing everyone to participate equally in society. It seeks freedom of cultural and religious practice, but does not fit easily with the more absolutist and exclusivist views of religion.

How does this relate to religious belief?

There are two possibilities:

- That each set of beliefs forms a self-contained view of the world, and must be accepted as being incompatible with the others. (The clash between Hinduism and Islam is the clearest example of this.)
- That there is a general sense of what religion is about, and it is recognized that individual religions – using different ideas and language – approach a single goal from different directions.

The second of these is exemplified in the work of John Hick, who, in various publications, has looked at the whole universe of faiths and has proposed definitions about what religion is really about. It can be seen as the 'transformation of human existence from self-centredness to Reality-centredness'. If so, then under this general heading of 'religion' the various world faiths are intellectual and practical frameworks that allow this process to take place.

On the other hand, from the perspective of each of those world faiths, their beliefs are experienced as being exclusive. Thus it is difficult to argue that a monotheist and a polytheist are 'really' approaching the same reality, but using different language. For a Muslim, any attempt to compromise monotheism and associate other gods with Allah is the very worst of sins.

Note

- An **exclusivist** holds that only the beliefs of his or her religion are true.

This is not a common position to hold, since it is clear that there are a good number of beliefs that are shared by more than one religion. On the other hand, it is commonly argued that a person's own religion is uniquely privileged in its understanding of religious truth. In other words, that it has the full truth whereas other religions have only partial truth.

- An **inclusivist** accepts that other religions may have true beliefs.

True, that is, provided that they are not incompatible with his or her own religion. This position still accepts that some are true and some not, but acknowledges those held in common.

Another option is to see the beliefs of different religions as each contributing in a partial way to an overall truth, taking into account the limitations of religious language and knowledge. This is a view more easily held by an academic studying religion, or by a humanist wanting to survey the contribution of religions to the sum total of human self-awareness. It is difficult to combine this with the commitment a believer is expected to give to the beliefs or his or her own religion.

Clearly, those religious traditions which embrace a great variety of beliefs and practices are going to be inclusivist. Hinduism and Buddhism would fall into this category, for both may almost be regarded as families of religions – and, of course, that is exactly what they are, for both 'Hinduism' and 'Buddhism' are Western terms for exactly those collections of faiths.

Any religion that accepts human reason as a valid source of religious truth is also going to accept some measure of inclusivism, simply because reason is equally available to those who belong to other religions or none. Hence, Catholic Christianity would allow that knowledge of the existence of God can come by reason alone – although then needing to be supplemented by its revealed doctrines.

The problem with going further and saying that all religions are 'really' dealing with the same reality is that this will inevitably be opposed by those who hold that their own perspective yields unique truths not available to others. What is more, without some **independent** knowledge of that 'reality', how can you judge whether others are speaking about the same thing?

This sort of debate would be productive if it were not for another difficulty, namely that religious beliefs may become used as tokens of cultural and political identity. Their literal truth is then defended on grounds that are unlikely to be either genuinely logical or religious. And this leads to the problem of fundamentalism.

Literalism and fundamentalism

'Fundamentalist' was originally used, in a Christian context, to describe those who would strip away the more superficial trappings of religion in order to reveal its fundamentals. In common usage today, however, it describes the tendency to take scriptures literally, and to implement a narrowly defined range of beliefs, rejecting theological or philosophical subtlety.

Given the on-going discussion in academic circles about religious belief, and the nature of religious language, one might assume that most believers would come to the conclusion that language about beliefs is best understood in a metaphorical or symbolic way. To pretend that literal language can be used for a concept such as 'God' is self-defeating, in that it makes the God who can be described literally into part of the universe, and therefore less than what was originally meant by the word 'God'. Literalism can be seen as leading to what, in old-fashioned language, is termed **idolatry**. And, of course, an idol is not necessarily a physical object of worship; there are plenty of mental idols, in the form of creeds, which are venerated in themselves rather than being used as pointers to that which is transcendent.

But it is a curious and – for some – disturbing feature of religion in the early twenty-first century, that there has been a rise in fundamentalism and the literal interpretation of scriptures and statements of belief. This is particularly true of Christianity and Islam.

Fundamentalism tends to be intolerant, often nationalistic, and angry in defence of what it sees as its own unique truth. It proclaims certainty and challenges both other faiths and secular society. In particular, fundamentalists oppose religious liberals, refusing to accept that religious doctrines are open to interpretation, or that there can be substantial agreement between faiths.

Islamic fundamentalism, following the character of Islam as a whole, has immediate social and political impact, whether through the imposition of strict Sharia law, intolerance of those who do not accept the strictest of beliefs, or militant opposition of all regimes that are seen either as opposing Islam or promoting values that are antithetical to Islam.

At its most extreme, this takes the form of terrorism. Now, it is perfectly understandable that a distinction should be drawn between, say, moderate Islam and fundamentalist Muslim terrorists. But we need to be clear that it is not simply a distinction between those who are prepared to use violence and those who are not. The distinction is between those who are able to accept the broad principles of their faith and interpret particular passages of scripture in the light of them, and those who seek to take each passage of scripture and interpret it literally. There are plenty of passages in the scriptures of the Christian and Jewish faiths also which, if taken literally and out of context, would be horrifying to most loyal believers.

Examples

If anyone comes to me and does not hate his father and mother, his wife and children, his brothers and sisters – yes, even his own life – he cannot be my disciple. (Luke 14:26)

The Lord said to Moses, 'Take vengeance on the Midianites for the Israelites ...' (Numbers 31:1.2) and after the battle in which all the Midianite men are killed and the officers return to Moses with the women and children, he asks 'Have you allowed all the women to live?' and then commands 'Now kill all the boys. And kill every woman who has slept with a man, but save for yourselves every girl who has never slept with a man.' (Numbers 31:15, 17, 18)

Any understanding of scriptures needs to take context and translation into account – and no passage can safely be taken and applied without a serious look at the intention of the writer. Perhaps the most obvious example of this is the refusal of Jehovah's Witnesses to accept blood transfusions, on the grounds that the Bible forbids the taking of blood. Here what is essentially a prohibition of murder (i.e. shedding the blood of another) is taken out of context, and is assumed to oppose the medical procedure for sharing blood, which can save life.

Liberals may rationalize away difficult passages of scripture, or allegorize them, or suggest that existing translations are inadequate, but scriptures are regarded by a large number of religious believers as literally the word of God, and therefore as their ultimate source for beliefs and moral principles. There is a constant danger that 'extremists' will take them literally.

But liberals too may come under severe criticism on the grounds that they do not sufficiently oppose those who take texts literally. Sam Harris argues that:

> By failing to live by the letter of the texts, while tolerating the irrationality of those who do, religious moderates betray faith and reason alike.

(*The End of Faith*, p. 21)

Not everyone would perhaps be quite so sweeping in their criticism, but a serious point has been made – that the crucial division today is not between the religious and the non-religious, or even between religions, but between the literalists and fundamentalists of all religions on the one hand and the liberal, religious moderates, along with secular humanists, on the other.

For reflection

There are many views expressed in scripture which, if printed in a newspaper or book today, would fall foul of the law, as being liable to incite religious or racial hatred, as well as discrimination on grounds of gender or sexual orientation. Yet religious texts are protected from challenge on these grounds – even given the danger that they may be taken literally and acted upon.

A secular agenda

We have already seen that multiculturalism is a recent and secular phenomenon. It is the attempt to acknowledge and celebrate diversity, and its impetus comes from a humanist appreciation of the right of every individual to self-expression.

To attempt a multi-faith equivalent is similarly secular; it suggests that we share a common humanity and can celebrate common values. Each religion can contribute to that common agenda, provided that it acknowledges the right of all other religions to contribute similarly. Schools are encouraged to provide assemblies that reflect the variety of world faiths – so that children become acquainted with all religions and are able to appreciate them.

In some ways this is a multicultural equivalent of the eighteenth-century attempt to strip religion of superstition and to promote a set of beliefs that could be justified by reason. And philosophy can contribute to this by examining beliefs and testing them out for logical coherence and conformity to existing beliefs and evidence.

The continuing difficulty here is that the secular and humanist nature of this agenda will always be visible to the religious fundamentalist. From a religious perspective it appears to be a dilution of absolute moral and metaphysical truths, delivered by revelation, in the interests of compatibility of the faith with those outside it who hold other beliefs or none. From the fundamentalist perspective, the task is to convert others, rather than seek with them a lowest common denominator of belief.

It is therefore difficult to see how a genuinely multicultural, multi-faith situation can be obtained unless there is a recognition that, over and above the self-understanding of each religion, there is an acceptance of the primary value of a common humanity – and that suggests that an overall secular humanism is needed in order to form a value structure within which the different belief systems can contribute their particular perspectives.

postscript

In the last chapter, we started to explore some broad issues relating to religion and society, and their importance highlights the danger of taking too narrow a view of the task of the philosophy of religion, for they all deserve the careful and balanced thought that philosophy encourages.

But philosophy is about logical argument, and the philosophy of religion should continue to test religious beliefs for logical coherence and conformity to evidence – that is clearly *part of* what it is about, but not the whole thing. Religion is a phenomenon, and that phenomenon needs to be examined and explained in whatever way is most appropriate. If philosophy attempts to deal with religion in the same way that it deals with, for example, science, politics or language, it is bound to come up against one of two crises:

- *Either* a failure to reach logically coherent conclusions, simply because the material with which it deals is not able to be fully appreciated through a process of logical analysis
- *Or* a failure to have such conclusions as it reaches accepted by those who practise religion.

This should not surprise us. Does anyone really think that the personal hopes and fears of an individual can be encompassed within the parameters of rational thought alone?

Religious intuitions (along with love, hate and fear and other powerful emotions) happen when we are engaged in the 'now' of experience. Hence it has been important to ground this book in experience. What is it that leads people to become religious? How do they express this? If religion persists, then it must benefit people; so how does it do that?

It is not enough, as some evangelical atheists seem to think, to show that religious beliefs are irrational, or that there is no satisfactory evidence for the existence of God. That is most unlikely to change anyone's views – for such beliefs seldom depend on reason or evidence, but on intuition and the interpretation of personal experience.

If you consider the whole range of ideas from the Enlightenment and the rise of science through to the radical thinkers of the nineteenth century – from Voltaire and Hume through to Feuerbach, Marx, Nietzsche, Darwin and Freud – it is amazing that we are still discussing the arguments for the existence of God, or the possibility of miracles. From the perspective of many of those thinkers, such questions were from a bygone age.

Then in the twentieth century, you have the hugely damaging secular ideologies of Nazism and Communism, presented with the ideological force of religion but causing death and destruction on a scale unmatched by earlier, equally brutal but less mechanized regimes. One might therefore expect that the twenty-first century would display a universal culture of cynicism, and secular materialism. And indeed, that is partly true. There is, however, a deeply engrained religious dynamic still in evidence, seen particularly in the fundamentalist branches of Christianity and Islam, in a resurgence of religion in former communist states, and in the vitality of religion in Africa.

Human nature changes only slowly, and the intuitions about meaning and purpose that initiated the great religious movements are still relevant. Faced with fragility and death, people still long for a perspective on life in which the individual counts for something; faced with beauty and the awe-inspiring power of nature, they somehow want to express amazement and joy and a sense of wholeness. These continue to fuel the fires of human spirituality. Religion itself, of course, is a human construct open to all the failings of humankind. But that should not blind the objective eye to its power and significance.

Never has critical reflection on religion been more important in terms of the global impact of belief systems on the future of humankind. Religious belief and ideology still has the power to unite or divide people. It can still stir up deep-seated rivalries between local communities, nations or whole cultures. Its beliefs therefore need to be taken seriously, not necessarily because they are true, but because they are powerful.

taking it further

Classic texts, available in a variety of translations and editions, not only present important arguments but also give a sense of the background and style of each of the thinkers. The following are particularly valuable:

Anselm *Proslogion* and *Monologion*
Aquinas *Summa Theologiae*
Descartes *Meditations*
Hume *Dialogues Concerning Natural Religion*
James *The Varieties of Religious Experience*
Kant *Critique of Pure Reason*
Kierkegaard *Philosophical Fragments* and *Concluding Unscientific Postscript*
Otto *The Idea of the Holy*
Plato *The Republic*
Schleiermacher *On Religion: Speeches to its Cultured Despisers*

The following is a personal selection of books, many referred to in the text, for those who want to follow up any of the issues in greater depth:

Appelbaum, D. and Thompson, M. (eds) (2002) *World Philosophy*, London: Vega

Argyle, M. (2000) *Psychology and Religion: an introduction*, London: Routledge

Ayer, A. J. (2001) *Language, Truth and Logic*, Harmondsworth: Penguin (originally published in 1936)

Clack, Beverley and Clack, Brian R. (1998) *The Philosophy of Religion: a critical introduction*, Cambridge: Polity Press

Craig, W. L. and Smith, Q. (1993) *Theism, Atheism and Big Bang Cosmology*, Oxford: Clarendon Press

Davies, Brian (1982) *An Introduction to the Philosophy of Religion* (3rd ed 2000), Oxford: Oxford University Press

Davies, Brian (2000) *Philosophy of Religion: a guide and anthology*, Oxford: Oxford University Press

Davies, Paul (2006) *The Goldilocks Enigma: why is the universe just right for life?* London: Allan Lane

Dawkins, R. (1990) *The Blind Watchmaker*, London: Penguin Books

Dawkins, R. (1997) *Climbing Mount Improbable*, London: Viking

Dawkins, R. (1999) *Unweaving the Rainbow*, London: Penguin

Dawkins, R. (2006) *The God Delusion*, London: Bantam Press

Dennett, Daniel (2006) *Breaking the Spell: Religion as a Natural Phenomenon*, London: Allen Lane

Dougherty, Jude P. (2003) *The Logic of Religion*, Washington: The Catholic University of America Press

Firth, R. (1996) *Religion: a humanist interpretation*, London: Routledge

Flew, Anthony (2005) *God and Philosophy* (2nd edition), New York: Prometheus Books

Griffiths, Bede (1989) *A New Vision of Reality*, London: Collins

Griffiths, Paul J. (2001) *Problems of Religious Diversity*, Oxford: Blackwell

Harris, Sam (2005) *The End of Faith: religion, terror and the future of reason*, New York: The Free Press (Simon & Schuster)

Helm, P. (ed) (1999) *Faith and Reason*, Oxford: Oxford University Press

Hick, John (1966) *Evil and the God of Love*, London: Macmillan

Hick, John (1993) *God and the Universe of Faiths*, Oxford: Oneworld Publications

Kenny, A. (1987) *Reason and Religion*, Oxford: Basil Blackwell

Kenny, A. (ed) *The Oxford Illustrated History of Western Philosophy*, Oxford: Oxford University Press

Kunin, Seth D. (2003) *Religion: the modern theories*, Edinburgh: Edinburgh University Press

Kung, Hand (1978) *Does God Exist?* London: Collins

Mackie, J. L. (1982) *The Miracle of Theism*, Oxford: Clarendon Press

Peacocks, A. (1990) *Theology for a Scientific Age*, Oxford: Basil Blackwell

Peterson, M., Hasker, W., Reichenback, B., Bassinger, D. (1991) *Reason and Religious Belief*, Oxford: Oxford University Press

Poidevin, Robin Le (1996) *Arguing for Atheism: An Introduction to the Philosophy of Religion*, London and New York: Routledge

Polkinghorne, J. (1998) *Science and Creation*, London: SPCK

Rorty, Richard (1980) *Philosophy and the Mirror of Nature*, Oxford: Basil Blackwell

Smart, Ninian (ed) (1962) *Historical Selections in the Philosophy of Religion*, London: SCM Press

Smart, Ninian (1999) *World Philosophies*, London and New York: Routledge

Stanesby, D. M. (1988) *Science, Reason and Religion*, London: Routledge

Stone, Martin (1998) 'Philosophy of Religion' in Grayling, A. C. (ed) *Philosophy 2*, Oxford: Oxford University Press

Swinburne, Richard (1979) *The Existence of God*, Oxford: Clarendon Press (a shortened version of which is available as *Is there a God?*) (1996) Oxford: Oxford University Press

Taliaferro, Charles (1998) *Contemporary Philosophy of Religion*, Oxford: Blackwell

Turner, Jonathan H. (2000) *On the Origins of Human Emotions*, Stanford, California: Stanford University Press

Vardy, Peter (1992) *The Puzzle of Evil*, London: HarperCollins

Vernon, Mark (2007) *Science, Religion and the Meaning of Life*, Basingstoke: Palgrave Macmillan

---

There are a good range of websites and blogs suitable for those wanting to follow up on the philosophy of religion, other areas of philosophy or world religions. New publications and sites are appearing all the time and a printed list is soon out of date. Readers are therefore invited to explore the on-line resources listed on the **Philosophy and Ethics** website, to be found at:

www.mel-thompson.co.uk

This site provides information on other books by the same author, additional material suitable for students taking AS and A2 level examinations in the United Kingdom, and a general listing of resources for philosophy and ethics.

a posteriori Latin phrase which denotes knowledge that is based on sense experience.

a priori Latin phrase which refers to thought or knowledge which is derived from a concept or principle, known prior to experience.

agnosticism An agnostic holds that we do not have sufficient evidence to decide whether a God exists or not.

analytic Used of a statement whose truth may be established by the definition of its terms, without reference to experience or evidence (for example, statements of logic and mathematics).

atheism The conviction that there is no god.

behaviourism The view that mental attributes are a way of describing bodily action (see particularly the work of Gilbert Ryle for 'logical behaviourism').

categorical imperative An absolute sense of moral obligation, which does not depend on the anticipated result of an action. It is particularly associated with the philosopher Kant, who used it as the basis for his ethical theory.

charismatic Used of those who claim divine inspiration during worship, being filled with the Holy Spirit.

cognitive language Language that claims to give factual information.

cosmological (arguments) Arguments for the existence of God, based on the fact of the world's existence.

deism The belief (generally seen as justified through human reason, rather than by revelation) in the existence of God as the designer and creator of the universe.

descriptive ethics The description of morals of a particular society, without making judgements about whether those morals are right or wrong (c.p. normative ethics).

design (argument from) The argument that the world appears to be designed, and therefore that God exists as its designer.

determinism The view that things are completely determined by their causes, and that freedom is an illusion.

dualism The view that body and mind are distinct and separate entities.

emotive theory The theory that moral assertions are simply the expression of emotions. (i.e. to say that something is wrong or bad, simply indicates that you dislike it).

empiricism The theory that all knowledge comes by way of the five human senses.

epiphenomenalism The view that the mind is merely a product of the complex physical processes going on in the brain.

epistemology The theory of knowledge.

exclusivist Used of the view that one's own religion alone has true beliefs.

existentialism A philosophy concerned with the individual and the problems of human existence.

fideism The view that God can only be known through faith or revelation, not through the unaided human reason.

final cause The 'end' or purpose of something; its essence or potential (from Aristotle).

Forms, the theory of Plato's theory of universals, in which particular things share, and from which they take their character.

fundamentalist Used to describe an approach to religion that claims to return to the fundamentals of belief; particularly associated with a literal interpretation of doctrine and scripture and sometimes involving a radical approach to social and political action.

hedonism The moral view that the quest for human happiness is paramount in assessing action.

humanism A philosophical and cultural movement, emphasizing the dignity of humankind and the primacy of reason. Although humanism does not require atheism, it is generally associated with the rejection of traditional religious beliefs.

idealism The view that reality (or our view of reality) is fundamentally mental rather than physical.

ideology The set of ideas that can form the basis for a social, political or economic system.

idolatry The association of a particular entity with God; used of the worship of physical images, or the veneration of ideas or dogmas in their own right.

immanence Used to describe God as being found within the world.

inclusivist The view that true beliefs of one's own religion are also to be found in other religions.

interactionism A general term (in the Philosophy of Mind) for theories in which mind and body act upon one another.

intuitionism The theory that 'good' is known by intuition, but cannot be defined.

Logical Positivism An approach to language, developed early in the twentieth century (particularly within the Vienna Circle) which equated the meaning of a statement with its method of verification, saw scientific language as ideal and dismissed religion and morality as meaningless.

materialism The view that reality is physical.

metaphysics The philosophical quest, beyond the world of the senses, to discover the fundamental structures of reality.

multiculturalism The view that different cultures can exist side by side within the same society and should be shown equal respect.

Natural Law A rational interpretation of the purpose of reality, used as a basis for ethics, originating in Aristotle but particularly associated (in Christian moral thought) with Aquinas.

normative ethics The study of the values (or 'norms') on the basis of which people act morally (as opposed to 'descriptive ethics', which records but does not evaluate behaviour).

numinous The term used by Otto to describe the particular sense of awe and dread associated with religious experience.

ontology/ontological The study of the nature of being itself; also used of one of the traditional arguments for the existence of God.

panentheism The belief that everything exists within God (but not that God is identified with everything).

pantheism The belief that the whole physical universe is God.

performative utterance A functional (rather than a descriptive) statement (for example, 'I baptize you.').

postmodernism An approach to culture and philosophy, developed in the latter part of the twentieth century, which emphasizes the autonomy of cultural symbols and texts, rather than relating them to a self-conscious author, or single authoritative meaning.

prescriptivism The theory that ethical assertions prescribe of a course of action (i.e. that to say something is 'good' is to recommend that it be done).

providence The belief that God, directly or through nature, provides for humankind.

reductionism The philosophical approach which sees complex entities as 'no more than' the various parts of which they are composed.

scepticism A view which challenges all claims to knowledge and certainty.

schematization The use of words to understand and describe the 'holy' (according to Otto).

secularism The view that humankind should be concerned primarily with this world.

synthetic Used of statements that depend upon empirical evidence to show that they are true or false.

teleological argument An argument for the existence of God based on the idea of the end or purpose of the world and everything in it, also known as the design argument.

theism Belief in the existence of God, as traditionally conceived in the major Western religions.

transcendence Used of the idea that God is above and beyond the ordinary physical things in the universe.

utilitarianism An ethical theory based on the desire to achieve 'the greatest benefit or happiness for the greatest number', thereby evaluating actions according to their expected results.

virtue ethics An ethical theory (originating in Aristotle) based on a consideration of those virtues or qualities that make for the 'good life' or human flourishing.

index

abductive argument 111
agnosticism 71, 110–11
al-Ghazali 83, 84
al-Kindi 83
Amish communities 187, 249
analogy 47–8
analytic statements 43
Anselm 75, 78, 79, 80
anthropic principle 207–9, 216
Aquinas, Thomas 39, 47, 48, 83, 89, 90–1, 125, 165, 166
Argyle, M. 252
Aristotle 39, 79, 99, 124, 203, 230
atheism 108–10, 111–12
atman 145, 146
Augustine of Hippo 165, 175
Augustinian approach (to evil) 165–7, 176
autonomy (in ethics) 229
Ayer, A. J. 42, 44, 45

Barth, K. 201
'basic beliefs' 66–7
behaviourism 132–5, 154–5
'being-itself' 14–15
Bentham, J. 53, 232
Berkeley, Bishop 135
Blind Watchmaker, The (Dawkins) 93, 220
Brahman 63, 146
British Humanist Association 116–17
Buber, M. 13–14, 15
Buddhism 120, 138–9, 141, 146–7, 159, 175, 236, 244, 256
  'eternal' 54–5
  and miracles 214
  non-theistic 65
  rational approach 41
  revelation 26
  suffering 179
Bunting, M. 253

Cameron, D. 253
categorical imperative (of Kant) 100, 234
Chance and Necessity (Monod) 93, 221
charismatic experiences 22–3
Christianity 172, 175, 176, 257
  rational approach 40
  revelation 26
  and science 193
  suffering 177–8, 183
  theism 64
  the Trinity 65–6
Cleanthes 93
Concept of Mind, The (Ryle) 126, 133
Concluding Unscientific Postscript (Kierkegaard) 12
constitutive concept (of Kant) 101
conversion 7, 251–2
Copernicus 192
Coplestone, F. C. 90
Coplestone–Russell debate 90
cosmological argument 69, 82–90, 106
creator (God as) 59–62, 218–19, 222
Critique of Pure Reason (Kant) 74, 76
Cupitt, D. 46–7, 67, 68, 108, 136–7, 138

Darwin, C. 92, 97, 218–20
Davies, B. 30–1, 61, 103, 144, 174, 212
Dawkins, R. 9, 93, 108, 109, 117, 118, 202, 220, 225–6
De Philosophia (Aristotle) 79
Death and Eternal Life (Hick) 144
degrees of quality (argument from) 85
deism 71, 163, 222
Dennet, D. 9
Descartes 28, 76–7, 126–7
descriptive ethics 229

design (argument from) **90–2, 94–8, 106, 172, 218–19, 222**
devil, the **175–6**
Dialogues Concerning Natural Religion (Hume) **91–2, 162, 206–7**
Dostoyevsky, F. **170**
double-aspect theory (mind/body theory) **129–30, 140**
dualism **123–30, 142, 148**
Durkheim, E. **115–16, 239**

Eckhart, M. **21**
education, religious **240–2**
efficient causes **230**
Einstein, A. **194**
emotive theory (of language) **42**
empiricists **43**
Enquiry Concerning Human Understanding, An (Hume) **43, 82–3, 198, 209–10, 214**
ens reallissum **76**
Epicurians **99**
epiphenomenalism **128–9**
Essay Concerning Toleration (Locke) **243**
eternal (quality ascribed to God) **14, 57–9**
eternal life **141–8**
ethics **229–38**
Euthyphro dilemma **238**

Evil and the Love of God (Hick) **164, 167–8**
evil, problem of **62, 115, 164–71, 173–6, 183–4**
    see also suffering
evolution **92–3, 97–8, 111–12, 203, 218–24**
ex nihilo (theory of creation) **59, 174, 183, 222**
exclusivism **254–5**
existence, of God **69–72, 75–9**
'experiencing as' **2–7, 38–9**
extremism **245–7**

factual/logical necessity **78–9, 106**
faith **37–8**
faith schools **241–2**
Feuerbach, L. **113–14**
fideism **37**
final causes **99, 230**
Firth, R. **117, 118**
Five Ways (Aquinas' argument) **83, 85–7**
Flew, A. **45**
forms (in Plato) **79–80, 130, 203**
free will defence **169–70**

freedom **139–41**
Frege, G. **52**
Freud, S. **151–2**
functionalism **115–16**
fundamentalism **251, 256–9**
funeral service **180–2**

Galileo **192**
Gaunilo **78**
genetics **92–3, 173, 202, 220**
God Delusion, The (Dawkins) **9, 93, 109, 118**
Greek terms (for self) **124**
Gregory of Nyssa **19**
Griffiths, B. **20, 55**

Happold, F. **21**
Harris, S. **246, 258**
hell **175–6**
heteronomy (in ethics) **230**
Hick, J. **38, 144, 164, 167–8, 255**
Hildegaard of Bingen **20**

Hindu
    rational approach **41**
Hinduism **145–6, 256**
    Brahman **63**
    polytheistic **64–5**
    suffering **178**
humanism **116–20**
Hume, D. **43, 82–3, 89, 91, 93, 94, 95, 138, 162, 198, 203, 206, 209–11, 214**
hypothetical imperative **100**

I and Thou (Buber) **13**
Idea of the Holy, The (Otto) **12**
idealism **43, 135**
identity hypothesis (mind/body theory) **129–30, 140**
idolatry **71, 256**
immanence **62, 66, 171–3**
immortality **141–8**
inclusivism **255–6**
induced experience **16–17**
induction **198–9**
Introduction to the Critique of Hegelian Philosophy of Right (Marx) **114**
Introduction to the Philosophy of Religion, An (Davies) **30, 61, 103, 144, 174**
intuitionalism **105, 173, 225**
Irenaean approach (to evil) **167–8, 176**
Irenaeus **167**
Islam **172, 175, 244–5, 253, 257**
    rational approach **40**
    revelation **26**

suffering 177
theism 64

James, W. 3, 7, 9–10, 21
John of the Cross 22, 25
Judaism 172, 236
  rational approach 41
  suffering 176–7
  theism 64
Julian of Norwich, Lady 20, 29
Jung, Karl 152–3

Kalam argument 83–4
Kant, I. 74, 76–8, 88, 96, 100, 101,
  140, 204, 234–5
karma 141, 146–7, 178, 179
Kierkegaard, S. 12–13, 15, 201
Kung, H. 94

language games (in Wittgenstein) 51–3
Language, Truth and Logic (Ayer) 44
Leibniz, G. 128, 183
life after death 141–8
lifestyle 247–52
literal interpretation 44–7, 256–9
Locke, J. 203, 242
Logical Positivism 39, 44

Mackie, J. L. 94
Malcolm, N. 77, 79
Malebranche, N. 127
Marx, K. 114–15, 182, 240, 244
materialism 130–5
metaphysical evil 164
metaphysics 237–8
Mill, J. S. 232
mind/body theories 123–30
miracles 209–15
models and qualifiers 48–9
Monod, J. 93
Monologion (Anselm) 79, 80, 85
moral argument 98–102, 106
moral evil 164
mourning 180–2
multiculturalism 247–9, 252–60
Murdoch, I. 81–2, 237–8
mysterium tremendum 11
mysticism 19–22, 55
myths 49–50

natural evil 164
natural law 230–2, 235
natural selection 92–3, 97, 219–21
near death experiences 10, 147–8
Newton Sir I. 192
Newtonian physics 192–3

Nietzsche, F. 111–12, 115, 233
Nirguna Brahman 63
nominalism 81
non-self 138–9
normative ethics 229
numinous 12

occasionalism 127–8
omnipotence 60
omniscience 60–2
On Religion (Schleiermacher) 8–9
ontological argument 69, 75–82, 106
Origin of Species, The (Darwin) 97,
  218
Otto, R. 11–12, 15, 48

Paley, W. 96
panentheism 63
pantheism 63, 71
Pascal, B. 105
Peacocke, A. 54, 173, 225
performance utterance 41
petitionary prayer 18–19
Phenomenon of Man, The (Teilhard)
  222
Phillips, D. Z. 52
Philosophical Investigations
  (Wittgenstein) 33–4, 38, 51, 52
Plantinga, A. 66, xv
Plato 79–80, 123, 126, 141, 165, 203
Platonism 81
political issues 242–5
Polkinghorne, J. 221
Popper, K. 199
possibility and necessity (argument
  from) 85, 88
postmodernism 67–9, 136–8
prayer 17–19
pre-established harmony (mind/body
  theory) 128
prescriptivism 42
privileged access (to mind) 133–4
progressive revelation 25–6
projected design 96
Proslogion (Anselm) 75, 78, 79, 80
providence 204–9
psychology 140, 150–7
Ptolemy of Alexandria 190

quantum theory 194

Ramsey, I. T. 48
rational and non-rational approaches
  38–41
re-becoming (Buddhist idea of) 146–7
realism 81
reductionism 131, 201–3

regulative concept (of Kant) **96, 101**
reincarnation **145–6**
relativity, theory of **194**
religious education **240–2**
religious experiences
    argument from **8–16, 102–4, 106, 200**
    concept of **4–6**
    interpretation of **23–9**
Republic, The (Plato) **80**
resurrection **144–5**
revelation **23–6, 200**
Rorty, R. **130, 131**
Russell, B. **90, 101, 108, 196**
Ryle, G. **126, 133–4, 137**

Saguna Brahman **63**
St Augustine of Hippo **165, 175**
St John of the Cross **22, 25**
St Teresa of Avila **22**
schematization **12, 48**
Schleiermacher, F. **8–9, 15, 69**
science **186–96**
scientific method **196–200**
sects **251–2**
secularism **111, 112–16**
self
    Buddhist view of **138–9**
    Greek terms for **124**
    postmodern **136–8**
self-transcending **29, 31, 50, 62, 119**
Sikhism
    suffering **179–80**
    theism **64**
skilful means (Buddhist idea of) **236, 248**
sociology **140, 238–42**
Spinoza, B. **129–30**
spiritual development **155–6**
Stoics **19, 99**

suffering
    Augustinian approach **165–7**
    and Buddhism **68, 138, 178–9**
    challenge **159–61**
    and Christianity **177–8**
    coming to terms with **180–2**
    free will defence **169–70**
    of God **171–2**
    and Hinduism **178**
    Irenaean approach **167–8, 170**
    and Islam **177**
    and Judaism **176–7**
    Marx on **115**
    problem of **161–4**
    and Sikhism **179–80**
    see also evil, problem of

Summa Theologiae (Aquinas) **89, 90, 125, 166**
superstition **225–7**
Swinburne, R. **60, 61, 183**
symbolism **49–50**
synthetic statements **43**
Systematic Theology (Tillich) **105**

Teilhard de Chardin **222–4**
teleological argument **90–2, 193, 216, 218–19**
Teresa of Avila **22**
terrorism **244–7, 257**
theism **62–3, 71, 163, 174, 175**
theodicy **163**
Theology for a Scientific Age (Peacocke) **54**
theonomy **236–8**
therapy, religion as **153–5**
Thus Spoke Zarathustra (Nietzsche) **111**
Tillich, P. **14–15, 105, 108**
Toynbee, Polly **241–2**
Tractatus Logico-Philosophocus (Wittgenstein) **44, 51**
transcendence **62**
    humanist **119**
    transcendence (of God) **171–2**
Trinity, Christian doctrine of **65–6**
Turner, J. H. **132**

ultimate concern **14, 15**
universe, origin of **215–17**
Upanishads **146**
utilitarianism **232–4**

Vardy, P. **164, 165**
Varieties of Religious Experience, The (James) **3, 7, 9, 21**
Verification Principle **44–5**
Vernon, M. **110**
Vienna Circle **44, 199**
virtue ethics **235**

Weber, M. **240**
Wittgenstein, L. **33, 38, 44, 51–2, 160, 199**
Wordsworth, W. **30**